AF696161

Contemporary Issues in Psychological Assessment

Series Editor
Randy W. Kamphaus
Georgia State University College of Education
Atlanta, Georgia
USA

For further volumes:
http://www.springer.com/series/7353

Amber E. Brueggemann Taylor

Diagnostic Assessment of Learning Disabilities in Childhood

Bridging the Gap Between Research and Practice

Springer

Amber E. Brueggemann Taylor
Special School District, St. Louis County
Ballwin, Missouri
USA

ISBN 978-1-4939-0334-4 ISBN 978-1-4939-0335-1 (eBook)
DOI 10.1007/978-1-4939-0335-1
Springer New York Heidelberg Dordrecht London

Library of Congress Control Number: 2014930308

© Springer Science+Business Media New York 2014
This work is subject to copyright. All rights are reserved by the Publisher, whether the whole or part of the material is concerned, specifically the rights of translation, reprinting, reuse of illustrations, recitation, broadcasting, reproduction on microfilms or in any other physical way, and transmission or information storage and retrieval, electronic adaptation, computer software, or by similar or dissimilar methodology now known or hereafter developed. Exempted from this legal reservation are brief excerpts in connection with reviews or scholarly analysis or material supplied specifically for the purpose of being entered and executed on a computer system, for exclusive use by the purchaser of the work. Duplication of this publication or parts thereof is permitted only under the provisions of the Copyright Law of the Publisher's location, in its current version, and permission for use must always be obtained from Springer. Permissions for use may be obtained through RightsLink at the Copyright Clearance Center. Violations are liable to prosecution under the respective Copyright Law.
The use of general descriptive names, registered names, trademarks, service marks, etc. in this publication does not imply, even in the absence of a specific statement, that such names are exempt from the relevant protective laws and regulations and therefore free for general use.
While the advice and information in this book are believed to be true and accurate at the date of publication, neither the authors nor the editors nor the publisher can accept any legal responsibility for any errors or omissions that may be made. The publisher makes no warranty, express or implied, with respect to the material contained herein.

Printed on acid-free paper

Springer is part of Springer Science+Business Media (www.springer.com)

To Jason, Mom, Dad, Nicole and all of my family for always believing I could do anything and making me feel as if I could. To Trinity for inspiring me to be the best me possible before I had even met you. To all the children and teachers I have worked with for making my profession the most enjoyable and rewarding there is.

Preface

When the possibility of writing this text was first introduced I was somewhat hesitant because of my uncertainty of others' interest in the topic. After consideration, the reason for my hesitancy became my motivation to complete the book. I first encountered the ambivalence and indifference surrounding learning disability diagnosis in graduate school when an instructor informed the class that she would not be discussing learning disability (LD) symptoms and identification because it was too boring. She did, however, invite us to read the chapter—not the most enticing introduction. Despite the threat of overwhelming boredom, I sought out other resources and began my own study of learning disabilities. I discovered that quite contrary to that less than lackluster introduction to the field, learning disability diagnosis was overflowing with intricacies and questions that appealed to my attraction to all things mysterious and neglected by the mainstream. All of these intricacies remain with me and make me gasp inwardly whenever I hear fellow clinicians speak about a simple or straightforward LD case. It seems impossible to be familiar with the learning disabilities literature and consider the diagnosis of a learning disability to be a simple matter. Even with what is considered a cut and dried discrepancy approach there are a myriad of variables to consider. If one uses a processing approach, it may become mindboggling. As I learned more, my graduate student peers began to come to me with their questions regarding LDs and seemed amazed by the depth of my knowledge, which was actually only a scratch on the surface. While I have continued to add to my treasure trove of LD tidbits, I have endeavored to keep this book from delving into the many details and controversies that fuel debates among academics and other professionals who share my interest in the field. Instead, my goal is to impart that introductory knowledge that my own colleagues found practical to provide a useful tool for those who want to know more without too many of those "boring" details that kept me coming back for more.

Amber E. Brueggemann Taylor

Acknowledgments

I wish to express my gratitude to Dr. Randy Kamphaus, my mentor and editor, first, for believing that my interests, ideas, and research were worthy of being shared in the lofty format of a manuscript, and second, for his feedback and encouragement in making the book a reality. Without his guidance, this book and my career in general would not have been possible.

Many other mentors and colleagues provided insight and inspiration that fueled my interest in assessment and learning disabilities, including Dr. Noel Gregg, Dr. Jonathan Campbell, Dr. Michele Lease, Dr. Roy Martin, and Dr. Allison Doerr.

I am also deeply grateful to the experts who contributed their knowledge and perspectives to this book. I was embarrassingly excited to have the distinguished Dr. Joseph K. Torgesen, Dr. Cecil R. Reynolds, Dr. Jack Naglieri, Dr. Scott Ardoin, Dr. Linda Siegel, and Dr. Stefan Dombrowski share the wisdom of their experience. I am particularly grateful that the late Dr. Kenneth Kavale enthusiastically and generously shared his ideas to carry on and inspire future researchers and practitioners.

Finally, I wish to express my gratitude to Judy Jones and Garth Haller of Springer for making this process smoother and simpler than I would have imagined possible.

Contents

About the Author

Amber E. Brueggemann Taylor, Ph.D., earned her doctoral degree from the University of Georgia with a specialization in learning disabilities. She is currently working as a full-time school psychologist with the Special School District of St. Louis County as well as a part-time supervising psychologist at Community Psychological Services of University of Missouri-St. Louis. Her previous work experiences include being a school psychologist for a program serving children with severe emotional and/or neurodevelopmental disorders, a staff psychologist providing therapy and evaluation for children and adolescents at St. Louis Behavioral Medicine Institute, and an evaluator for the Fetal Alcohol Spectrum as part of the St. Louis University Partners for Success grant project. Dr. Taylor is a Missouri licensed psychologist, Missouri certified school psychologist, and nationally certified school psychologist.

Chapter 1
Introduction/History of Learning Disability Assessment

Introduction

Many books and articles focus on various aspects of learning disabilities (LD), including history, identification, characteristics, remediation, and so on. Given the broad range of topics within the field of LD, this chapter aims to delineate the different approaches to the identification of LD in children in a clear and concise manner. LD exist across the lifespan and may not be addressed until adulthood; however, this is not usually the case. The focus of this book is specifically on the identification of LD in children and adolescents, because LD typically surface and are diagnosed during the school years. Many examples and research studies cited also focus on reading disabilities due to the greater amount of available research, although research regarding mathematics disabilities is increasing as evidenced by the August 2005 special issue of the *Journal of Learning Disabilities*. This introduction presents the varying definitions of LD and an overview of historically accepted diagnostic practices. The chapters that follow delve into the different methods of identification and their contemporary application in greater depth. Before turning to these issues, an important question remains to be answered: Why all the fuss about identifying youth with LD?

Why Diagnose Learning Disabilities?

The category of specific LD accounts for half of the students being served by the Individuals with Disabilities Education Act (IDEA; U.S. Department of Education 2002), and approximately 6% of students in public schools are identified as having an LD, with identification varying across states (U.S. Department of Education, National Center for Education Statistics 2006). There was a 28.5% increase in LD diagnosis between the 1991–1992 and 2000–2001 school years. A major factor contributing to the large proportion of students receiving the LD label is hypothesized to be due to confusion regarding the appropriate definition and diagnostic procedures for the disorder (Stanovich 2005).

A. E. B. Taylor, *Diagnostic Assessment of Learning Disabilities in Childhood*, Contemporary Issues in Psychological Assessment, DOI 10.1007/978-1-4939-0335-1_1,

© Springer Science+Business Media New York 2014

Diagnosis of LD and other disorders is a form of classification that serves five primary purposes: communication, information retrieval, description, prediction, and theory formulation (Blashfield 1998). In the service of the first purpose, classification provides a common language so that various individuals, such as educators, clinicians, and physicians, can communicate with one another. This allows professionals to quickly form at least a rough conceptualization of presenting problems rather than requiring laborious descriptions each time a symptom constellation is encountered. Diagnosis also serves as a method of information retrieval for treatment and the scientific study of specific disorders. When an educator is told that he/she will be working with a student with an LD, this allows him/her to access intervention ideas that have been shown to be successful with other such students. Similarly, classifying individuals based on similar characteristics and behaviors allows researchers to more easily focus on groups of interest. Through classification, a shorthand description of co-occurring "symptoms" or problems is established, allowing professionals to quickly understand a given situation and formulate hypotheses. This leads to the fourth purpose, which is often the primary focus of attention, prediction of course and treatment. The final purpose of classification, concept formation, implies that organization of characteristics of disorders should lead to theories of disorder that guide research.

In the case of LD, the lack of a common definition has prevented the goals of classification from being met. The term LD as it has been applied in past and current practice refers to a large heterogeneous group that may include individuals who genuinely cannot perform certain learning tasks despite average intellectual functioning, individuals who have not been exposed to appropriate academic opportunities, and individuals who are considered gifted in some areas yet perform within the average range in another, among others. The resulting lack of information organization impedes research efforts, which has a further negative impact on progress in prevention, identification, and remediation.

In addition to the need for accurate diagnosis to meet the purposes of classification, the act of classification itself may produce benefits. For example, the practice of diagnosing individuals with mental retardation and the increased attention paid to diagnostic accuracy contributed to the beginning of the deinstitutionalization movement (Kamphaus 2001). A more recent example of the necessity for classification is attention-deficit/hyperactivity disorder (ADHD). Prior to the publication of the *Diagnostic and Statistical Manual of Mental Disorders Third Edition*, individuals with the constellation of symptoms characteristic of ADHD (or ADD as it was known at the time) were not recognized as having a disorder. Due to the classification of these individuals as having ADHD, it is now understood that ADHD has a biological basis, and great progress is being made in treatment research. If children with LD are not identified as such, it is likely that much-needed advances in prevention and treatment will not be made.

Identifying children as having an LD usually involves considerations that differ from other disorders due to its primacy in educational settings. Often, clinicians and educators are presented with a choice to either diagnose the construct of LD or identify a child as having an LD so that he or she may receive a desired school placement (Shepard 1989). Diagnosing the disorder involves the inference of a theoretical construct while school placement is concerned only with the behavioral manifestation of a disorder. While behavior may be enough for pre-referral intervention, the very nature of diagnosis requires that the construct be present, otherwise classification will not serve to enhance communication, prediction, or research.

It is also necessary for educators and psychologists to weigh the benefits of special services with the stigma of a special education label and the cost of assessment. Some individuals lean heavily toward a needs-based definition of LD that would allow any struggling child to receive services without a costly assessment (Shepard 1989). In addition, labeling a child as having an LD is often viewed as more desirable than classifying him/her as suffering from mental retardation (MR) due to the history of ethnic minority overidentification in the latter diagnosis and resulting pressure to avoid disproportionate MR diagnoses. However, by inappropriately classifying students as having an LD, we fail to reap the beneficial aspects of a classification system and threaten the credibility of the LD construct. If students inappropriately receive special services for LD when they should be receiving services for MR or less intense interventions, the LD label becomes meaningless and the quality of its associated special services suffers.

In a seminal study, Shepard et al. (1983) examined the special education files for a stratified sample of 800 students who had been identified as having LD. They found that fewer than half of the sample met diagnostic criteria for LD as defined in federal law or the professional literature at that time. Most of the students in the category did have some sort of learning problems, but they were due to other causes, such as MR, emotional disturbance, and language interference. The researchers suggested that the overidentification may have been due to educators' desire to explain their failure to educate students, confusion about definitions, and bureaucratic and parental pressure to identify and provide services for low-achieving students.

If the magnitude of LD misidentification in the Shepard et al. (1983) study is representative of practices across the USA, research concerning LD will be confounded and the construct could be rendered meaningless in public perception. If the LD label is applied to low achievers, such as nonnative English speakers and ethnic minorities who may require services for different reasons than learning-disabled students, questions of bias similar to those surrounding mild MR placements are likely to surface. In the most optimistic scenario, if misidentification flourishes, labeling a child as having an LD will continue to be viewed as more beneficial than harmful, allowing it to continue as a catchall category that will ultimately become meaningless and be abolished in public policy (Shepard 1989). If this is the eventual outcome, then students who truly have LD will be unable to gain access to much needed interventions.

Overview of Learning Disabilities Definitions

The identification of children with LD in schools is governed by the Individuals with Disabilities Education Improvement Act (IDEIA 2004). The conceptual definition of LD presented by IDEIA has not changed since the passage of P.L. 94–142 in 1975. The definition states that, "The term 'specific learning disability' means a disorder in one or more of the basic psychological processes involved in understanding or in using language, spoken or written, which disorder may manifest itself in imperfect ability to listen, think, speak, read, write, spell, or do mathematical calculations." The definition continues to specify that several labels previously applied to children with LD are included, while learning difficulties resulting from visual, hearing, or motor disabilities, mental retardation, emotional disturbance, or environmental, cultural, or economic disadvantage are excluded (IDEA, S.1248, 2003, sec.602(29)).

While most attention is given to LD in school-age children, the condition persists across the life span. Thus, the conceptual definition and identification procedures set forth by IDEIA are not the only approaches endorsed in the field of LD. The National Joint Committee on Learning Disabilities (NJCLD), a committee representing organizations concerned about individuals with disabilities, disagreed with several points in the federal definition and released the following definition in 1990: "Learning disabilities is a general term that refers to a heterogeneous group of disorders manifested by significant difficulties in the acquisition and use of listening, speaking, reading, writing, reasoning, or mathematical abilities. These disorders are intrinsic to the individual, presumed to be due to central nervous system dysfunction, and may occur across the life span. Problems in self-regulatory behaviors, social perception, and social interaction may exist with learning disabilities but do not by themselves constitute a learning disability. Although learning disabilities may occur concomitantly with other handicapping conditions (for example, sensory impairment, mental retardation, serious emotional disturbance), or with extrinsic influences (such as cultural differences, insufficient or inappropriate instruction), they are not the result of those conditions or influences." The NJCLD's goal was to eliminate difficult-to-define terms, while highlighting that LD do not cease to exist after childhood and are intrinsic to the individual. They have also released more recent related policy and research recommendations in an attempt to ensure that LD remain a distinct eligibility category (NJCLD 2011).

Kavale et al. (2009) pointed out many difficulties with the definition of LD similar to those discussed previously. They proposed the following definition based upon the responsive revision of MR criteria, the questions guiding that revision: "Specific learning disability refers to heterogeneous clusters of disorders that significantly impede the normal progress of academic achievement in 2–3 % of the school population." The lack of progress is exhibited in school performance that remains below expectation for chronological and mental ages, even when provided with high-quality instruction. The primarily manifestation of the failure to progress is significant underachievement in a basic skill area (i.e., reading, mathematics, writing) that is not associated with insufficient educational, interpersonal, cultural/familial, and/or sociolinguistic experiences. The primary severe ability–achievement discrepancy is coincident with deficits in linguistic competence (receptive and/or expressive), cognitive functioning (e.g., problem solving, thinking abilities, maturation), neuropsychological processes (e.g., perception, attention, memory), or any combination of such contributing deficits that are presumed to originate from central nervous system dysfunction. The specific LD is a discrete condition differentiated from generalized learning failure by average or above (>90) cognitive ability and a learning skill profile exhibiting significant scatter, indicating areas of strength and weakness. The major specific LD may be accompanied by secondary LD that also may be considered when planning the more intensive, individualized special education instruction directed at the primary problem (Kavale et al. 2009, pp. 45–46). While this definition has not been accepted within the LD community, it was intended to generate more useful and specific revised definitions of LD and, ultimately, consensus.

Overview of Learning Disabilities Identification

While there is some disagreement regarding the appropriate definition of LD, the more acrimonious debate relates to how LD are identified. Once again, IDEIA (formerly IDEA) determines what constitutes an LD in educational settings. The 1997 reauthorization of IDEA instructed educators to operationalize the definition as failure to achieve commensurate with age and ability as evidenced by a severe discrepancy between academic achievement and intellectual ability in one or more of seven academic areas. Additionally, the evaluation had to rule out the exclusionary factors listed in the definition (U.S. Department of Education 1999, p. 12457). The most recent reauthorization of the special education law in 2004, known as the IDEIA, allows state education agencies to choose between the standard discrepancy model and response to evidence-based intervention, or other unspecified research-based approaches. An additional academic area was also added for a total of eight. The eight areas include the following: oral expression, listening comprehension, written expression, basic reading skill, reading comprehension, mathematical calculation, mathematical reasoning, and reading fluency. Table 1.1 lists subtests of academic achievement tests commonly used to evaluate each of these areas.

Outside of academic settings, the *Diagnostic and Statistical Manual of Mental Disorders Fourth Edition* (DSM-IV; APA 2000) has provided the standard criteria for diagnosing LD. These criteria also employ the discrepancy approach. More specifically, achievement in reading, mathematics, or written expression as measured by an individually administered standardized achievement test must be substantially below expectation based on chronological age, measured intelligence, and age-appropriate education. The discrepancy must interfere with activities in academics and daily living that require the skill in question. Further, the difficulties in the academic skill must be in excess of those usually associated with any sensory deficit that may be present. Individuals with disorders who do not meet criteria for Reading Disorder, Mathematics Disorder, or Disorder of Written Expression, as well as problems in all three areas are classified as having Learning Disorder Not Otherwise Specified.

With the recent release of the *Diagnostic and Statistical Manual of Mental Disorders Fifth Edition* (DSM-5; APA 2013), the clinical diagnosis of what is now

Table 1.1 Instruments and subtests typically used to evaluate the eight areas of the IDEIA definition of specific learning disability

Oral expression	*Reading comprehension*
KTEA-II[a] oral expression	GORT-4[e]
OWLS[b] oral expression	KTEA-II reading comprehension
WJ-III ACH[c] story recall	TORC-IV[f]
WIAT-II[d] oral language	WIAT-II reading comprehension
	WJ-III ACH passage comprehension
Listening comprehension	*Reading fluency*
K-TEA II listening comprehension	K-TEA II word recognition fluency
OWLS listening comprehension	WJ-III ACH reading fluency
WJ-III ACH understanding directions	GORT-4
WIAT-II listening comprehension	Curriculum-based measures (e.g., DIBELS[g])
Written expression	*Mathematical calculation*
K-TEA II written expression	K-TEA II mathematics computation
OWLS[h] written expression	KeyMath3[j]
TOWL-4[i]	WJ-III ACH calculation
WIAT-II written expression	WIAT-II numerical operations
WJ-III ACH writing samples	
Basic reading skill	*Mathematical reasoning*
K-TEA II letter and word recognition	K-TEA II mathematics concepts and applications
WIAT-II word reading	KeyMath3
WJ-III ACH letter-word identification	WIAT-II mathematics reasoning
WJ-III diagnostic reading battery[k]	WJ-III ACH applied problems

[a] Kaufman Test of Educational Achievement-Second Edition (Kaufman & Kaufman 2004)
[b] Oral and Written Language Scales: Listening Comprehension and Oral Expression (Carrow Woolfolk 1995)
[c] Woodcock–Johnson III Tests of Achievement (Woodcock et al. 2001)
[d] Wechsler Individual Achievement Tests-Second Edition (The Psychological Corporation 2001)
[e] Gray Oral Reading Tests (Wiederholt and Bryant 2001)
[f] Test of Reading Comprehension, Third Edition (Brown et al. 1995)
[g] *DIBELS* Dynamic Indicators of Basic Early Literacy Skills, Sixth Edition (Good et al. 2003)
[h] Oral and Written Language Scales: Written Expression (Carrow Woolfolk 1996)
[i] Test of Written Language-Third Edition (Hammill & Larsen 1996)
[j] KeyMath-3 Diagnostic Assessment (Connolly 2007)
[k] Woodock–Johnson III Diagnostic Reading Battery (Schrank et al. 2004)

termed “specific learning disorder” includes consideration of an individual’s history, formal assessment results, and response to intervention (APA 2013; see Fig. 1.1). Additionally, rather than three distinctive disorders for different academic areas, the new criteria indicate the necessity of difficulty acquiring and using reading, writing, arithmetic, or mathematical reasoning skills for 6 months, despite interventions with at least one of six specific deficits. The deficits include difficulties in the following areas: word reading, reading comprehension, spelling, written expression, mathematics concepts and/or calculation, and mathematics reasoning.

Diagnosis also requires performance below age expectations with associated functional impairment inception during the early school years and rule-out of

A. Difficulties learning and using academic skills, as indicated by the presence of at least one of the following symptoms that have persisted for at least 6 months, despite the provision of interventions that target those difficulties:

   1. Inaccurate or slow and effortful word reading (e.g., reads single words aloud incorrectly or slowly and hesitantly, frequently guesses words, has difficulty sounding out words).
   2. Difficulty understanding the meaning of what is read (e.g., may read text accurately but not understand the sequence, relationships, inferences, or deeper meanings of what is read)
   3. Difficulties with spelling (e.g., may add, omit, or substitute vowels or consonants)
   4. Difficulties with written expression (e.g., makes multiple grammatical or punctuation errors within sentences; employs poor paragraph organization; written expression of ideas lacks clarity).
   5. Difficulties mastering number sense, number facts, or calculation (e.g., has poor understanding of numbers, their magnitude, and relationships; counts on fingers to add single-digit numbers instead of recalling math facts as peers do; gets lost in the midst of arithmetic computation and may switch procedures).
   6. Difficulties with mathematical reasoning (e.g., has severe difficulty applying mathematical concepts, facts, or procedures to solve quantitative problems).

B. The affected academic skills are substantially and quantifiably below those expected for the individual's chronological age, and cause significant interference with academic or occupational performance, or with activities of daily living, as confirmed by individually administered standardized achievement measures and comprehensive clinical assessment. For individuals age 17 years and older, a documented history of impairing learning difficulties may be substituted for the standardized assessment.

C. The learning difficulties begin during school-age years but may not become fully manifest until the demands for those affected academic skills exceed the individual's limited capacities (e.g., as in timed tests, reading or writing lengthy complex reports for a tight deadline, excessively heavy academic loads).

Fig. 1.1 Specific learning disorder criteria as presented in the DSM-5 (*Diagnostic and Statistical Manual of Mental Disorders Fifth Edition*; APA 2013)

D. The learning difficulties are not better accounted for by intellectual disabilities, uncorrected visual or auditory acuity, other mental or neurological disorders, psychosocial adversity, lack of proficiency in the language of academic instruction, or inadequate educational instruction.

Specify if:

315.00 (F81.0) Reading

Word reading accuracy

Reading rate or fluency

Reading comprehension

315.2 (F81.81) Written expression

Spelling accuracy

Grammar and punctuation accuracy

Clarity or organization of written expression

315.1 (F81.2) Mathematics

Number sense

Memorization of arithmetic facts

Accurate or fluent calculations

Accurate math reasoning

Fig. 1.1 (continued)

exclusionary factors. Information is obtained from a combination of history, school reports, and psycoeducational assessment. Further specifiers for each of the three main academic areas are also included for actual diagnosis as well as severity specifiers.

In response to the proposed DSM-5 criteria presented in spring of 2012 (APA 2012), Fletcher et al. (2012) praised the improved alignment with IDEIA; however, they expressed concerns with the academic classes, or subtypes, of specific learning disorder included, which at that time included seven due to separate mathematics fact memory and calculation subtypes. Fletcher et al. (2007) provided an extensive review of research in support of five subgroups of LD. These include three forms of reading disabilities, namely word recognition, fluency, and comprehension; plus written expression disorders; and mathematics disabilities. While they point out that there is unclear evidence for mathematics problem solving as a disorder distinct from reading and language deficits, Fletcher et al. (2012) amend the five subtypes to six by considering mathematical calculation and mathematical problem solving separately. The authors also applaud the exclusion of oral expression and listening comprehension in DSM-5, as these do not directly involve academic achievement. This situation highlights the probability that not only do the definitions and identification methods vary, but the types of LD that are identified also depend upon the setting and diagnostic criteria.

As discussed previously, the differing identification criteria lead to a variety of difficulties regarding LD research that also impact intervention and prognosis. In addition to different decision-making rules across situations, the individuals making decisions may vary across location and setting. In many educational settings, school psychologists conduct psychoeducational assessments and share their results with teachers, parents, and administrators who decide as a team whether a child meets the criteria for LD.

These decision-making teams also consider student observations, work samples, and other classroom data with the weight given to each type of evidence depending upon the specific state, school, or team. For example, in some schools, a response to intervention procedure may be used with a review of progress monitoring data being the primary consideration to determine the presence of disability. At the same time, in private settings, clinical psychologists or other qualified clinicians may use the comparison between a child's achievement and intelligence test scores to unilaterally determine whether a child has an LD. Depending upon a school district's policy, independently obtained evaluation results and diagnoses may not be sufficient to qualify for special education services as a student with an LD.

Dissatisfaction with currently endorsed classification approaches has prompted the proposal of various identification methods since the advent of the LD category. The methods have included the standard aptitude–achievement discrepancy, cognitive processing, various intraindividual discrepancies, response to intervention, and low achievement cut scores. As discussed later, strengths and weaknesses have been pointed out and debated for each of these identification procedures. Before proceeding to these specific diagnostic methods, a review of the history of the LD field will shed some light on their origins.

Origins of LD and Early Practices

The basic concept of LD originated with early nineteenth-century European physicians. Joseph Gall is recognized as the first to study disorders that would today be considered language disorders and categorized as LD (Hammill 1993). He attributed these problems to specific areas of the brain, leading to Pierre Broca and Carl Wernicke's independent observations later in the century that expressive and receptive speech functions reside in the left frontal lobe and superior temporal gyrus, respectively (Hallahan and Mock 2003). Soon after these developments, a

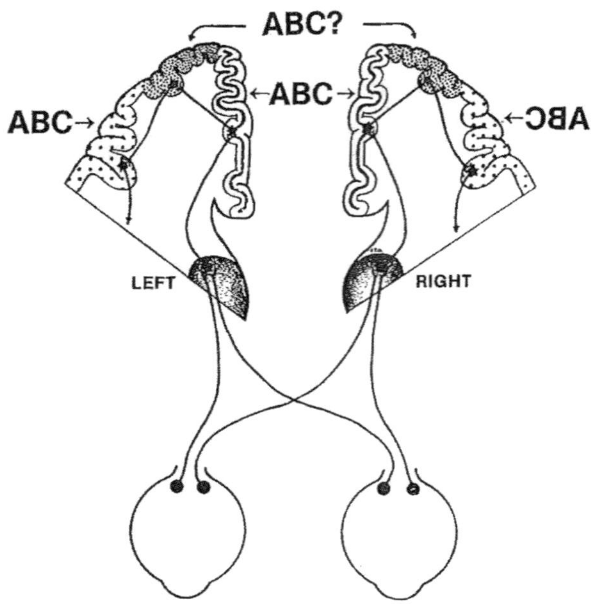

Fig. 1.2 Illustration of Orton's hypothesis that normal reading occurs by focusing attention on dominant hemisphere's correct order and overriding the nondominant hemisphere's reverse order. (Orton 1989. Copyright 1989 by The International Dyslexia Association. Reprinted with permission)

German ophthalmologist, Rudolf Berlin, introduced the term "dyslexia," which continues to be used in contemporary settings with a more neurological or medical influence. Inspired by these events, James Hinshelwood, a French physician, began to study cases of children who had difficulty acquiring reading skills, although they demonstrated average performance in other skill areas (Torgesen 1991). In 1917, he postulated that reading disability, which he called congenital word-blindness, was a heritable condition caused by faulty visual memory for words and letters that could be remediated through one-to-one training (Hallahan and Mock 2003).

An American neuropathologist, Orton (1925), expanded on Hinshelwood's work through his own observations of students referred by teachers as "defective." He found that most of these children actually functioned in the normal range of intelligence and felt they most likely had above average ability that was masked by a reading disability. He further theorized that letter and word images are stored in both hemispheres in beginning readers, with one hemisphere becoming dominant to match the customary left-to-right orientation of print. Reading disability, according to Orton, results when one hemisphere fails to become dominant, causing distraction due to the presence of mirror images in one hemisphere and leading to reversals in speech and writing (see Fig. 1.2).

Due to the presumed neurological basis for reading difficulties and his fear that word-blindness implicated an acquired disorder, Orton labeled the condition strephosymbalia to emphasize reversals of symbols. This is the likely origin of the popular conception of dyslexia as a disorder in which people read words and numbers backwards. Orton suggested a multisensory method of explicit phonics

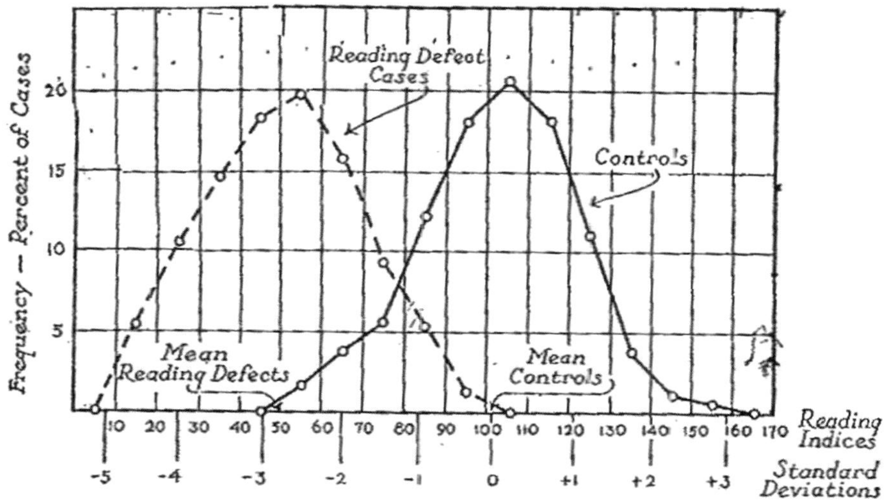

Fig. 1.3 Distributions of reading indices. (Source: Monroe 1932. Copyright 1932 by University of Chicago Press. Reprinted with permission)

and sound-blending instruction to help educators reach their struggling students (Hallahan and Mock 2003), but teachers were not receptive to brain dysfunction hypotheses (Torgesen 1991).

Orton's fellow researcher, Monroe (1932), suggested a discrepancy approach that was more acceptable to educators for determining which students had reading difficulties and would benefit from intervention. This procedure involved calculating a reading index based on the difference between actual and expected reading achievement, with actual achievement being quantified as the average of reading comprehension, word analysis, word discrimination, and word recognition score and expected achievement computed by the average of chronological age, mental age, and arithmetic grade equivalent. Figure 1.3 illustrates the distribution of reading indices for individuals with reading disabilities and those with typical reading ability. Hallahan and Mock (2003) described Monroe's approach as the earliest model for the discrepancy method in widespread use today. Kavale (2002), however, attributed the origin of discrepancy to Franzen's (1920) conception of the "Accomplishment Quotient" that was derived from the ratio of a student's age equivalent on an academic test, or "Educational Quotient," to the student's Intelligence Quotient. In other words, the Accomplishment Quotient quantified a student's actual educational progress given his or her learning potential.

The Beginning of the LD Movement

One of Monroe's colleagues, Samuel Kirk, made a lasting contribution to the study of learning difficulties by providing the foundation—a label—that would create a recognized discipline. Kirk coined the term LD, which he defined as a deficit in a school subject resulting from a psychological handicap that is not a result of mental retardation, sensory deprivation, or cultural or instructional factors. In 1963, a group of parents formed the Learning Disabilities Association of America based on Kirk's ideas (Hallahan and Mock 2003), stimulating the formation of other organizations and the beginning of the LD movement (Hammill 1993).

At this same time, the 1960s and 1970s, parents became active advocates for their children with learning difficulties, and the government began to sponsor research on LD in order to reach a definitional consensus. Medical professionals preferred the term "minimal brain dysfunction," while educators stressed on intraindividual differences and discrepancy between ability and achievement, the idea of which was reintroduced by Bateman (1965) despite being absent from Kirk's influential definition. In contrast to Franzen's (1920) and Monroe's (1932) well-defined approaches to discrepancy, Bateman did not provide a model for quantifying discrepancy. Several researchers aligned with the medical model, focusing on visual and visual–motor disabilities with laterality training as remediation rather than academic intervention (Hammill 1993). The US government, however, favored the educators' position.

With the passage of the Education for All Handicapped Children Act (EAHCA) in 1975, all disabled students, including those with LD, were guaranteed a free and appropriate public education. In 1977, the US Office of Education updated EAHCA, providing a definition of LD similar to Kirk's from the previous decade and recommending the use of a discrepancy model to determine which students were eligible for services under the LD category (Hallahan and Mock 2003). The federal regulations did not specify how a significant discrepancy should be calculated, instead leaving this decision to individual states.

Unfortunately, the discrepancy regulation led to identification problems. Without guidelines for specifying how to determine whether a discrepancy existed, different methods were being employed across states and school districts. Not only were schools identifying different numbers of children as learning disabled, but they were also identifying different children, such that a child could have LD in one district and be problem-free in another. Some schools even used grade-level discrepancy models, treating ordinal scores as interval data so that resulting calculations were meaningless and "slow learners" without actual disabilities were overidentified (Reynolds 1984).

Disagreement regarding optimal diagnostic practices in the field of LD has existed for decades. The debate has been stimulated by concerns regarding overidentification as well as misidentification of students as having LD in schools. In response to these concerns, researchers have proposed various classification techniques, each with its own strengths and weaknesses. Some of these methods suggest diagnosing LD based upon the hypothesized underlying cause of the disability, the simple evidence of underachievement relative to some standard or expectation, or the presence of a particular profile that is assumed to indicate the optimal remediation technique. Some diagnostic methods employ more than one of these principles, and certain supporters and detractors of a given diagnostic approach may differ in their claims as to the primary basis of that approach.

The argument surrounding LD diagnosis has intensified due to recent regulations allowing states and school districts to choose between the standard discrepancy model and response to intervention. The relevant literature has focused on the reliability and validity of the various proposed models, yet underlying the debate is an often unmentioned preoccupation with the classification methods' ability to capture the essence of what it is to have an LD. This complicates matters when the core of an LD is not completely agreed upon. For instance, some may feel that substantial underachievement is the defining characteristic of LD, while others may believe that it is an "unexplained" failure in a certain type of academic pursuit.

Stanovich (1999) has pointed out that the concept of "unexplained" underachievement is unfounded, since students with LD have deficits, such as poor phonological awareness, that do in fact explain their academic performance. Based on this logic, academic underachievement must be the unifying distinction in LD. Other researchers and practitioners, however, may argue that because underachievement is due to identifiable deficits, often referred to as cognitive processes, the presence of a process deficit is the unifying characteristic of LD. Many respond to this assertion with the fact that most individuals' profiles consist of significant strengths and weaknesses across areas. Thus, the debate continues and the field of LD continues its search for a diagnostic panacea.

The diagnostic confusion and resulting high identification rate are likely to continue and become more problematic given the recent changes to IDEA, or now IDEIA (Dombrowski et al. 2004). This latitude will undoubtedly result in differing diagnostic practices, prevalences, and symptom constellations across geographic locations as has been noted for decades (Shepard et al. 1983). More importantly, diagnostic confusion will threaten the viability of the very construct of LD, which would be a disservice to children and adults who genuinely have learning differences that require specialized instruction and services (Stanovich 2005).

While researchers continue to search for the gold standard of LD diagnosis, children continue to be referred to practitioners for evaluations due to learning difficulties. The question of how to best assess a child for an LD, taking into account the definition of LD and sound measurement techniques, remains Of course, the appropriate method of assessment will be determined to some extent by the practitioner's type of setting and location. Clinicians in private practice are not governed by IDEA education law, but should take this law into account in order for their findings and recommendations to be considered and implemented by schools. School psychologists and other practitioners in the public school setting must be familiar with their state's interpretation of the federal law as well as their district's implementation of the state interpretation. It is up to the individual practitioner to conduct the best assessment possible within those guidelines.

This book proposes to assist professionals conducting LD assessments for school-age populations by introducing various popular methods of evaluation and identification. Chapters 2–5 each describe a different diagnostic approach and its associated strengths and weaknesses as well as providing a case example. The approaches include the aptitude–achievement discrepancy model, cognitive processing, response to intervention, and low achievement. Chapter 6 attempts to integrate the research and practice presented in the previous chapters with original research conducted by the author to propose best practice in LD identification. The final chapter, Chap. 7, discusses commonly comorbid disorders and differential diagnosis.

Summary of Key Points

- A significant proportion of American school children are diagnosed with an LD due to various factors influencing the accuracy of identification.
- Classification of LD is important because it allows for a common definition for accurate diagnosis for communication, intervention planning, and research.
- The federal definition of LD has remained unchanged since its conception with the NJCLD offering an alternate definition highlighting the lifelong nature of LD.
- The 2004 reauthorization of IDEA allows for states and schools to choose between use of ability–achievement discrepancy, response to intervention, or other research-based methods to identify LD in one or more of the eight following areas: oral expression, listening comprehension, written expression, basic reading skills, reading comprehension, mathematics calculation, and mathematics reasoning.
- The DSM-IV (APA 2000) continues to use discrepancy criteria for LD diagnosis with the differing definitions between organizations resulting in differing diagnostic approaches across settings.
- The DSM-5 (APA 2013) integrates a variety of information, including the individual's history, school performance, and psychoeducational assessment to determine whether the individual is underachieving in comparison to same-age peers along with exclusionary criteria.
- The concept of conditions similar to those currently known as LD dates back to nineteenth-century European physicians' work, such as Gall, Berlin, Broca, and Wernicke, then progressed to the work of Orton and Monroe in the early twentieth-century USA.
- The LD movement began in the 1960s based on Kirk's LD work, and the EAHCA incorporated his definition in 1977 and recommended the use of an ability–achievement discrepancy formula to identify LD.
- Disagreement regarding varying identification methods for LD began with the discrepancy formula and continues till date.

Questions and Answers with the Expert: Joseph K. Torgesen

Meet the expert: Joseph K. Torgesen, PhD, is currently appointed as the W. Russell and Eugenia Morcom Chair of Psychology and Education at Florida State University and serves as the director emeritus of the Florida Center for Reading Research. He is well known for his research with children who have learning problems and is the author of many articles, book chapters, books, and tests related to reading and learning disabilities. He has served on the editorial boards of professional research journals, participated in the efforts of the National Institute of Child Health and Human Development related to reading problems and remediation, and currently serves on the Board of Directors of the National Institute for Education Sciences. His current interests include the psychology of reading and prevention of reading disabilities, cognitive characteristics of children with learning disabilities, assessment practices with children, and computer-assisted instruction in basic academic skills. For more information, go to http://www.psy.fsu.edu/faculty/torgesen.dp.html.

Question 1 Who do you believe was most influential in establishing LD disability diagnostic practices?

Answer 1 A number of individuals have played an important role in establishing current LD diagnostic practices. The early work of Heinz Werner and Alfred Strauss at the Wayne County Boy's Training School laid the foundation for explanations of academic learning difficulties in terms of deficient or underdeveloped psychological processes, and they also pioneered the idea that significant intraindividual differences in processing strengths and weaknesses could lead to specific learning difficulties. So, their work was important in laying the foundations for current diagnostic practices. Other individuals who elaborated on these ideas in important ways were Newell Kephart and Helmer Mykelbust. The work of Samual Kirk, in particular his work on the assessment of intraindividual differences in psycho-linguistic abilities, was also extremely important in laying the foundations of current diagnostic practices that involve a search for patterns of intraindividual differences in cognitive abilities.

Finally, the committees involved in developing federal regulations in the area of LD had the most direct influence in determining current practices. Their discussions acknowledged that there was insufficient agreement and evidence about the utility of assessing psychological processes (the work of Donald Hammill is important here) as a required part of the diagnosis of disabilities, and they settled essentially on the idea that one important sign of LD was a significant discrepancy between broad intellectual potential or capacity (intelligence quotient (IQ)) and actual achievement in reading, mathematics, etc.

The work of Jack Fletcher has been particularly important in helping to move the field beyond discrepancy-based approaches to methods involving analysis of the child's response to instruction (RTI).

Question 2 What misconception(s) regarding LD have originated from the field's history?

Answer 2 Perhaps the most important misconception is that a discrepancy between broad intelligence (as determined by an IQ test) and academic achievement is a primary sign of LD. This discrepancy-based approach was arrived at because understanding of the specific cognitive limitations responsible for LD was very limited at the time it was established. For example, advances in research over the past 25 years have established that the primary cause of most early reading difficulties involves a disability or weakness in the phonological component of language. This disability makes it more difficult to understand the alphabetic principal or to acquire the phonological decoding skills that are necessary for the normal development of reading accuracy and fluency. Students with either high or low general verbal abilities, or verbal intelligence, can have phonological disabilities. Under current regulations, only students with relatively higher broad verbal ability qualify for LD services, in spite of the fact that all students with severe phonological disabilities (without regard to general IQ) require essentially the same kind of intensive, explicit, and systematic instruction in order to master early reading skills.

Another important misconception that arose from some of the early foundational work was that instruction and practice devoted to improving basic learning processes would be helpful to students with LD. As we now know, the most helpful instruction for these students involves intensive, systematic, and explicit direct instruction in academic skills. The one current exception to this rule may be instruction in phonemic awareness as an oral language skill in preparation for, or during, reading instruction. Even in this case, though, instruction in phonemic awareness should be closely integrated with phonics instruction in order to help students directly apply what they are learning to decoding words in print.

Question 3 What practices have you seen in LD definition and diagnosis?

Answer 3 During course of my career in the study of learning disabilities, which began in about 1974, I have seen many practices come and go. In my early years as a graduate student at the University of Michigan, I was aware of classes for learning disabled students that still focused on training in "perceptual-motor skills" in order to improve the learning ability of these students. We also spent considerable time assessing "psycho-linguistic" abilities that were only loosely linked to academic achievement. I wrote an early paper called "What shall we do with Psychological Processes?" in which I used research from developmental psychology to show that training in psychological processes that were not directly part of academic tasks was not likely to be effective. Rather, what we needed was a better understanding of the academic tasks (such as reading and mathematics) themselves so we could develop a more explicit sequence of instruction for students who struggled to learn in these areas.

I have also seen an overreliance on discrepancy-based diagnostic procedures to the exclusion of clinical judgment. In connection with this diagnostic approach, I have observed school psychologists give one test after another until they achieved the "discrepancy" or "pattern of intraindividual differences" required to qualify a student for LD services.

Although any diagnostic procedure is subject to distortion and misapplication at the local level, I am hopeful that approaches that diagnose the need for LD services on the basis of response to instruction may be useful because they involve the direct assessment of progress in acquiring important academic skills. Although this approach has its own set of challenges (what is adequate progress? When should instruction be changed?), its primary focus is on finding instruction that works for individual students, which is the right focus.

Question 4 What do you consider best practice for LD identification?

Answer 4 At the moment, I consider that an approach involving careful analysis and documentation of a child's response to well-specified instruction or intervention, coupled with clinical analysis of the child's history and assessment of other language and cognitive skills, to be the best, and most scientifically defensible approach to the diagnosis of LD. The diagnosis should not be made on the basis of any single score or piece of information, but rather should be based on clinical judgment by experienced professionals who consider a variety of information about the child.

Question 5 What do you see in the future for the identification of LD and the LD disabilities field in general?

Answer 5 As we come to understand more about the precursors and early signs of learning difficulty, I am hoping that we can learn to make accurate judgments earlier about the *level* of intervention that might be required for individual children to prevent them from falling behind in early academic development. If we wait for a child to "fail" at several different levels of intervention before we provide the kind of instruction that is actually required in order to maintain adequate progress in school, we will have missed many of the advantages of prevention over remediation. I am hoping that current work in both neurobiology and psychology will allow us to develop more accurate early assessment practices that can lead to powerful interventions in preschool or kindergarten.

As a general development for the field, I would hope that we can convince schools and school districts that LD are real, and that many children with this disability require much more intensive and skillful interventions early in their academic career than they are currently receiving. This, of course, is not a problem that's limited to the school level. Schools must have additional resources, primarily in the form of greater numbers of highly skilled intervention specialists, if they are to provide the type of powerful instruction that many students with LD need in order to acquire foundational academic skills in elementary school. I would also hope that we can develop a better understanding of the types of additional supports that students with LD may need as they move into more complex middle and high school settings. I would urge the field to focus on prevention of early academic deficits in foundational skills, and then to provide the kinds of additional supports that some LD students may need as they encounter increasingly complex academic challenges after elementary school.

I agree with Torgesen, but how can we get to a point of successful integration of diagnostic methods when a beruacratic system pushes back against progress?

rhetorical Appeal to time

Chapter 2
Aptitude–Achievement Discrepancy

The aptitude–achievement discrepancy approach to learning disabilities (LDs) diagnosis is likely the most well known and most controversial identification method. This is due to many factors, including its historical connection to the original definition of LDs, its apparent simple elegance in describing and identifying individuals with LDs, and the underlying technical difficulties underlying its surface simplicity. Since its inception as a recognized exceptionality, the LD field has proven to be remarkably resistant to change (Stanovich 2005) with the discrepancy formula being just one instance of this invariability.

Origin of Discrepancy Criteria

The currently employed diagnostic criteria remain very similar to Kirk's 1963 definition focusing on exclusions and Bateman's discrepancy (Dombrowski et al. 2004), with changes reflected in the Individuals with Disabilities Education Improvement Act (IDEIA) diagnostic regulations threatening to leave the LD field without the consistent and uniform diagnostic approach it has been in need of for over 30 years. As defined by Kirk, an LD continues to be defined as "a disorder in one or more of the basic psychological processes involved in understanding or using language, spoken or written, which may manifest itself in an imperfect ability to listen, think, speak, read, write, spell, or do mathematical calculations." The term does not include "a learning problem that is primarily the result of visual, hearing, or motor disabilities, of mental retardation, of emotional disturbance, or of environmental, cultural, or economic disadvantage (Individuals with Disabilities Education Act Amendments of 1997, Sect. 602 (26), p. 13). According to the new regulations, a state may not require the use of a discrepancy formula, although schools may still use it, and must permit the use of a process that determines if the child responds to scientific, research-based intervention as part of the evaluation procedures or the use of other alternative research-based procedures for determining whether a child has an LD (IDEA 2004).

The concept of severe discrepancy spread as a result of attempts to operationalize LDs when the construct was introduced into law with the Education for All

A. E. B. Taylor, *Diagnostic Assessment of Learning Disabilities in Childhood*, Contemporary Issues in Psychological Assessment, DOI 10.1007/978-1-4939-0335-1_2,

© Springer Science+Business Media New York 2014

Handicapped Children Act (PL 94–142). According to Reynolds (2003), the only consensus to be found regarding LD in the documents and debates when the education law was originally developed was that it was characterized by a discrepancy between expected academic achievement and actual achievement. Several formulas were developed to determining discrepancy, but they used age and grade equivalents and treated them as if they were interval- and even ratio-scale data. Hence, the formulas were mathematically incorrect.

Discrepancy Within Identification Criteria

Despite the apparent simplicity and clarity of a discrepancy definition of LD, development of an accurate discrepancy formula is more difficult than it appears on the surface. For instance, quantifying severe discrepancy using the standard deviation between intelligence quotient (IQ) and achievement seems to make sense, but because the two scores are positively correlated the new distribution of scores results in a smaller standard deviation, thus identifying fewer children than would be expected. Additionally, it is necessary to take into account regression to the mean when using multiple scores in decision-making models.

The difficulty in developing an appropriate formula has led to different states and agencies using different methods of determining what constitutes a significant discrepancy. As noted above, the definition of LDs has remained the same since they were first described in federal law. This means that the exclusionary criteria, psychological processes, and failure to achieve also remain factors in determining whether a student has an LD in addition to determining whether that student exhibits a discrepancy between achievement and aptitude. Exclusionary criteria include visual, hearing, or motor disabilities, mental retardation, emotional disturbance, and environmental, cultural, or economic disadvantage.

How each state and school district interprets and incorporates all the various definitional factors into LDs identification varies, as do the discrepancy formulas, making a concise description of the actual practice of discrepancy assessment difficult. This lack of uniformity has also led to a lack of reliability in terms of who is diagnosed as having an LD across locations, which is one of the criticisms of the discrepancy model of LD diagnosis. Given the many variations of discrepancy criteria, not all of the possible combinations used for identification can be presented here. Instead, various widely used discrepancy formulas will be described.

Calculating Severe Discrepancy

Simple Standard Score Discrepancy

Discrepancy formulas typically utilize standard score differences. In a simple standard score model, a child is considered to exhibit a significant discrepancy when

Table 2.1 Reynolds' (2003) example of discrepancy calculation

Step 1: Test for reliable difference between ability and achievement scores	$z = \frac{X_i - Y_i}{\sqrt{2 - r_{xx} - r_{yy}}}$ If $z > 1.65$, the discrepancy is reliable
Step 2: Choose value for severity and correct for unreliability	$s = z_a - SE_{\wedge y - yi}$
Step 3: Calculate severe discrepancy	
Simple difference model	$SD_{xy} z_a \left(\sqrt{2 - 2r_{xy}}\right)$
Regression model	$\wedge Y - Y_i > SD_y z_a \left(\sqrt{1 - r_{xy}^{\ 2}}\right)$

X_i = child's intelligence score, Y_i = child's achievement score, z_a = point on normal curve representing frequency for severe discrepancy, r_{xx} = internal-consistency reliability for intelligence test, r_{yy} = internal-consistency reliability for achievement test, $\wedge Y$ = mean achievement score for all children with IQ = X_i, SD_{xy} = standard deviation of intelligence and achievement scales, SD_y = standard deviation of Y formulas for classification provided tables, rxy = correlation between achievement and intelligence tests

her intelligence standard score is higher than her achievement standard score by a predetermined number of standard score points (with both measurements on the same scale). The standard score points criteria is usually chosen by calculating the percentage of children in the population expected to have a discrepancy of that magnitude. The discrepancy score representing the percentage of the population expected to have an LD can then be selected. This sounds simple, but as with any method of identifying LDs, there is no agreed-upon standard for how many individuals should be considered to have an LD. Once this percentage is agreed upon, reliability must also be taken into account as well as preference for under- versus over-identification, but further discussion of the mathematical issues is beyond the scope of this text. See Table 2.1 for an illustration of the formulas used to calculate discrepancy.

In practice, a simple difference discrepancy model typically specifies only the standard score difference required between an intelligence score and an achievement score. For example, in Georgia, a difference of 20 standard score points between performance on a cognitive measure and achievement measure is required for a child to initially be identified as having an LD. This type of approach does not take into account the correlation between the two instruments.

As mentioned previously, the main difficulty associated with a simple difference discrepancy model is that it does not account for regression effects when comparing achievement and intelligence scores. Given the positive correlation between the two constructs, this model will, therefore, overidentify individuals with above-average IQs and underidentify individuals with below-average IQs as having LDs.

Regression Models of Discrepancy

In order to overcome the problems associated with a simple difference model, regression models of discrepancy have been used. In addition to the obvious advantage of taking regression effects into account, other advantages include determining whether discrepancies are reliable or are the result of chance, accounting for the correlation between the achievement and intelligence tests, and considering measurement error. Unfortunately, regression discrepancy formulas require choosing the severity level considered to indicate the presence of LDs, allowing variability in who is identified as having an LD. This also complicates research using a discrepancy method since an actual prevalence rate for LDs has been unable to be established.

While there are equations for determining the average achievement score associated with a certain IQ score based upon the correlation, in the majority of states that use, or used, regression, the procedure (Table 2.1) described by Reynolds (2003) involves converting all scores to a standard z-score metric. The first step, whether using a simple difference or regression discrepancy model, is to test for significance between the obtained achievement and intelligence scores. When $p=0.05$, the critical value of $z=1.65$. Next, one must determine the frequency of the discrepancy score that is necessary to be severe. This value depends upon preference for minimizing false negatives versus minimizing false positives. Reynolds (2003) recommends using a z value of 2 to represent a severe discrepancy because of the precedent of using 2 standard deviations and.05 confidence levels in other areas of diagnosis and research. The value chosen to represent severity should then be corrected for unreliability, although this is not always done. For a simple difference model, the standard deviation of the achievement and intelligence scales and the correlation between the scales can be entered into the formula to determine the percentage of the population with a discrepancy considered to be severe. For a regression model, the mean achievement score of all children with a given IQ, the standard deviation of the child's achievement score, and the squared correlation between the achievement and intelligence tests are entered into the formula to determine a severe discrepancy.

For example, Washington state regulations (WAC-392-172-130) developed a table based upon the regressed standard score discrepancy with a criterion level of 1.55 standard deviations. In order to use the example table (Table 2.2), the student's overall intellectual standard score is obtained. Next, the age-based achievement standard score is determined. The student's overall intelligence score is located in the left-hand column of the chart and the criterion discrepancy, or cutoff, score is found. The student's achievement score is compared to this criterion. If the achievement score is equal to or less than the criterion score, a severe discrepancy is considered to be present. In order to obtain accurate estimates, however, the correlation between the specific IQ and achievement tests used must be known. Some states developed broader guidelines and explicitly included consideration of test intercorrelations. For an example, see Table 2.3, which is similar to a version previously used in Maryland. There is also an online tool, Test Score Discrepancy Analyzer 2.0 (TSA2) (available at http://www.interventioncentral.org/tools.php),developed by the Syracuse, New York school district to calculate discrepancies. The New Jersey Department of Education developed a similar program called ESTIMATOR-NJ.

Table 2.2 Criterion discrepancy scores (1.55 standard deviations) table for ages 6–21 years

Overall IQ	Criterion score	Overall IQ	Criterion score
69	62	97	80
70	62	98	81
71	63	99	82
72	64	100	82
73	65	101	83
74	65	102	84
75	66	103	84
76	67	104	85
77	67	105	86
78	68	106	86
79	69	107	87
80	69	108	88
81	70	109	88
82	71	110	89
83	71	111	89
84	72	112	90
85	73	113	91
86	74	114	91
87	74	115	92
88	75	116	93
89	75	117	93
90	76	118	94
91	76	119	95
92	77	120	95
93	78	121	96
94	78	122	97
95	79	123	97
96	80	124	98
		125	99

Table 2.3 Guidelines for comparing expected achievement with actual achievement

IQ score range	Expected achievement range	Discrepancy range
130–139	118–123	95–100
120–129	112–117	89–94
110–119	107–111	83–88
100–109	100–106	77–82
90–99	94–99	71–76
80–89	88–93	65–70
70–79	82–87	59–64

Psychometric Considerations

When making any diagnostic decisions utilizing test data, it is crucial to use quality data, and making decisions using the discrepancy model is no exception. If instruments used have poor technical and/or psychometric properties, the result of the discrepancy method employed will be flawed and meaningless. Reynolds (2003, pp. 487–494) provides the following useful guidelines for test selection:

1. *A test should meet all requirements stated for assessment devices in the rules and regulations for implementing IDEA* (p. 487).
2. *Normative data should meet contemporary standards of practice and should be provided for a sufficiently large, nationally stratified random sample of children.*
    a. *The psychological trait being assessed must be amenable to at least ordinal scaling.*
    b. *The test must provide an adequate operational definition of the trait under consideration.*
    c. *The test should assess the same psychological construct throughout the entire range of performance.*
    d. *The normative reference group should consist of a large random sample that is representative of the population to whom the test will be administered or performance compared.*
    e. *The sample of examinees from the population should have been tested using standard conditions.*
    f. *The population sampled must be relevant to the test and to the purpose for which the test is to be employed.*
    g. *Normative data should be provided for as many different groups as may be useful for comparisons of an individual (pp. 488–489).*
3. *Standardization samples for tests whose scores are being compared must be the same or highly comparable (pp. 490).*
4. *For diagnostic purposes, individually administered tests should be used (pp. 490).*
5. *In the measurement of aptitude, an individually administered test of general intellectual ability should be used (pp. 490).*
6. *Age-based standard scores should be used for all measures, and all should be scaled to a common metric (pp. 490).*
7. *The measures employed should demonstrate a high level of reliability, which should be documented in the technical manual accompanying the test (pp. 493).*
8. *The validity coefficient* r_{xy}, *which represents the relationship between the measures of aptitude and achievement, should be based upon an appropriate sample (pp. 494).*
9. *The validity of test score interpretation should be clearly established (pp. 494).*
10. *Special technical considerations should be addressed when one uses performance-based measures of achievement (e.g., writing skill) (pp. 494).*
11. *Bias studies on the instruments in use should be reported (pp. 494).*

Several of the psychometric issues addressed by Reynolds (2003) are particularly important when using the discrepancy model of LD diagnosis because results from two instruments are being compared. The guidelines regarding appropriate normative samples are especially relevant. It would be ideal for the intelligence and achievement tests to have been conormed, meaning that they were standardized using exactly the same children. Table 2.4 provides examples of some conormed

Table 2.4 Conormed intelligence and achievement tests

Intelligence instrument	Conormed achievement instrument
Wechsler Intelligence Scale for Children, Fourth Edition (WISC-IV; Wechsler 2003)	Wechsler Individual Achievement Test, Second Edition (WIAT-II; The Psychological Corporation 2001)
Kaufman Assessment Battery for Children, Second Edition (KABC-II; Kaufman and Kaufman 2004)	Kaufman Tests of Educational Achievement, Second Edition (KTEA-II; Kaufman and Kaufman 2004)
Woodcock–Johnson III Tests of Cognitive Abilities (WJ-III COG; Woodcock et al. 2001)	Woodcock–Johnson III Tests of Achievement (WJ-III ACH; Woodcock et al. 2001)
Wide Range Intelligence Test (WRIT; Glutting et al. 2000)	Wide Range Achievement Test 3 (WRAT3; Wilkinson 1993)

intelligence and achievement measures. When conormed tests are not available, it is important to ensure that standardization of the measures used took place within the same time period across age and grade levels, since the correlations may change as a function of development, and achievement domains, since correlations may differ across academic areas. If an achievement scale is used that has a very different normative sample from the intelligence scale that is being used, the resulting discrepancy, or lack of discrepancy, may be attributable to the time period or characteristics of the sample when the tests were normed.

Dissatisfaction with Discrepancy

Several researchers have pointed out problems with the discrepancy approach and called for new diagnostic methods (Francis et al. 2005; Shepard et al. 1983; Siegel 2003; Stanovich 2005). Some of the most widely cited shortcomings of the discrepancy model are its lack of reliability and validity, lack of relevance to treatment, and inability to identify children in need of remediation versus those who are not. Each of these issues will be discussed below.

Intelligence as a Controversial Concept

Before considering discrepancy, the use of IQ itself is controversial. What is intelligence? According to the *Oxford English Dictionary*, intelligence is the ability to acquire and apply knowledge and skills. The construct of intelligence became integral to the conceptualization and identification of LDs because of its ability to serve as a comparison in determining unexpected underachievement. Linda Siegel (1989) identified four basic assumptions inherent in intelligence–achievement discrepancy.

First, IQ tests measure intelligence. Second, intelligence can be measured independently of academic achievement. Third, there is a strong correlation between reading and IQ and, fourth, cognitive processes differ between individuals with LD who have low versus those who have high IQ scores. As can be seen from the discussion below, these assumptions factor into several related and unrelated criticisms of the use of intelligence in identifying students as having LDs.

Effect of LDs on Intelligence Test Performance

Siegel (1989) argues that tasks found on intelligence tests will be more difficult for children with LDs. For example, if a child has a reading disability, that child will have had less exposure to print material and verbal information and will perform poorly on verbal reasoning tests such as those measuring vocabulary. Similarly, a child with a mathematics disability will have difficulty completing tasks requiring visual–spatial skills. Thus, these children's scores on IQ tests measure aspects of their disability and not pure reasoning ability, or intelligence.

The Matthew Effect

A related criticism has been referred to as the Matthew effect (Stanovich 1986). The Matthew effect describes the process whereby strong readers gain more knowledge and vocabulary through access to text allowing them to perform better on reading and cognitive tasks. Poor readers do not have access to more information and fall farther behind peers in reading skills, vocabulary, and knowledge, leading to further declines in reading as well as in cognitive abilities. Thus, poor readers' intelligence scores will be lower as a result of poor reading ability and their similarly poor performance on achievement and intelligence tasks will make them less likely to exhibit the required discrepancy (Dombrowski et al. 2004).

Global IQ May be Less Meaningful for Individuals with LD

Some critics argue that global IQ should not be used because the deficits that characterize LDs lead to a different factor structure than that derived for the general population (Hale et al. 2007). Thus, this group would suggest interpreting intelligence tests at the factor level, which leads to further contention because this would result in clinicians using different factors within a discrepancy level resulting in great diagnostic variability. Hale and colleagues (2007) argue that subtest and factor scores account for more achievement variance than full-scale IQ, making them preferable when interpreting intelligence test results. They go onto describe full-scale IQ as meaningless because it represents the average of many different cognitive functions. They suggest interpretation of global intelligence is only justified when results are consistent across cognitive domains.

One must be cautious when interpreting the above recommendations. Psychometrically sound interpretation of test results requires making inferences from the most reliable and valid scores obtained. In general, this means interpreting overall composite scores due to their greater reliability due to a larger sample of behavior and greater evidence of validity from numerous research studies. Kamphaus (2001, p. 476) cautions that "a clinical diagnosis should never be made solely on the basis of a subtest profile." Many practitioners are hesitant to interpret a global composite score when significant scatter exists among factor scores. All evidence should be considered in every case before drawing conclusions and there may be instances when a global score is not the best description of an individual's performance. Some researchers (Watkins et al. 2007), however, have determined that full-scale IQ remains a strong predictor of achievement in both general and clinical samples despite factor variability.

Variability in Identification

The debate regarding the appropriate intelligence score to be used highlights yet another difficulty inherent in the discrepancy approach. Should a practitioner use the full-scale, composite scores, or other factor scores when calculating the discrepancy between intelligence and achievement? As discussed above, different individuals have varying opinions on this topic. Generally, states provide guidelines for when it is acceptable to use a score other than the full-scale intelligence score. State departments of education, however, tend to have different interpretations of special education law, so that recommendations across states likely vary just as the actual implementation of recommendations by professionals is likely to vary. Just as using different discrepancy models causes different students to be identified as having an LD across locations, using different scores within the same discrepancy model also results in different students being identified. It should be noted that significant variability across states also exists for many other disability categories, indicating that it is not only an issue for LD identification and may be more related to fidelity of implementation than the actual model of identification used (McKenzie 2009).

IQ Does Not Equal Potential

The use of intelligence in a discrepancy approach assumes that IQ measures "potential" that is unaffected by other skill areas—high IQ should equal high reading ability and low IQ should equal low reading ability (Siegel 1992). Some critics of this assumption still support a discrepancy definition, but suggest using chronological age to determine expected reading level. Children with low IQs and consistently low reading that is below expectation for age are then considered to be "garden variety" poor readers, while children with high IQs and unexpectedly low reading ability are termed "dyslexic."

Garden Variety Poor Readers vs. Reader with Dyslexia

Keith Stanovich (2001) summarized the two main experimental methods for determining whether the distinction between dyslexia and poor reading ability is valid. The first method is to compare children with dyslexia to younger children without dyslexia matched on reading level. If their reading skills profile is found to be similar, then the differentiation between unexpected poor readers and expected poor readers would not be valid. The second method is to compare dyslexic children to same-age children reading at the same level, which is consistent with expectation given their IQ. Again, if the reading skills of the two groups match, then it would not make sense to assume different underlying causes for their reading difficulty. Unfortunately, the definition of reading level in such studies has been unclear and/or has differed across studies. The mixed results of the various studies have not been enough to answer this question satisfactorily, although Stanovich (2001) integrated his own research to develop the "Phonological-Core Variable-Difference Model." This framework suggests that the underlying cause of reading disability is poor phonological ability, regardless of IQ, and that low-IQ poor readers simply do not have the compensatory mechanisms of high-IQ poor readers.

Intelligence Does Not Predict Reading Ability

Later studies using more clearly defined criteria have determined that more similarities than differences have been found between IQ-discrepant poor readers and low reading achievement test score poor readers (Shaywitz et al. 1992), suggesting that discrepancy is not a valid indicator of learning (e.g., reading) disability. Further, it has been indicated that skills for which differences have been found between individuals considered to have dyslexia and those considered to be typical poor readers are less related to the key processes involved in reading than to skills for which no differences have been identified (Siegel 1992). Perhaps more importantly, it has been shown that both poor readers and strong readers exist throughout the intelligence continuum, such that an individual with a very high IQ and an individual with a below-average IQ may both be average readers.

"Wait to Fail" Model

The discrepancy approach has also been accused of delaying children's access to remediation, leading to its alias—the "wait to fail" model (Stuebing et al. 2002). This is because a child is often not referred for intervention until his or her achievement scores are low enough to evidence a discrepancy from teacher expectations of performance for that child. While a teacher may begin to notice that a child is not performing commensurate with expectations based upon comparison to peers or achievement in another academic area, a young child will likely fail to be identified as having an LD through the discrepancy approach. As a result, the child may not receive access to interventions available outside the classroom. This delay results because children's achievement scores do not begin to decline until the content of achievement tests becomes increasingly complex and abstract, which generally begins to occur around the third grade (Dombrowski et al. 2004).

Intelligence Does Not Guide Treatment

It also fails to provide relevant treatment information because IQ and reading ability are not linearly related, meaning that low- and high-IQ readers do not require different forms of remediation (Vellutino et al. 1996). More information regarding global intelligence is necessary to make classification and intervention decisions (Hale et al. 2007).

In Defense of Intelligence

Other researchers, while not necessarily supporting the discrepancy method, have argued that intelligence is an important part of LDs assessment. For some, intelligence is necessary to identify intraindividal profiles of strengths and weaknesses (e.g., Mather and Gregg 2006). This approach will be discussed further in the chapter addressing cognitive processing assessment. For others, IQ represents a predictor of response to intervention. A review of existing studies was carried out to indicate that IQ influences the effectiveness of reading instruction (Fuchs and Young 2006). This was primarily true in studies of comprehensive reading interventions utilizing intelligence tests with well-established reliability and validity and more complex reading achievement measures, such as reading comprehension, for children in grades two and above. Hence, an aptitude–treatment interaction was suggested in which intelligence is more likely to impact responsiveness to a multicomponent reading intervention than to a strictly phonological intervention. The authors, however, were careful to note the inconsistencies and difficulties in the history of aptitude–treatment interaction research.

In spite of all the criticisms regarding the use of IQ for diagnosing LDs, the reader should not take away the idea that the general intelligence, or Spearman's *g*, is a meaningless concept. Countless studies have shown that global intelligence is an important predictor of many outcomes, such as achieved socioeconomic status, creativity, crime delinquency, mate selection, health risk behavior, quality of life and longevity, educational–vocational choice, and positive psychological adjustment. According to Lubinski (2004, p. 100), "*g* is clearly the most important dimension of individual differences in the study of cognitive abilities to date." Studies conducted using different statistical methodologies (e.g., Dana and Dawes 2007) determined that based on their calculations, the full-scale IQ factor structure for groups with disabilities, including LDs, does not differ from the factor structure for the general population. Perhaps more importantly, it is unwise to discount global intelligence simply because it is a psychological construct rather than an objective entity. One must keep in mind the fact that many psychological and even medical phenomena of interest are not tangible, but are still considered to exist and are given great importance.

Gifted Individuals with LD

Gifted LD is a label applied to individuals who are believed to be capable of high performance, but do not achieve to expectations in a certain area. Given this conception of gifted LD, the discrepancy approach is typically used in identification. Even when the discrepancy approach is not explicitly espoused when discussing gifted LD, the constructs involved require some comparison and reference to high intelligence. An IQ score is obtained and considered a measure of the child's potential. When a child does not meet that potential, i.e., a discrepancy exists between aptitude and achievement, in a given academic subject, they are considered to have a specific LD. Whether formally calculated or not, a discrepancy comparison is conducted when making this judgment.

One can imagine that when combining two groups, such as those considered to have a gifted level of ability and those considered to have an LD, the result can be rather confusing. The ambiguity of LD definitions has been discussed previously. To further complicate matters, the definition of giftedness has not been agreed upon either. Giftedness has been defined as high general intelligence, high ability in a specific academic area, talent in one of multiple intelligences, and above average aptitude in any human endeavor. Of course, conceptualizations of giftedness that depend upon IQ are fraught with issues similar to those of using IQ in LD diagnosis. Brody and Mills (1997) pointed out that while definitional agreement has not been reached, federal definitions of giftedness do not prevent identifying children as having dual exceptionalities of giftedness and LDs, because the definitions do not require that a child be gifted in all areas, do not set lower limits of ability in other areas, and state that a child can be gifted even if they are not performing at a high level. Based on this, it follows that it is possible for a gifted child to also have a disability. Even Lewis Terman (1931), often considered the father of the study of intellectual giftedness, stated that "superiority of one kind does not *necessarily* imply superiority in everything" (p. 568).

It is not uncommon for gifted students who achieve only in the average range in one academic area to be identified as having an LD. While proponents of gifted LD recognize the inherent drawbacks of using an intelligence–achievement discrepancy to identify LD, they tend to cling to it as the only way to identify such dually exceptional students. If the discrepancy model is agreed to be inappropriate for average and below-average achievers, then it must not continue to be applied to gifted individuals. Kavale (2005) points out that discrepancy indicates only the possibility of a disability. In line with this, the gifted LD camp does also often recommend assessing cognitive processing, which will be discussed in more detail in the next chapter. Reluctance to part with the notion of gifted LD stems in part from the idea of an "unexpected" academic failure. As noted above, however, research has shown that, in reading, an idea of some type of unexplained reading failure being different from reading failure with an explanation is simply "folk psychology" (Stanovich 1999).

As stated previously, there is great variability in the students who are identified because different discrepancy methods are used. For instance, it is not stated whether clinicians should use full-scale scores, verbal composites, or processing composites and it is possible to compare any of these scores to several achievement composites or subtests.

Another Type of Discrepancy

Some have proposed an alternative to the discrepancy model that uses only achievement data to determine if a child's low reading achievement is indicative of a disability (Aaron et al. 2008; Joshi 2003). The Component Model of Reading and its associated identification process is based upon Gough and Tunmer's (1986) assertion that reading consists of the abilities to decode words and comprehend text. They represented their view with the formula: $R = D \times L$. R represents reading comprehension, D represents decoding, and L represents linguistic comprehension, which is typically assessed through a test of listening comprehension.

In this model, listening comprehension basically replaces IQ in the typical discrepancy approach. Listening comprehension is considered superior to IQ because it is a key part of linguistics, listening comprehension is a good predictor of reading comprehension, tests of listening comprehension are easy to administer and do not require intensive training as do IQ tests, and findings based on listening comprehension inform intervention (Joshi 2003).

In order to use the Component Model for diagnosis, an achievement profile consisting of listening comprehension, reading comprehension, and decoding must be obtained. If a child's listening comprehension is within the average range or above, but reading comprehension is significantly lower, the reading difficulty is attributed to a word recognition, or sight word decoding, deficiency. If a child's word recognition score is in the average range or above, but the listening and reading comprehension scores are significantly below the word recognition ability, the child is considered to have a deficit in comprehension.

Once the area of deficit has been identified, intervention is developed to specifically address that area. This ability to design interventions targeting the deficient component in the reading equation is considered the primary advantage of this approach to identifying LDs. It is assumed that within the IQ-achievement discrepancy model, assessment ceases once a discrepancy in any area has been identified without concern for determining the key deficit in order to inform remediation strategies. A research study showed that training in the specific area of deficit was more effective than undifferentiated instruction for individuals with identified deficits in each of the reading components (Aaron et al. 2008). The issue of whether targeted instruction provided after identifying deficits through another assessment model would be equally effective was not addressed, but logic would lead one to assume that other assessment methods may yield equally informative information for intervention implementation. Indeed, in the following chapter we will learn about the cognitive processing model of assessment, which some may argue is ideal for discovering the best interventions and accommodations for a particular individual with an LD.

Below are two sample written reports. The first presents an initial evaluation while the second presents a reevaluation. The first uses the Wechsler Intelligence Scale for Children, Fourth Edition (WISC-IV; Wechsler 2003) and the conormed Wechsler Individual Achievement Test, Second Edition (WIAT-II; The Psychological Corporation 2001) as part of a clinic-based evaluation conducted in accordance with the Diagnostic and Statistical Manual of Mental Disorders, Fourth Edition (DSM-IV) (APA 2000). The second sample report uses the Reynolds Intellectual

Assessment Scale (RIAS; Reynolds and Kamphaus 2003) and WIAT-II (The Psychological Corporation 2001), which were both normed during approximately the same time period.

Case Examples

Union Educational Psychology Clinic

Psychoeducational Evaluation

Confidential

Name: Tess Howard
School: Union Middle School
Gender: Female
Age: 11 years, 1 month
Grade: 6th

Assessment Instruments

Intellectual Functioning
Wechsler Intelligence Scale for Children, Fourth Edition (WISC-IV)

Achievement
Wechsler Individual Achievement Test, Second Edition (WIAT-II)

Social–Emotional
Behavior Assessment System for Children—Parent Rating Scales (BASC-2-PRS)
Behavior Assessment System for Children—Teacher Rating Scales (BASC-2-TRS)
Behavior Assessment System for Children—Self-Report of Personality (BASC-2-SRP)

Additional Information
Parent Interview
Child Interview

Referral Question and Background

Referral Question

Tess was referred to the Union Educational Psychology Clinic by her mother, Dana Howard, whose older son had previously been evaluated at the clinic. Mrs. Howard was concerned about difficulty reading since Tess was in kindergarten. She noted that Tess normally earned A's in school but her grades had begun to decline as the curriculum became more reading intensive across academic areas. Ms. Howard also reported that it takes Tess longer than her classmates to complete assignments, which might be contributing to feelings of low self-esteem. Mrs. Howard wanted a comprehensive psychoeducational evaluation to get a complete picture of Tess' current functioning and to determine whether her reading difficulties are indicative of "dyslexia."

Family History

Tess is an 11-year, 1-month-old Caucasian female who has resided in Union since birth. She lives with her mother, father, and older brother, Jack, who is 15. Mrs. Howard described the relationship between all family members as "pretty good," despite some sibling rivalry with Jack.

Mrs. Howard reported a significant family history of depressive disorders for Mr. Howard's relatives. This includes a grandfather diagnosed with bipolar disorder, an aunt with severe depressive episodes, and a great-grandfather who was placed in a mental health facility. Mrs. Howard stated that she had been hospitalized for post-partum depression after Jack's birth, but this depressive episode was related to systemic lupus. Tess' brother, Jack, has been diagnosed as having Asperger's disorder which has contributed to Tess experiencing feelings of resentment.

Developmental History

Mrs. Howard reported a difficult pregnancy with Tess due to her age, 40 years, and a large fibroid tumor. Tess was delivered prematurely by Caesarean section at about 35 weeks at normal weight but with a collapsed lung and spent a week in intensive care. She received oxygen for several days as a result of her lung problems. Tess reached developmental milestones within normal limits, with the exception of speaking in sentences. She spoke in sentences at about 2–3 years of age. Tess suffered from migraine headaches when she was younger, but Mrs. Howard stated that she had "since outgrown them."

Educational History

Tess learned to write and read at home before starting kindergarten in the Union public school system. She did well in all academic subjects in the early grades, but according to Mrs. Howard his teachers expressed concern about her ability to identify novel words beginning in kindergarten. As Tess got older, her difficulty with decoding began to affect homework completion time, although she still understood what she read and earned good grades. Mrs. Howard attended school support team meetings for reading fluency difficulties in second and third grade but was dismissed from further services.

Previously, Tess had been earning A's and B's in late elementary school, but Mrs. Howard reported that she had not been participating as much in sixth grade because she feels discouraged by her slower reading rate. She stated that in earlier grades she used to want to do well and made an effort, but it now seems as if she is no longer motivated. She is currently performing below average in literature and history, although according to Mrs. Howard she is in the advanced mathematics class and enjoys the work. Her apparent reluctance to begin and inability to complete longer reading assignments and projects has a great negative impact on her grades in all academic subjects.

Affect and Social Characteristics

Mrs. Howard described Tess as having a "mellow disposition" but also as a young woman who is curious, compassionate, bright, and funny with a love of learning. She also believes that she has poor self-esteem because of her difficulty completing reading assignments. Mrs. Howard reported that Tess has one best friend whom she has been close to for a few years. She expressed the belief that Tess is not interested in forming more friendships because she feels she has different interests from other children her age. She also noted that Tess feels somewhat embarrassed because her friend is a voracious reader. Tess enjoys karate lessons, band, and using the computer.

Mrs. Howard expressed concern about Tess' tendency to shut down when things do not go her way or she is disciplined. Typically, discipline involves making use of the computer contingent on finishing homework assignments, and in these instances she simply goes to bed without comment or completing the task. She reported that she has also expressed belief in the fact that she cannot change situations she does not like by saying things such as, "I am not going to try, because it will take forever and I would not finish anyway."

General Behavioral Observations

Tess was evaluated at the Union Educational Psychology Clinic. She reported that she had not gotten a good night's rest, but felt as well as she would on a normal school day. Tess was quiet and reserved during test administration and often hung her head or rested it on the table. She worked quickly initially but when tasks became more difficult, took her time and was very persistent. During the interview, she rarely made eye contact with the interviewer, but was willing to answer and expand on any questions. She appeared anxious during reading tasks, often saying, "I am sorry this is taking me so long," and "I am not good at reading."

Cognitive Functioning

The WISC-IV was administered to assess Tess' overall intellectual ability. The WISC-IV is an individually administered clinical instrument for assessing the intellectual ability of children aged 6 years through 16 years, 11 months. The child's performance on ten subtests is summarized in an overall intelligence score called the

Full Scale standard score. The WISC-IV also yields Verbal, Comprehension, Perceptual Reasoning, Working Memory, and Processing Speed scores.

Tess earned a Verbal Comprehension Index score of 121 (92nd percentile, Superior), a Perceptual Reasoning Index score of 127 (96th percentile, Superior), a Working Memory Index score of 102 (55th percentile, Average), and a Processing Speed Index of 85 (16th percentile, Low Average). Based on these results, Tess has relative strengths in verbal and perceptual reasoning skills. While her Working Memory Index is in the average range, it is significantly lower than her Verbal Comprehension and Perceptual Reasoning indexes. Also, Tess' Processing Speed Index is significantly lower than her Verbal Comprehension, Perceptual Reasoning, and Working Memory indexes. Both of these differences are likely to occur in less than 5 % of her same-age standardization sample and should be considered a true difference that did not occur by chance. Due to these significant differences, the Full Scale IQ may not be reliably interpreted. The Verbal Comprehension IQ and Perceptual Reasoning IQ are considered better estimates of Tess' intellectual functioning because they assess higher-level cognitive and reasoning abilities.

The subtest scaled scores of the WISC-IV have a mean of 10 with a standard deviation of 3. Scores between 7 and 13 are considered average.

Verbal comprehension	Scaled score
Similarities	13
Vocabulary	15
Comprehension	13
Perceptual reasoning	
Block design	13
Picture concepts	13
Matrix reasoning	17
Working memory	
Digit span	10
Letter–number sequencing	11
Processing speed	
Coding	6
Symbol search	9
Cancellation	12

Academic Functioning

Reading Achievement

Tess' skills in single-word decoding, nonsense word decoding, and reading comprehension were assessed using the WIAT-II. She earned a standard score of 84 (14th percentile, Below Average) on the Reading composite. She performed in the below average to average range on all Reading subtests.

The WIAT-II yields standard scores with a mean of 100 and a standard deviation of 15.

WIAT-II subtests	Standard scores	Percentile
Word reading	87	19
Reading comprehension	90	25
Pseudoword decoding	82	12

Written Language Skills

Tess' ability to construct individual sentences, spell words, and write paragraphs was assessed by the WIAT-II. Tess received a standard score of 115 (84th percentile, High Average) on the Written Language Composite. She demonstrated spelling abilities above her age level and responded appropriately to an essay prompt. However, her essay was average in terms of persuasion tactics, supporting arguments, and vocabulary usage.

The WIAT-II yields standard scores with a mean of 100 and a standard deviation of 15.

WIAT-II subtests	Standard scores	95 % band	Percentile
Spelling	117	111–123	87
Written expression	109	100–118	73

Oral Language

Tess' oral language was assessed using the WIAT-II. The WIAT-II Listening Comprehension scale assesses the ability to listen for detail by selecting a picture that matches a word or sentence and the ability to generate a word that matches a picture or oral description. The Oral Expression scale assesses the examinee's ability to use oral language to effectively communicate with others through listing several members of a category, telling stories about pictures, and giving specific directions to complete everyday tasks. Tess earned an Oral Language Composite standard score of 139 (99.5 percentile, Very Superior).

The WIAT-II yields standard scores with a mean of 100 and a standard deviation of 15.

WIAT-II subtests	Standard scores	95 % Band	Percentile
Listening comprehension	126	116–136	96
Oral expression	136	126–146	99

Mathematics

Tess' mathematics achievement was assessed with the WIAT-II. The Numerical Operations subtest assesses the ability to solve written mathematics problems using basic operations such as addition, subtraction, multiplication, and division. The Math Reasoning subtest requires solving single- and multiple-step word problems using whole numbers, fractions, and graphs. Tess earned a Mathematics Composite standard score of 128 (97th percentile, Very Superior).

The WIAT-II yields standard scores with a mean of 100 and a standard deviation of 15.

The WIAT-II yields standard scores with a mean of 100 and a standard deviation of 15.

WIAT-II subtests	Standard scores	95% band	Percentile
Numerical operations	129	122–136	97
Mathematics reasoning	118	112–124	88

Behavioral and Social–Emotional Functioning

Parent Reports

Tess' mother, Mrs. Howard, completed Behavior Assessment System for Children-Parent Rating Scales, Second Edition (BASC-2-PRS) to provide an overview of Tess' behavioral, social, and emotional functioning. Mrs. Howard did not endorse any difficulties within the home environment.

The BASC-2-PRS yields T-scores with a mean of 50 and a standard deviation of 10. Scores above 70 on the clinical scales are considered to be indicative of significant problems. On the Adaptive scales, scores below 30 are considered significantly low. Scores that represent significant problems are marked with two asterisks and scores that represent possible problems are marked with a single asterisk.

Clinical scales	Mother T-scores
Hyperactivity	39
Aggression	46
Conduct problems	37
Externalizing problems	*40*
Anxiety	47
Depression	45
Somatization	36
Internalizing problems	*41*
Attention problems	–
Learning problems	–
School problems	–
Atypicality	41
Withdrawal	47
Attention Problems	51
Behavioral Symptoms Index	*43*
Adaptive Scales	
Adaptability	55
Social Skills	50
Leadership	46
Activities of daily living	49

Clinical scales	Mother T-scores
Study skills	–
Functional communication	50
Adaptive skills composite	*50*

Teacher Reports

Tess' literature teacher, Ms. Paxton, completed the BASC-2-TRS to provide information pertaining to Tess' behavioral, emotional, and academic functioning at school. Ms. Paxton's ratings indicated that Jaden is having difficulty succeeding in school and that she displays signs of anxiety and depression when working on reading-related tasks. The Withdrawal scale was also in the at-risk range because Ms. Paxton endorsed that Tess prefers to work alone.

The BASC-2-TRS is a questionnaire completed by teachers to obtain ratings of adaptive skills and behavior and emotional problems of students. The BASC-2-TRS yields T-Scores with a mean of 50 and a standard deviation of 10. Scores above 70 are considered to be indicative of significant problems. Scores that are indicative of significant problems are marked with two asterisks and scores that indicate possible problems are marked with a single asterisk.

Clinical scales	Teacher T-score
Hyperactivity	49
Aggression	46
Conduct problems	45
Externalizing problems	*46*
Anxiety	65*
Depression	66*
Somatization	47
Internalizing problems	*62**
Attention problems	62*
Learning problems	78**
School problems	*72***
Atypicality	59
Withdrawal	66*
Attention problems	–
Behavioral symptoms index	*60**

Adaptive scores below 30 are considered to indicate significant difficulties.

Adaptive scales	Teacher T-score
Adaptability	45
Social skills	42
Leadership	42
Activities of daily living	–
Study skills	38*

Adaptive scales	Teacher T-score
Functional communication	41
Adaptive skills	*40*

Self Report

While at the clinic, Tess completed the Behavior Assessment System for Children-Self-Report of Personality, Second Edition (BASC-2-SRP). Tess indicated that she experiences a significant Sense of Inadequacy. The Sense of Inadequacy scale assesses perceptions of low achievement expectations, a tendency to not persevere, and a perception of being unsuccessful, particularly in academic endeavors. Specifically, Tess expressed her perception that she should be able to do better in reading, but regardless of her effort she cannot do so. Tess' ratings also resulted in an at-risk Attitude to School scale due to her negative feelings related to her reading experiences. Despite these difficulties, Tess expressed satisfaction with her relationships as well as a positive self-concept.

The BASC-2-SRP yields T-Scores with a mean of 50 and a standard deviation of 10. Scores above 70 on the clinical scales are considered to be indicative of significant problems. Scores below 30 on the personal adjustment scales are considered significantly low. Scores representing significant problems are marked with two asterisks and scores representing possible problems are marked with a single asterisk.

Clinical scales	T-Score
Attitude to school	68*
Attitude to teachers	40
School problems	*55*
Atypicality	47
Locus of control	42
Social stress	46
Anxiety	58
Depression	46
Sense of inadequacy	77**
Internalizing problems	*53*
Attention problems	53
Hyperactivity	40
Inattention/hyperactivity	*46*
Emotional symptoms index	*55*
Personal adjustment scales	
Relations with parents	60
Interpersonal relations	59
Self-esteem	58
Self-reliance	47
Personal adjustment	*58*

Summary and Diagnostic Impressions

Tess is an 11-year, 1-month-old female who was referred to the Union Educational Psychology Clinic by her mother for a psychoeducational evaluation. Results of the evaluation indicate that Tess' verbal and perceptual cognitive abilities are in the superior range, while her working memory and processing speed are average and low average, respectively. Her academic abilities range from below average to very superior. It is apparent that she is quite capable academically, but her reading ability, particularly her reading decoding, is lower than her ability in other academic subjects and within the below average range. When comparing her reading composite score to her WISC-IV Verbal Comprehension Index, it is clear that Tess' reading performance is significantly lower than expectations given her cognitive ability. Based on results from parent interview, rating scales, and psychoeducational testing, and the DSM-IV criteria, Tess' ipsative weakness in reading warrants a diagnosis of Reading Disorder.

Axis I	Reading disorder (315.00)
Axis II	None
Axis III	None
Axis IV	None
Axis V	GAF=70 (current)

Recommendations

1. Tess' parents should share the results of this evaluation with Union Middle School so that appropriate interventions and accommodations may be implemented in the school setting.
2. Teach Tess a specific method for identifying and decoding unfamiliar words.
3. Use word banks and flash cards to assist Tess in developing a sight word vocabulary.
4. Tess' parents may wish to seek professional consultation in assisting her with homework completion as her classes across the curriculum require more reading.

OAKVILLE ACADEMY

CONFIDENTIAL
PSYCHOEDUCATIONAL REPORT

This report is provided to school personnel for professional use in planning an appropriate educational program. Access is to be limited to those identified as appropriate under state and federal guidelines. Duplication of this report is prohibited without appropriate authorization of release to the Psychological Services Department.

NAME: Shari Gage
BIRTH DATE: 06/15/1992

AGE: 16 years, 5 months
SEX: Female
PARENT/GUARDIAN: Mary Gage
REFERRED BY: IEP Team (REEVALUATION)
SCHOOL: Oakville Academy
GRADE: 10
VISION: 11/19/2008
HEARING: 11/19/2008
CONSENT FOR EVALUATION: 11/24/2008
DATES EVALUATED: 12/01/2008, 12/02/2008, 12/05/2008, 02/15/2009

Evaluation Instruments Administered

Shari was administered a battery of tests which included the following instruments:
Reynolds Intellectual Assessment Scales (RIASs)
Wechsler Individual Achievement Test, Second Edition (WIAT-II)
Wide Range Achievement Test–4 (WRAT-4)
The Behavior Assessment System for Children, Second Edition (BASC-2)

- Parent Rating Scales (PRS)
- Teacher Rating Scales (TRS)
- Self-Report of Personality (SRP)

Clinical Interview
Review of Records

Reason for Referral

Shari was referred for a comprehensive psychoeducational evaluation in order to evaluate academic progress, to determine instructional needs, and to determine possible eligibility for future special education services. Shari has been being served through the Learning Disability program.

Background Information

According to a December 3, 2004 report by Ms. Privitera, a school psychologist for the School District Office of Psychological Services, Shari was initially referred for evaluation in preschool and was determined to be eligible for services through the Significantly Developmentally Delayed program. In March of 1997, as a kindergarten student, Shari was reevaluated and found eligible for Emotional and Behavioral Disorder services due to distractibility, difficulty transitioning, and verbal and physical outbursts. After reevaluation in 1999, Shari's emotional control was considered improved enough that she was no longer considered eligible for the Emotional and Behavioral Disorder program and she was found eligible for Learning Disabilities services. Ms. Privitera's evaluation revealed that Shari's reading and mathematics skills were in the borderline range and writing skills were in the low average range as measured by the Diagnostic Achievement Battery–3. Shari's intellectual functioning was measured by the Wechsler Abbreviated Scale of Intelligence and results indicated low average verbal abilities, average nonverbal ability, and low average overall ability.

Social History

Shari's mother, Ms. Mary Gage, completed a social history update questionnaire on November 1, 2008. Ms. Gage noted that Shari lives at home with her mother and 17-year-old sister, Jeri. She also indicated that she was biologically Shari's maternal grandmother but adopted Shari when she was 3 years old. She reported that she and her husband divorced when Shari was 11 years old. Ms. Gage indicated that Shari is involved in the community by regularly attending church.

General Description/Testing Observations

Shari is a 16-year-old female who is noted to be of average height and above average weight for her chronological age. She was tested at Oakville Academy over four sessions. Shari entered the testing situation willingly and rapport was easily established and maintained. Her affect was appropriate to the testing situation and her mood was pleasant and cooperative. Shari attempted all tasks and put forth adequate effort, although her first statement to the examiner was, "I am probably going to fail everything." At times, Shari required extra encouragement to persevere with difficult tasks. The quality of Shari's expressive language was considered to be within the average range. She was alert and appeared oriented throughout the evaluative sessions. Her eye contact was appropriate and no disturbances in her thought processes were observed. Overall test results appear to be a valid estimate of Shari's current level of functioning.

Test Results and Interpretation

Intelligence

Shari was administered the *RIAS* in order to provide an estimate of her cognitive ability. The RIAS is an individually administered test designed to provide subtest and composite scores that represent intellectual functioning in specific cognitive domains. The RIAS also yields a co-normed, supplemental measure of memory. The RIAS includes a two-subtest Verbal Intelligence Index (VIX) and a two-subtest Nonverbal Intelligence Index (NIX). The scaled sums of T scores for the four subtests are combined to form the Composite Intelligence Index (CIX), which is a summary estimate of global intelligence. Her score on the Verbal Intelligence Index suggested low average verbal reasoning ability and crystallized intellectual functioning. Shari's performance on the NIX suggested average nonverbal reasoning ability and fluid intellectual functioning. Shari's overall performance was within the low average range of intellectual functioning. Her CIX score was a standard score of 84, which corresponds to the 14th percentile, which means that Shari is functioning at the same level as or better than 14% of children her same age. The chance that the range of scores from 79 to 90 includes Shari's true IQ is 95 out of 100.

The various indexes yielded by the RIAS are scaled to a mean of 100 and a standard deviation of 15. Composite scores that fall between 90 and 109 are considered average. Shari's scores were as follows:

Index score	Standard score	Percentile
Verbal intelligence index (VIX)	82	12
Nonverbal intelligence index (NIX)	90	25
Composite intelligence index (CIX)	84	14
Composite memory index (CMX)	79	8

The following scores reflect Shari's performance on individual subtests. Each subtest score is scaled to a mean of 50 and a standard deviation of 10. Subtest scores that fall between 45 and 54 are considered average.

Verbal subtest	T-score
Guess what (GWH)	31
Verbal reasoning (VRZ)	41
Nonverbal subtest	
Odd-item out (OIO)	39
What's missing (WHM)	48
Memory subtest	
Verbal memory (VRM)	34
Nonverbal memory (NVM)	41

In the area of memory, Shari obtained a Composite Memory Index (CMX) composite score of 79 (eighth percentile), which is in the borderline range. Shari's VIX and NIX are fairly consistent with her CIX and this indicated that Shari's verbal and nonverbal abilities are similarly developed. When compared to her overall intelligence, Shari's memory score (CMX) indicates a slight weakness in working memory skills both in the verbal and nonverbal areas.

Academic Achievement

Shari was administered selected subtests of the *WIAT-II* to determine her current level of academic achievement. These tests are individually administered, norm-referenced tests that assess performance in the essential academic areas of reading and mathematics. Standard scores are based upon a mean of 100 and a standard deviation of 15. Scores that fall between 85 and 115 are considered to be within the average range.

	Standard score	Percentile
Word reading	68	2
Reading comprehension	60	0.4
Pseudoword decoding	80	9
Reading composite	*65*	*1*
Numerical operations	66	1
Math reasoning	66	1
Mathematics composite	*62*	*1*
Spelling	88	21
Written expression	87	19
Written language composite	*86*	*86*
Listening comprehension	71	3
Oral expression	87	19
Oral language composite	*76*	*5*

Shari obtained a Reading Composite score of 65 (first percentile), which is in the Extremely Low range of functioning. This composite included three subtests—Word Reading, Reading Comprehension, and Pseudoword Decoding. On the Word Reading subtest, which requires quickly reading through a list of words, Shari obtained a standard score of 68, which is in the Extremely Low range. When reading through the list, Shari only sounded out unfamiliar words when prompted, and sometimes substituted words similar in appearance to the target word. Based on these observations, it appears that Shari tends to rely on a sight word approach to reading, but may not be familiar with a wide range of words. On the Reading Comprehension subtest, Shari obtained a standard score of 60, which is also in the Extremely Low range. The Reading Comprehension subtest requires reading sentences and short passages and then answering questions about the main idea, specific details, or the order of events. Shari was unable to respond to the first set of items for her grade level and, thus, was administered the previous set of items. She demonstrated difficulty recalling information she had just read, was often unable to identify the necessary details by looking back at the passage, and sometimes did not appear to understand the main point of the passage. Finally, on the Pseudoword Decoding subtest, Shari was able to correctly sound out several "fake" words, earning a standard score of 80, which is in the Low Average range. Based on these results, Shari appears to have a stronger phonemic decoding ability than sight word vocabulary.

In the area of mathematics skills, Shari obtained a Math Composite score of 62 (1st percentile), which is in the Extremely Low range of functioning. This composite included two subtests—Numerical Operations and Math Reasoning. On the Numerical Operations subtest, Shari obtained a standard score of 66, which is in the Extremely Low range. Shari successfully completed multi-digit addition and subtraction with regrouping and division with a single digit divisor. She was unable to correctly perform various operations on fractions and decimals. On the Math Reasoning subtest, Shari obtained a standard score of 66, which is also in the Extremely Low range. Shari solved word problems requiring reading a graph, using patterns, and stating fractions. She was unable to solve problems that required geometric reasoning, ordering quantities less than a whole, and complex multiplication and division problems.

Within the area of written language, Shari obtained a standard score of 88 on the Spelling subtest, which is in the Low Average range, and a standard score of 87 on the Written Expression subtest, which is also in the Low Average range. Her Written Language composite score was 86 (18th percentile), which is within the Low Average range. On four of the spelling items, Shari substituted the incorrect homonym (e.g., absents for absence) and appeared to attempt to use spelling conventions, i.e., an orthographic approach, to spell unfamiliar words. Shari was able to combine sentences into one complete sentence, but sometimes incorrectly communicated the original meaning or made punctuation or word omission errors.

Shari earned a standard score of 76 on the Oral Language composite, which is within the Borderline range. On the Listening Comprehension subtest, she obtained a score or 71, which is in the Borderline range. On this subtest, Shari was better able to identify pictures that matched words or sentences spoken by the examiner than to produce words that corresponded to a picture. In other words, her receptive ability appeared better developed than her expressive ability in this context. On the Oral Expression subtest, Shari earned a score of 87, which is within the Low Average range. Shari correctly described stories and gave directions, but tended to leave out specific details and descriptive elements.

Shari was also administered the Wide Range Achievement Test, Fourth Edition (WRAT-IV) in August 2007 as standard school procedure. The WRAT-IV measures academic functioning, rendering a Word Reading score and Math Computation score.

	Standard score	Percentile
Word reading	79	8
Sentence comprehension	78	7
Reading composite	*76*	*5*
Math computation	76	5

Shari's scores on the WRAT-IV were within the Borderline range for reading and mathematics, which are slightly higher than her WIAT-II results.

Social/Emotional/Behavioral Rating Scales

Shari's mother and teacher completed the *BASC-2*, a measure that evaluates levels of behavioral, emotional, and social competencies relative to adolescents of the same age and gender. On the clinical scales and composite scores of the BASC-2, T-scores of 70 and above are considered clinically significant, scores between 60 and 69 are in the at-risk range, and scores of 41–59 are in the average range. Adaptive scale scores of 30 or less are considered clinically significant, scores of 31–40 are at-risk, and scores between 41 and 59 are average.

Skill area	T-score (mother)	T-score (teacher)
Hyperactivity	54	60*
Aggression	50	70**
Conduct problems	55	63*
Externalizing problems	*53*	*65**
Anxiety	46	68*
Depression	49	86**
Somatization	41	96**
Internalizing problems	*44*	*89***
Attention problems	–	61*
Learning problems	–	76**
School problems	–	*70***
Atypicality	52	48
Withdrawal	47	66*
Attention problems	56	–
Behavioral symptoms index	*52*	*69**
Adaptability	56	48
Social skills	62	55
Leadership	46	51
Activities of daily living	43	–
Study skills		40*
Functional communication	57	36*
Adaptive skills	*53*	*46*

*At-risk; **Clinically significant/high level of maladjustment

The F, Response Pattern, and Consistency indexes were all within the acceptable range for Dr. Decker's report. Teacher results indicated clinically significant scores for Aggression (e.g., sometimes engages in several forms of verbal aggression, loses temper easily), Depression (e.g., seems lonely, is negative, is sad), Somatization (e.g., several physical complaints resulting in frequent visits to the school nurse), and Learning Problems (e.g., had difficulty keeping up in several academic areas). Results also indicated that Shari was at risk for Hyperactivity (e.g., sometimes has problems seeks attention while working, gets out of seat, or interrupts), Conduct Problems (e.g., sometimes disobeys and sneaks around), Anxiety (e.g., worries and is nervous, particularly about tests), Attention Problems (e.g., easily distracted with short attention span), Withdrawal (e.g., does not always join group activities or seek companionship), Study Skills (e.g., does not consistently complete tasks necessary for academic success), and Functional Communication (e.g., does not always clearly communicate). As a result of the significant Depression and Somatization scales and the at-risk Anxiety scale, the Internalizing Problems composite was also elevated. Similarly, the School Problems composite score reflects the at-risk levels of Attention Problems and significant Learning Problems.

Ms. Gage's F and Response Pattern indexes were within the acceptable range, but her Consistency index fell in the caution range, indicating that her responses differed for similar items perhaps due to not carefully reading item content or changing perspective during the completion of the form. An inspection of the inconsistent items revealed that pairs of items differed slightly, for example, applying to slightly different circumstances, or were rated similarly although not exactly the same. Ms. Gage indicated that she did not perceive Shari's behavior as being problematic in the home environment.

Thus, ratings indicated that Shari appears to have significant difficulty with aggression, depression, somatization, and academics at school and she has some problems with impulse control, disobeying, anxiety, inattention, withdrawal, academic task completion, and functional communication in the school environment, but does not demonstrate similar difficulties at home. It may be hypothesized that Shari's behavioral and emotional difficulties at school are related to her learning challenges.

Shari also completed the BASC-2-SRP to provide her perception of her behavioral, emotional, and social functioning. Shari's F, Response Pattern, V, L, and Consistency Indexes were within the acceptable range. Specific T-scores obtained on the BASC are listed below:

Skill area	T-score
Attitude to school	65*
Attitude to teachers	53
Sensation seeking	60*
School problems	*62**
Atypicality	45
Locus of control	57
Social stress	51
Anxiety	54
Depression	49
Sense of inadequacy	56
Somatization	60*
Internalizing problems	*54*
Attention problems	70**
Hyperactivity	48
Inattention/hyperactivity	*60**
Emotional symptoms index	*55*
Relations with parents	51
Interpersonal relations	36*
Self-esteem	45
Self-reliance	44
Personal adjustment	*42*

*At-risk; **Clinically significant/high level of maladjustment

Shari rated herself as being within the at-risk range for School Problems and Inattention/Hyperactivity. Within the School Problems scale, Shari endorsed disliking school because she believes it is boring and enjoying high excitement activities like playing rough sports and daring other to do things resulting in scores in the at-risk range for Attitude to School and Sensation Seeking. The Inattention/Hyperactivity scale was elevated due to Shari endorsing clinically significant Attention Problems. Shari also rated herself as being at-risk for Somatization and difficulties in Interpersonal Relations due to various body aches and her perception that others do not always like her, respectively.

Clinical Interview

In a separate interview, Shari described her perception of events in her life as well as her thoughts and feelings on several issues. According to Shari, she was held back in kindergarten and people picked on her from first through ninth grade. Shari described herself as outgoing, hardworking, and smart, although she noted that she often makes self-deprecating comments when experiencing frustration with schoolwork. She endorsed doing her best to remind herself that she is smart, but just has a problem with certain subjects.

Classroom Observation

Shari was observed on December 13, 2007, by Dr. Decker, while in tenth grade literature. During the observation, Shari was completing an open book lesson quiz and tended to complain about the difficulty level, saying that she did not understand the story she had read because being in class was "too much." Shari left the classroom once during this time for a restroom break and had difficulty resuming the task when she returned. When given the opportunity for free time, she then laid her head down and fell asleep. Ms. Simpson reported that this was typical behavior for Shari and expressed concern that she gives up on tasks too easily.

Shari was also observed on January 15, 2008, by the examiner, while in Mr. Griffin's class for mathematics. Shari was the only student in the classroom studying mathematics at the time and, therefore, did not interact with other students in the room. Shari began working on her mathematics assignment, which involved calculating repeating digits and multi-operation problems, with assistance from Mr. Griffin. She attempted all items, but required a great deal of assistance, particularly if some aspect of the task was different from the items demonstrated by Mr. Griffin. Throughout the period, Shari was engaged in the assignment and instruction, although she did briefly leave the room at one point. She did, however, come back to her desk and immediately resumed her work. Mr. Griffin stated that Shari's behaved in the typical manner while in his classroom and praised her willingness and ability to seek assistance.

Summary

Shari is a 16-year-old, tenth-grade student who was referred for a comprehensive psychoeducational evaluation to assist in determining continuing eligibility for special education services. Current test results suggest that Shari is functioning intellectually in the below-average range. She displayed below-average abilities associated with language development and acquired knowledge. Her nonverbal reasoning ability was just within the average range. Academically, Shari's performance in mathematics and reading was in the extremely low to borderline range. Her oral language ability was within the borderline range, while her written language performance was within the low average range. Her oral language score was not considered an accurate representation of her actual communication ability. Behavioral ratings indicated that Shari has some difficulties at school that are likely related to her academic frustration.

Results of the current assessment indicate that Shari exhibits a significant discrepancy between her ability and reading and mathematics achievement, indicating that she continues to meet criteria for the Specific Learning Disability category. The eligibility team is encouraged to take these results and all other pertinent information into consideration when determining Shari's eligibility for special education services.

Summary of Key Points

- The concept of severe discrepancy originated with the introduction of the LDs into law with Education for All Handicapped Children Act (EAHCA) and was based upon a combination of the Kirk's and Bateman's work.
- Measurement issues of the discrepancy method, including regression to the mean and positive correlation between intelligence and achievement resulting in a smaller standard deviation, affect the accuracy of identification.
- Different discrepancy formulas are used across locations, resulting in different identification rates. Simple standard score discrepancy requires intelligence scores to be a certain number of standard score points higher than achievement scores and results in overidentifying students with average and above intelligence and underidentifying students with below-average intelligence. Regression methods account for regression to the mean and are a psychometric improvement to standard score methods; however, regression methods still require choosing a level to represent significant discrepancy.
- Several researchers have questioned the use of intelligence in identification of LDs. Issues discussed have included the effect of LDs on intelligence scores, the Matthew effect, decreased meaningfulness of global IQ for individuals with LD, the various intelligence scores available to use, the idea the IQ is equal to potential, the lack of IQ's ability to predict reading ability, and irrelevance to treatment.
- Some researchers have argued that intelligence may influence individual's response to intervention and general intelligence, or "g", is a good predictor of many life outcomes.
- The discrepancy formula allows the questionable practice of identifying gifted individuals with average or better achievement scores to be classified as having an LD.
- An alternative but similar model called the Component Model of Reading has been proposed. The equation $R = D \times L$ replaces IQ with listening comprehension (L) to determine if a student has a deficit in reading decoding (D) or reading comprehension (R).

Questions and Answers with the Expert: Cecil R. Reynolds

Meet the expert: Cecil R. Reynolds, PhD, ABN, earned his doctoral degree from the University of Georgia in 1978 under the tutelage of Dr. Alan S. Kaufman, with a major in School Psychology and minors in Statistics and in Clinical Neuropsychology. He served an internship divided between the Medical College of Georgia (Pediatric Neurology section and Neurological Surgery section) and the Rutland Center for Severely Emotional Disturbed Children. Prior to joining the Texas A & M University faculty in 1981, Dr. Reynolds was a faculty member at the University of Nebraska Lincoln, where he served as Associate Director and Acting Director of the Buros Institute of Mental Measurement, after writing the grants and proposals to move the Institute to Nebraska following the death of its founder, Oscar Buros. His primary research interests are in all aspects of psychological assessment with particular emphasis on assessment of memory, emotional and affective states and traits, and issues of cultural bias in testing. He is the author of more than 300 scholarly publications and the author or editor of over 50 books and several widely used tests of personality and behavior. He maintained a clinical practice treating trauma victims and individuals with traumatic brain injury for 25 years before retiring from clinical work at the end of 2003. Dr. Reynolds holds a diplomate in Clinical Neuropsychology from the American Board of Professional Neuropsychology, of which he is also a past president, and he was a diplomate in School Psychology of the American Board of Professional Psychology, prior to retiring his diplomate in 2004. He has served in a variety of prestigious positions for professional organizations and has been the recipient of many awards and recognition for his professional contributions.

Question 1: How would you describe the key elements of the discrepancy approach to learning disabilities (LDs) diagnosis?

Answer 1: Establishing unexpected levels of underachievement has always been central to the concept of an LD. Simple difference (SD) analysis does that but it requires care and consistency. To do it properly requires: (1) use of an intelligence measure that is not adversely confounded by the student's disability, (2) highly reliable achievement measures that appropriately sample the curriculum to which the student has been exposed, (3) proper (i.e., effective) instruction that has been demonstrated to work with nondisabled students, (4) knowledge of the statistical relationship between the intelligence and achievement measures, and (5) application of a regression-based prediction method such as recommended in the Federal task force report I authored in 1984. One must also realize that the presence of a severe discrepancy should be treated as a necessary but insufficient condition for the diagnosis of an SLD—this is often overlooked. There are additional criteria that must be applied.

Question 2: What are the positive and negative aspects of the discrepancy approach to LDs identification?

Answer 2: Some of the negative aspects are related to the method itself but most are related to inconsistencies in practice. The SD model has never been consistently applied; so, it has never been truly tested. This is a huge issue and will become over time an even bigger issue in RTI models. The other difficulties with the SD approach center around the difficulties in locating and using appropriate measures that possess the qualities described above and knowing and applying the mathematical models accurately. The strengths lie in the fact that we know no superior way to determine that unexpected underachievement exists and that the method, as I have presented it, is objective.

Question 3: What role, if any, should intelligence assessment play in LD diagnosis?

Answer 3: It is central to determining unexpected underachievement. Intelligence is related to academic learning and to deny this is nonsensical

Question 4: What do you consider best practice for LD identification?

Answer 4: Once a student has failed to respond adequately in an RTI model, best practice for me dictates the use of a true comprehensive assessment that evaluates and documents the criteria as present or absent in the Federal definition. No short-cuts, no subjective appraisals, no assumptions that if RTI fails a student must be SLD, but rather a comprehensive evaluation that assesses the criteria in the definition using instruments with the qualities I have described above to determine if a SD exists and then the use of strong tests of processing as well as measures of academic learning skills. There are many reasons why a student may fail in RTI and the presence of an SLD is but one possible reason. We must then rule out emotional and behavioral disorders, or determine they are comorbid with the SLD, rule out mental retardation (MR), rule out health-related issues, other developmental disorders, and then move forward with accurate diagnosis and the development of effective instructional programs for an SLD child that are driven by student characteristics.

Chapter 3
Cognitive Processing

Several researchers in the area of learning disabilities (LD) have suggested that the methods used to identify LD should be more closely aligned with the definition, i.e., should assess cognitive processes (Mather and Gregg 2006; Kavale et al. 2005). The concept of processing deficits, however, originated with Kirk's foundational work in LD regarding intraindividual differences and, yet, the concept seems no clearer now than it was at the time of its formulation. Recognizing this difficulty, the national Joint Committee on Learning Disabilities actually chose to delete the phrase "basic psychological processes" from their definition of LD released in 1990. This highlights the fact that before clinicians and educators can determine whether a process deficit is responsible for a student's LD, they must have a clear definition of what a process is. According to the *Oxford English Dictionary*, a process is a series of actions or steps toward achieving a particular end, but what the actions and the end consist of are open to interpretation.

Siegel (1988), on the one hand, pointed out the problematic nature of cognitive processes posited to contribute to or cause LD due to their ambiguity, lack of definition, and domain specificity. Torgesen (2001), on the other hand, suggested that processes may be the most useful way to differentiate between specific learning disabilities (SLD) and general learning weaknesses. A brief history of the various hypothetical concepts that have been posited and reified for centuries may help clarify the lack of clarity that appears inherent in process theories. Following this historical overview, current processing practices, support for and against use of processing assessment, and case studies are provided.

A Brief History of Processes

Processes have been postulated since at least the sixth century BC by Greek philosophers, and since that time, they have had numerous labels and functions bestowed upon them (Mann 1979). Process theories have experienced shifting tides of favor and disfavor, with the so-called charlatans of psychology, phrenologists, being the earliest modern psychologists to espouse process training beginning in the early

A. E. B. Taylor, *Diagnostic Assessment of Learning Disabilities in Childhood*,
Contemporary Issues in Psychological Assessment, DOI 10.1007/978-1-4939-0335-1_3,

© Springer Science+Business Media New York 2014

nineteenth century. Later in the nineteenth century and into the beginning of the twentieth century, educators adopted a focus on processes, or faculties, with an emphasis on the senses and perception. For example, some of the processes deemed of most importance by theorists were the senses (e.g., smell, taste, touch, etc.), memory, imagination, judgment, and reason, with instruction targeting each of these areas. Such instruction was assumed to strengthen the mind through exercise, which would result in a positive effect on academic performance and general life outcomes.

Interest in the faculties eventually declined in psychology and general education because training the senses without a connection to real-world experience was deemed to be of little value. Despite the dip in popularity, process diagnosis and training continued to be used in special education rather than directly targeting academic problems. Despite the ill-defined nature of processes and the lack of support for their use, processes and process training were embraced in special education as a means of revitalizing a model of remedial education that had so far delivered lackluster results (Mann 1979).

One example of such an approach to LD assessment and intervention is Samuel Kirk's Illinois Test of Psycholinguistic Abilities (ITPA). Kirk developed the ITPA so that specific abilities could be assessed and interventions could be designed based upon the results (Minskoff 1998). Kirk posited two types of LD—those with core academic problems and those with core developmental deficits in cognitive processes. The ITPA measured three major processes based upon a model of communication, including reception, organization, and expression. Several remedial programs were developed based upon the ITPA and Kirk's belief that in addition to training in specific skill areas, deficient processes should also be trained, although critics cited lack of validity, particularly instructional relevance, as one of ITPA's major shortcomings (Towne 2004). Research examining process training based upon ITPA items was taken out of the academic context and did not transfer to actual achievement (Wong 1992). It should be noted that, despite criticisms of the ITPA, successful phonological training programs are also a result of Kirk's work (Minskoff 1998).

What Are Psychological Processes?

Different researchers, theorists, and practitioners have delineated and defined various processes. Dehn (2006) describes 13 processes in his concise and informative work, *Essentials of Processing Assessment*. These processes include the following: Attention, Auditory Processing, Executive Processing, Fluid Reasoning, Long-Term Retrieval, Phonemic Awareness, Planning, Processing Speed, Short-Term Memory, Simultaneous Processing, Successive Processing, Visual Processing, and Working Memory. Each of these processes can be measured with many different standardized tests. Table 3.1 lists two examples for each of these processes. For a more comprehensive list, the reader is referred to Dehn's (2006) work.

Table 3.1 Examples of instruments commonly used to assess various processes

Cognitive process	Instruments
Attention	NEPSY, second edition (NEPSY-II) (Korkman et al. 2007)
	Conners' Continuous Performance Test-II (CPT-II) (Conners and MHS staff 2000)
Auditory processing	SCAN-C: a test of auditory processing disorders in children-revised (Keith 1999)
	Woodcock-Johnson III Tests of Cognitive Abilities (WJ-III COG) (Woodcock et al. 2001)
Executive processing	Behavior Rating Inventory of Executive Functions (BRIEF) (Gioia et al. 2000)
	Delis-Kaplan Executive Function Systems (D-KEFS) (Delis et al. 2001)
Fluid reasoning	Kaufman Assessment Battery for Children, Second Edition (KABC-II) (Kaufman and Kaufman 2004)
	Wisconsin Card Sorting Test, Revised and Expanded (WCST) (Heaton.et al. 1993)
Long-term retrieval	Kaufman Assessment Battery for Children, Second Edition (KABC-II)
	Wide Range Assessment of Memory and Learning, Second Edition (WRAML-2) (Sheslow and Adams 2003)
Phonemic awareness	Comprehensive Test of Phonological Processing (CTOPP) (Wagner et al.1999)
	Woodcock Diagnostic Reading Battery (WDRB) (Schrank et al. 2004)
Planning	NEPSY-II
	WISC-IV Integrated (Wechsler. et al 2004)
Processing speed	Differential Ability Scales, Second Edition (DAS-II) (Elliott 2007)
	Wechsler Intelligence Scale for Children, Fourth Edition (WISC-IV) (Elliott 2007)
Short-term memory	California Verbal Learning Test, Children's Version (CVLT-C) (Delis et al. 1994)
	Reynolds Intellectual Assessment Scale (RIAS) (Reynolds and Kamphaus 2003)
Simultaneous processing	Cognitive Assessment System (CAS) (Naglieri and Das 2007)
	Kaufman Assessment Battery for Children, Second Edition (KABC-II)
Successive processing	Cognitive Assessment System (CAS)
	Kaufman Assessment Battery for Children, Second Edition (KABC-II)
Visual processing	Universal Nonverbal Intelligence Test (UNIT) (Bracken and McCallum 1998)
	Stanford-Binet Intelligence Scales, Fifth Edition (SB5) (Roid 2003)
Working memory	Wechsler Intelligence Scale for Children, Fourth Edition (WISC-IV)
	Woodcock-Johnson III Tests of Cognitive Abilities (WJ-III COG)

Another example of processes can be derived from the Woodcock-Johnson III (Woodcock et al. 2001), which includes the *Woodcock-Johnson III Tests of Cognitive Abilities* (WJ-III COG) and the *Woodcock-Johnson III Tests of Achievement* (WJ-III ACH). The WJ-III was designed to correspond to the Cattell-Horn-Carroll

Fig. 3.1 Planning, Attention, Simultaneous, Successive (PASS) theory diagram. (Source: Naglieri 1999. Copyright 1999 by John Wiley & Sons, Inc. Reprinted with permission)

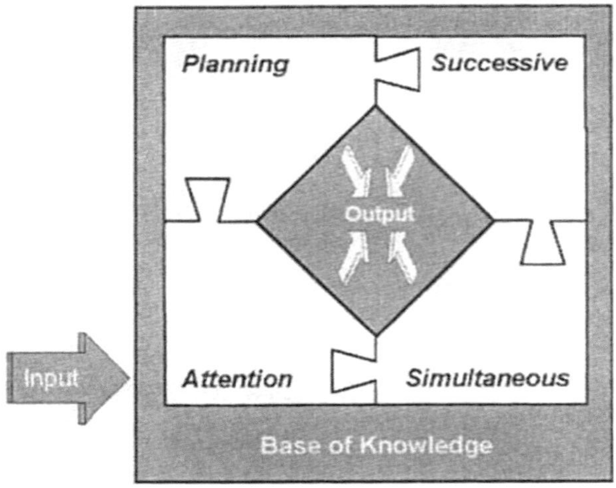

theory of intelligence. Gregg et al. (2003) described the use of the WJ-III clinical clusters within what they describe as a clinical model of LD diagnosis. The authors expanded on the areas assessed by the clinical clusters and noted that they include Phonological Awareness and Phoneme/Grapheme Knowledge, Cognitive Fluency, Working Memory, Executive Processes (including Representation, Planning, Execution, Evaluation), and Broad Attention (including attentional capacity, divided attention, attention to speech sounds, sustained attention, and interference control). Gregg et al. (2003) also described the Cognitive Performance Model, which provides further information regarding processing strengths and weaknesses, including verbal abilities, thinking abilities, and cognitive efficiency.

Contemporary Assessment of Cognitive Processes

Most recent efforts at process assessment have focused specifically on identifying children with LD. Naglieri has proposed the application of the Planning, Attention, Simultaneous, Successive (PASS) model of intelligence (see Fig. 3.1) to the diagnosis of LD because the assessed simultaneous, successive, and planning processes have been shown to be related to achievement and are assumed to provide more insight into underlying cognitive processes, thus allowing for targeted strategy training (Naglieri 1989). In response to Siegel's (1989) claim that pseudoword decoding scores are more accurate diagnostic tools than intelligence tests, Naglieri and Reardon (1993) examined the relationship between PASS components and specific measures of reading ability. They found that pseudoword scores were significantly predicted by successive processing scores and that word recognition scores were significantly predicted by successive scores as well as a combination of successive and planning scores. Further investigation showed that a group of children with reading disabilities earned a lower mean score than a control group on the successive scale of the Cognitive Assessment System (CAS; Naglieri and Das 1997), which requires repeating words and sentences in a certain order (Naglieri et al. 2004). In effect, Naglieri and colleagues are attempting to measure the cognitive processes underlying reading disabilities so that individuals can be identified based upon their cognitive profile, and interventions can be developed to remediate the cognitive deficit thought to result in the disability.

Those who align themselves with certain tests may also describe the reasoning and methods of processing assessment differently. For example, the clinical model, which consists of integrating various types of qualitative and quantitative data related to learning in order to make a diagnostic decision, has been described in detail within the framework of the Woodcock–Johnson III (Gregg et al. 2003). The WJ-III is described as providing important information regarding processing abilities across a range of cognitive, linguistic, and achievement tasks. The test results for these areas are compared and strengths and weaknesses are identified. Based on the individual's profile of strengths and weaknesses, difficulties within an academic area are then determined to be related to underlying deficits in language and/or cognitive processes. Note that rather than requiring a certain discrepancy between cognitive and achievement scores or scores below a certain cutoff, professional judgment is the primary tool to determine whether the obtained pattern is representative of an LD.

Similarly, as briefly mentioned above, Naglieri (1999) espouses a "Discrepancy/Consistency Model" of LD identification. Using this method, consistencies between cognitive and academic deficits and discrepancies between academic and processing weaknesses and academic and processing strengths are identified. More specifically, this is accomplished by comparing each cognitive process score with each academic area score. If both scores are low, it may be hypothesized that the processing deficit underlies the academic achievement deficit. When both an academic skill and a related processing skill are consistent and other unrelated areas are discrepant, then an LD in that academic skill can be diagnosed. If, however, a pattern is obtained that does not correspond with the expected pattern for an LD, then other factors, such as general cognitive ability, environment, and other "rule-outs," are examined. Fiorello et al. (2006) Cognitive Hypothesis Testing takes a similar approach that occurs after response to intervention; however, they refer to establishing concordance between cognitive and reading deficits and discordance between cognitive strengths and weaknesses in processing and reading.

Many tests purport to measure cognitive processing and suggest how to interpret the results. In most cases, this consists of comparing the various factors and subtests to determine strengths and weaknesses based upon performance on a single instrument. To demonstrate, consider the well-known tests and subtests of the Wechsler Intelligence Scale for Children, Fourth Edition (WISC-IV). Starting at the level of more psychometrically defensible level of index scores, one can determine a pattern of strengths and weaknesses among fluid reasoning, general learning and memory, working memory, and processing speed based upon the Fluid Reasoning, Verbal Comprehension, Working Memory, and Processing Speed indexes, respectively. In order to delve deeper into the processing abilities, a clinician may look at individual subtest scores by comparing scores to one another or comparing each score to the mean subtest score. For example, if a child earns a score of 5 on the Block Design subtest, but a score of 10 on the remaining Fluid Reasoning subtests, the clinician may hypothesize that the child has a visual-motor coordination weakness with intact fluid reasoning abilities. The reader is again cautioned that subtest interpretation is not recommended given the lower reliability and lack of validity evidence as compared to index and full-scale scores (Kamphaus 2001). It should also be noted that the WISC-IV Integrated (Wechsler et al. 2004), which consists of an additional 16 optional subtests in addition to the WISC-IV core subtests, was developed expressly to identify underlying processing problems.

Of course, in practice, many clinicians using process assessment compare results from different instruments in an approach that is sometimes referred to as cross-battery assessment. An example of a specific approach to processing assessment is outlined in Dehn's (2006) *Essentials of Processing Assessment*. First, subtest, factor, and composite scores from the various instruments administered are calculated. Any subtests or factors that do not measure a processing component are excluded from analysis. Second, clinical factor scores for each processing ability are computed if not supplied by the test's structure. Dehn (2006) specifies that at least two subtest scores are necessary to obtain a clinical factor score. In order to do this, subtest scores on a common standard score metric are added to obtain the mean and then rounded to the nearest whole number. After obtaining the clinical factor scores, they are arranged in a list that specifies the process that was assessed, the instrument and subtests used to assess the process, and the factor score. Dehn (2006) provides a worksheet to organize this process. Then, the average of all of the clinical factor scores is computed to provide the individual's processing factor mean. Each clinical factor score is then subtracted from the processing factor mean. Next, the clinical factor scores are assessed for normative patterns, noting strengths if they are above 109, weaknesses if they are below 90, and average abilities if they are within the range from 90 to 109. Then, ipsative strengths and weaknesses are determined by considering the number obtained by subtracting the clinical factor scores from the processing factor mean. When a factor score is 15 points or more lower than the processing factor mean, it is considered an ipsative weakness, while a factor score 15 points or higher than the processing factor score is considered an ipsative strength. Dehn (2006) then specifies that processing deficits or assets are recorded for those processing factors that are both normative and ipsative weaknesses or strengths. Dehn (2006) goes on to suggest that the subtest scores used to compute each factor be examined to determine if there are outliers as well as to compare scores of related processes to assess face validity.

As Dehn's (2006) processing assessment model makes clear, it is necessary to distinguish between ipsative and normative comparison. Ipsative profile analysis refers to comparing an individual's scores in one area to scores in another area, or to the overall average of the various scores. In other words, ipsative comparisons are intraindividual comparisons. These are the types of comparisons most often being made in processing assessment in order to determine an individual's strengths and weaknesses. Normative comparison, on the other hand, involves comparing an individual's scores to those obtained by the general population. While much of the focus is on ipsative profiles, it is also necessary for normative comparisons to be made in order to make the information meaningful in context. For instance, an ipsative strength or weakness may be identified, but still be within the average range. If this is the case, it is unlikely that the strength or weakness is diagnostic in and of itself.

The importance of interindividual versus intraindividual analysis also raises the issue of significance. Often, clinicians use a variety of instruments within an assessment battery to determine the current levels of functioning. When comparing scores across different tests, there is frequently no normative information for determining the statistical significance of a discrepancy. While general guidelines may be provided, this leaves room for significant variability in practice between clinicians and varying test batteries.

Support for Processing Assessment

Flanagan, Ortiz, and Alfonso (2008) suggest that cognitive tests are useful within a diagnostic framework, such as response to intervention, not just in order to diagnose LD, but also to identify strengths and weaknesses in areas that have been empirically linked to academic skills in order to hypothesize why a student may not have responded to an intervention, contribute to intervention selection or modification, and suggest necessary accommodations. Others have also pointed out that while process training may not generalize to other tasks, those that are known to be related to specific academic tasks, such as phonological awareness to reading, make processing assessment worthwhile (e.g., see Torgesen 1979). Fuchs et al. (2011) point out that while use of cognitively focused interventions is not currently supported by research, the research also suggests that these interventions should not yet be completely ruled out.

Torgesen (2001) proposed a specific framework in which processing could defensibly be the primary characteristic assessed for direct diagnosis of LD. In this framework, a description of the basic psychological processes that cause learning difficulties is identified allowing identification of the locus of the neurological impairment at the second level of explanation. The final level of explanation is the etiology of the neurological impairment. Torgesen (2001) points to reading disabilities that have a phonological basis as support for this model. For example, the first level would be the description of phonological processing. The second level is the neurobiological evidence that poor readers primarily show abnormalities in the left hemisphere. Finally, the third level consists of evidence of heritability of the brain abnormalities and associated phonological difficulties. Within this framework, Torgesen (2001) argues that LD could be identified very early in individuals' schooling, individuals who do not demonstrate IQ discrepancies will not be excluded from intervention, and identifying the core process leading to learning problems will improve instruction for all learners.

Psychological processes are also the main component of the federal definition of LD. Examination of the definition suggests that the "basic psychological processes" are the core feature of the disability, and the manifestation of the said disability in the "imperfect ability to listen, think, speak, read, write, spell, or do mathematical calculations" is simply a symptom. Given this presentation of what an LD actually is, it logically follows that assessing psychological processes is necessary in order to accurately identify an LD. It has been reasoned from this conclusion back to the premise, such that because tests of cognitive processes are so widely used in identifying students with LD, cognitive processes are considered a central feature of LD (Minskoff 1998). This relates to the intuitive appeal of processing assessment and brings diagnosis of LD closer to the medical model. For example, just as a physician uses blood tests to identify an underlying infection that causes observable symptoms and then cures the symptoms by targeting the infection, processing assessment, in theory, allows a clinician to identify the underlying cause of observable learning difficulties and then ameliorate the learning problems by "curing" the underlying processing deficit.

Critique of Processing Assessment

Critics of processing assessment have pointed out that research does not support the validity, reliability, or utility of positing and assessing processes for identification or treatment (Vaughn and Linan-Thompson 2003; Reschly and Wilson 1990). While supporters assert the necessity of cognitive processing measures, citing the federal definition, federal LD classification criteria have never required cognitive processing assessment. When the Individuals with Disabilities Education Act (IDEA) was being revised, several researchers recommended that eligibility requirements include documentation of a basic psychological processing disorder. In response, the government concluded that "there is no current evidence that such assessments are necessary or sufficient for identifying SLD" (CFR pp. 46651). They went on to state that processing assessment typically adds to the testing burden without adding benefit to interventions. The response goes on to quote the Office of Special Education Programs (OSEP) Learning Disability Summit (Bradley et al. 2002), "Although processing deficits have been linked to some SLD (e.g., phonological processing and reading), direct links with other processes have not been established. Currently, available methods for measuring many processing difficulties are inadequate. Therefore, systematically measuring processing difficulties and their link to treatment is not yet feasible * * *. Processing deficits should be eliminated from the criteria for classification * * *." (p. 797).

In terms of identification, profiles do not provide a sound basis for diagnosing LD because such score differences commonly occur in the general population. Kavale and Forness (1984) conducted a meta-analysis of studies using Wechsler scale profiles, including the Wechsler Intelligence Scale for Children (WISC), Wechsler Intelligence Scale for Children- Revised (WISC-R), and Wechsler Preschool and Primary Scale of Intelligence (WPPSI). Through consideration of the various intelligence quotients, verbal and performance subtests, factor scores, and recategorization schemes, the researchers concluded that no manner of grouping or regrouping led to a significant indicator of LD. In fact, the LD group did not significantly differ from controls and actually demonstrated less variability than that of the average group. Additional psychometric drawbacks related to profile analysis have included low reliability and specificity of subtests, lack of increased predictive power above full scale IQ for academic outcomes, differing psychometric properties of ipsative versus normative scores, and varying profiles within a diagnostic category (Gresham et al. 2008).

Further, process training lacks treatment validity (Fuchs et al. 2011; Reschly and Wilson 1990), whereas specific instruction in academic skills has received support (Vellutino et al. 2006; Swanson 1999). This issue was addressed by Cronbach's (1975) discussion of Aptitude x Treatment Interaction (ATI) in which an outcome measure is regressed on some prerecorded characteristic, in this case a psychological process. If the slopes of regression lines of two treatments being compared differ, then an ATI is considered to exist. However, Cronbach (1975) pointed out that upon examining, ATI applied to cognitive aptitudes generalizations could rarely be made due to moderating variables. He wrote, "Once we attend to interactions, we enter a hall of mirrors that extends for eternity" (pp. 119).

In acknowledgment of arguments that studies have shown cognitive processes to be correlates of achievement (see Mather and Gregg 2006), it remains to be seen why clinicians should assess a correlate of achievement for LD diagnosis when achievement can be reliably, validly, and directly measured. As Wong (1992) points out, the key is to identify the component processes that underlie performance in certain areas of achievement and directly teaching these to students. For example, if some believe that working memory is a process involved in mathematics performance, engaging in exercises to improve a student's working memory will not actually lead to improved mathematical computation because working memory is not a proven component of successful mathematics calculation. A clear connection has been established between phonological processing and reading, but numerous well-designed research studies are necessary before the same claim can be made for other psychological processes and achievement domains (Gresham et al. 2008). Additionally, there is a frequent lack of consensus regarding the underlying processes for certain task areas and the definitions of those processes that are identified (Dean and Burns 2002). Furthermore, the effect size for direct instruction is considerably larger than that for linguistic process training (Kavale and Forness 2002).

Long ago, Mann (1979) summed up the seductiveness and dangers of processing models when he wrote, "Modern authors seem also to be incapable of abandoning the idea that they can train the mind and its parts. I must admit, myself, to being prejudiced in this direction. The problem is, as far as I am concerned, that when I am training the mind and its parts, I am not sure of exactly what I am training. And I am always in danger of believing what I do" (p. 540).

Case Examples

Below are two sample written reports utilizing processing assessment. The first presents an initial evaluation conducted in a private setting, while the second presents a reevaluation completed within a school setting. Both use a variety of instruments to determine processing strengths and weaknesses.

Associated Assessment Services
Confidential Psychological Report

Name: Christina Ward Parents: Peter and Tammy Ward
Date of Birth: 05/30/1999 Address: 12 Whitlock Circle
Age: 8 years, 9 months Telephone: 573–555-2439
Gender: Female
Dates of Evaluation: 04/12 and 04/13/2008
Report Date: 04/20/2008
Sources of Information:
Wechsler Intelligence Scale for Children, Fourth Edition (WISC-IV)
The Beery-Buktenica Developmental Test of Visual-Motor Integration (VMI)
Woodock-Johnson III Tests of Cognitive Ability (WJ-III COG)
Wide Range Assessment of Memory and Learning, Second Edition (WRAML-2)
Delis-Kaplan Executive Function System (D-KEFS)
Trail Making Test, Verbal Fluency Test, Design Fluency Test, Color–Word Interference Test, Twenty Questions Test, Tower Test
Behavior Rating Inventory of Executive Function (BRIEF)
Parent Form
Teacher Form
Comprehensive Test of Phonological Processing (CTOPP)
Test of Auditory Processing Skills, Third Editions (TAPS-3)
Auditory Comprehension and Auditory Reasoning subtests
Clinical Evaluation of Language Fundamentals—Screening Test (CELF-4)
Wechsler Individual Achievement Test, Second Edition (WIAT-II)
Kaufman Test of Educational Achievement, Second Edition (KTEA-II)
Test of Word Reading Efficiency (TOWRE)
Gray Oral Reading Test, Fourth Edition (GORT-IV)
The Behavior Assessment System for Children, Second Edition (BASC-2)
Parent Rating Scales (PRS)
Teacher Rating Scales (TRS)
Self-Report of Personality (SRP)
Structured Clinical Interview
Review of Records

Background Information

Christina was referred twice to her school's resource and support team, once in first grade and again in second grade, due to difficulties in reading and writing. She was described by her teacher as needing many repetitions to grasp new concepts. Her classroom grade averages were reported as being a 68 in grammar, 66 in spelling, and 65 in math. After interventions, Christina was reported to have made some improvement in math, but concerns were beginning to be noted with self-motivation. Christina's parents referred her to Associated Assessment Services for evaluation due to her continuing academic difficulties and frustration.

In an interview, Ms. Ward reported that Christina lives with her mother, father, and 12-year-old sister. Christina was the product of a full-term, uncomplicated pregnancy and was delivered normally at a weight of 8 pounds, 2 ounces. The family was noted to have lived in Juniper, SD, at the time of Christina's birth. Christina met all developmental milestones within normal limits and was reported to be in good health and to have not had serious illnesses or injuries. Ms. Ward cared for Christina at home during infancy and she does not currently receive after-school care. Main Street Elementary is the only school Christina has attended and she repeated kindergarten for a second year. Ms. Ward noted that she helps Christina with her homework, which takes about 1.5 h per night, and described homework time as "a battle."

Ms. Ward described Christina as being friendly, trustworthy, and happy with herself. Christina's chores were reported to include picking things up inside and outside and occasionally doing the dishes. Christina's bedtime hour is 9:00 p.m. and her hour of waking is 7:30 a.m. Family activities were noted to include playing outside, watching movies, and working with ceramics. Ms. Ward endorsed being most concerned about Christina's reading levels, her grades, and friends at school. She reported that Christina's main interests are karate and school, and that she has a good relationship with family, classmates, and friends. When asked what she enjoys most about Christina, she stated "everything—she's a good kid."

Testing Observations

Christina is an 8-year-old second grader who is noted to be of average height and weight for her chronological age. Christina entered the testing situation willingly, and rapport was easily established and maintained. Her affect was appropriate to the testing situation, and her mood was pleasant and cooperative. She appeared motivated, attempted all tasks, and put forth adequate effort. When Christina felt confident that she knew an answer, she responded quickly, but she took her time and carefully considered items of which she was less certain. The quality of Christina's expressive language was considered to be within the average range. When reading words or passages of varying difficulty across evaluation tasks, Christina tended to add an extra syllable that sounded like "uh" to the end of some words. At times, Christina had difficulty following directions and understanding questions she was asked. Christina was alert and appeared oriented throughout the evaluative sessions. She approached tasks in an organized and logical manner, although she sometimes had to stop and regroup after beginning an impulsive response. Her eye contact was appropriate and no disturbances in her thought processes were observed. Overall test results appear to be a valid estimate of Christina's current level of functioning.

Evaluation Results

Christina was administered the WISC-IV in order to provide an estimate of her cognitive ability. The WISC-IV is an individually administered test designed to provide subtest and composite scores that represent intellectual functioning in specific cognitive domains. Christina's performance on this test was compared to that of similar-aged children in a standardization sample.

The following scores reflect Christina's performance on the WISC-IV. Each subtest score is scaled to a mean of 10 and a standard deviation of 3. The various composite scores are scaled to a mean of 100 and a standard deviation of 15. Composite scores that fall between 90 and 109 are considered average.

	Composite score	Percentile rank
Verbal Comprehension Index (VCI)	112	79
Perceptual Reasoning Index (PRI)	115	84
Working Memory Index (WMI)	94	34
Processing Speed Index (PSI)	112	79
Full Scale IQ (FSIQ)	112	79

Verbal comprehension subtests	Scaled score	Percentile rank
Similarities	16	98
Vocabulary	11	63
Comprehension	10	50
Perceptual reasoning subtests	*Scaled score*	*Percentile rank*
Block design	10	50
Picture concepts	13	84
Matrix reasoning	14	91
Working memory subtests	*Standard score*	*Percentile rank*
Digit span	9	37
Letter-number sequencing	9	37
Processing speed Index	*Standard score*	*Percentile rank*
Coding	10	50
Symbol search	14	91

Christina was administered ten subtests of the WISC-IV from which her composite scores are derived. The Full Scale IQ (FSIQ) is derived from a combination of the ten subtest scores and is considered the most representative estimate of global intellectual functioning. Christina's general cognitive ability is within the High Average range of intellectual functioning as measured by the FSIQ. Her overall thinking and reasoning abilities exceed those of approximately 79 % of children her age. Christina's FSIQ would be expected to fall between 107 and 117 across 95 % of test administrations.

Christina's verbal reasoning abilities as measured by the Verbal Comprehension Index (VCI) are within the High Average range and above those of approximately 79 % of her peers. The VCI is designed to measure verbal reasoning and concept formation. Christina excelled at a task that required her to describe how two objects or concepts are similar, scoring two standard deviations above the mean. She performed within the Average range on the two other verbal subtests contributing to the VCI. This degree of variability is unusual for a child her age and may be noticeable to adults who know her well.

Christina's nonverbal reasoning abilities as measured by the Perceptual Reasoning Index (PRI) are in the High Average range and above those of 84 % of her peers. The PRI is designed to measure fluid reasoning in the perceptual domain with tasks that assess nonverbal concept formation, visual perception and organization, simultaneous processing, visual-motor coordination, learning, and the ability to separate figure ground and visual stimuli. Christina scored one standard deviation higher on the Picture Concepts and Matrix Reasoning subtests, than on the Block Design subtest. The former tests require selecting appropriate figures presented on paper that match a concept or complete a matrix, while the Block Design test requires using two-color cubes to construct replicas of two-dimensional geometric patterns. These results suggest that Christina's fluid visual information processing and abstract reasoning skills are better developed than her ability to analyze spatially presented part-whole relationships. The Block Design subtest may also be influenced by visual-spatial perception, visual perception-fine motor coordination, and planning ability.

Christina's ability to sustain attention, concentrate, and exert mental control is in the Average range. She performed better than approximately 34 % of her age mates in the area of Working Memory.

Christina's ability in processing simple or routine visual material without making error is in the High Average range when compared to her peers. She performed better than approximately 79 % of her peers on the processing speed tasks.

Overall, Christina's cognitive ability appears to be evenly developed and within the High Average range. She demonstrated a relative weakness in the area of working memory, suggesting that her abilities to sustain attention, concentrate, and exert mental control may make complex information processing more time consuming and difficult for Christina. It should be noted that while clearly weaker than her verbal and nonverbal reasoning skills, her working memory is still within the average range and comparable to same-age peers.

Christina was administered the WJ-III COG in order to assess various cognitive processing skills. The WJ-III is an individually administered instrument consisting of 20 tests that each measures a different aspect of cognitive ability. The tests are combined to provide various cluster scores representing broader aspects of cognitive functioning. Christina's performance on this test was compared to that of similar-aged individuals in a standardization sample.

The following scores reflect Christina's performance on the WJ-III. Each subtest score is scaled to a mean of 100 and a standard deviation of 15. Standard scores between 85 and 115, which include 68 % of the general population, are considered to be within the average range.

Test/cluster	Standard score	Percentile rank
Verbal comprehension	98	43
General information	110	74
Verbal ability	*103*	*59*
Visual-auditory learning	84	14
Retrieval fluency	98	44
Long-term retrieval	*86*	*18*
Concept formation	104	62
Sound blending	111	76
Thinking ability	*101*	*53*
Spatial relations	92	30
Picture recognition	95	37
Visual-spatial thinking	*92*	*31*

As expected, based upon WISC-IV results, Christina displayed average verbal ability. Within Long-Term Retrieval, which is the ability to store and retrieve information, Christina performed differently on two different tasks resulting in a long-term retrieval standard score within the very low range. Her performance was average on tasks requiring fluent retrieval of previously learned information that required her to name as many examples as possible from a given category within a 1-min time period. Christina demonstrated a relative and normative weakness in Visual-Auditory Learning, which measures her ability to learn, store, and retrieve a series of visual-auditory associations. On this test, she was required to learn and recall the names of rebuses (pictographic representations of words). Her paired-association learning, storage, and retrieval skills were within the very low range. This may also have implications for Christina's orthographic awareness, or ability to appropriately associate a mental representation with a letter, word, or other symbol, which includes spelling patterns, orthographic rules, inflectional and derivational morphology, and etymology.

Thinking ability measures Christina's ability to reason, form concepts, and solve problems using unfamiliar information or novel procedures, which is sometimes called fluid reasoning. Christina's thinking ability was within the average range.

Christina performed within the average range on Visual-Spatial Thinking tasks. Visual-spatial thinking is the ability to perceive, analyze, synthesize, and think with visual patterns, including the ability to store and recall visual representations.

Processing Speed is the ability to perform simple and automatic cognitive tasks rapidly, particularly when under pressure to maintain focused attention. Christina's processing speed standard score was within the low range indicating that she will have difficulty with tasks requiring cognitive speediness.

The Beery-Buktenica Developmental Test of VMI is an evaluation tool, which was designed to assess the extent to which individuals can integrate their visual and motor abilities. The VMI is a developmental sequence of geometric forms to be copied with paper and pencil. Standard scores from 83 to 117 are considered average.

Christina obtained a standard score of 85 on the VMI, which is within the below average range of functioning. This score placed her at the 16th percentile, when comparing her performance to other children her same age. Results of the VMI suggest that Christina's visual/perceptual-motor skills are somewhat less developed than what is expected given her chronological age and intellectual ability.

The *Wide Range Assessment of Memory and Learning, Second Edition (WRAML-2)* is an instrument that is designed to assess memory ability, including evaluation of immediate and/or delay recall, as well as differentiating between verbal, visual, or more global memory deficits. The WRAML-2 is comprised of six core subtests that yield three indexes: a Verbal Memory Index, a Visual Memory Index, and an Attention/Concentration Index. These three indexes together form the General Memory Index. Standard scores obtained on the WRAML-2 composites are based upon a mean of 100 and a standard deviation of 15. Standard scores on the subtests of the WRAML-2 are based upon a mean of 10 and a standard deviation of 3. The following scores were obtained on the WRAML-2.

Index score	Standard score	Percentile
Verbal memory	91	27
Visual memory	109	73
Attention/concentration	82	12
General memory	91	27

Verbal memory subtests	Scaled score
Story memory	8
Verbal learning	9
Visual memory subtests	*Scaled score*
Design memory	10
Picture memory	13
Attention/concentration subtests	*Scaled score*
Finger windows	9
Number letter	5
Additional subtests	*Scaled score*
Sound symbol	6
Sentence memory	9

Results of the WRAML-2 suggest that Christina's Verbal Memory is within the average range. Her Visual Memory is over a standard deviation higher, but also within the average range. Christina's Attention/Concentration score fell within the below average range of functioning. Christina's score on the Number Letter subtest was within the borderline range and lower than her Finger Windows score, which was within the average range. The Number Letter subtest requires repeating a sequence of single digits and letters orally presented by the examiner. Christina's General Memory score fell within the average range of functioning. Christina was also administered two supplemental subtests. Her score on the Sentence Memory subtest was within the average range, while her score on the Sound Symbol subtest was within the below average range. The Sound Symbol subtest is a paired-associate task requiring the learner to recall sounds associated with various abstract figures, and it is thus a cross-modal task (i.e., verbal-visual), and one that taps important aspect involved in the acquisition of the mechanics of reading or "word-calling." Christina's poorer performance on this task suggests that she has a deficit in orthographic memory.

Christina was also administered several tasks from the D-KEFS. The first test Christina completed was the D-KEFS Trail Making Test. Christina's scores are shown below:

Condition/composite	Completion time scaled score
Condition 1: visual scanning	6
Condition 2: number sequencing	10
Condition 3: letter sequencing	9
Condition 4: number-letter switching	3
Condition 5: motor speed	11
Combined number + letter switching	10

Primary contrast measure	Contrast scaled score
Switching vs. Visual scanning	8
Switching vs. Number sequencing	3
Switching vs. Letter sequencing	4
Switching vs. Combined LS + NS	3
Switching vs. Motor speed	2

Christina's visual scanning score suggests she may have some difficulties. Indeed, Christina's visual scanning contrast score indicates similar levels of impairment in visual-scanning/attention and cognitive flexibility abilities. Christina's completion time for Number Sequencing was equal to a scaled score of 10, which places her within the average range. The Switching vs. Number Sequencing contrast score of 3, which is within the extremely low range, suggests that Christina has a deficit in cognitive flexibility that is unaffected by her number sequencing ability. Christina's letter sequencing was average, while her letter sequencing contrast score again suggested a cognitive shifting deficiency unrelated to letter sequencing ability. On Number-Letter Switching, Christina tended to stop after reaching a letter and then count on her fingers to determine that letter's position in the alphabet and then continue onto the appropriate number. Her motor speed was within expected limits. Overall results of the D-KEFS Trail Making Test suggest that Christina has a cognitive flexibility deficit and some visual-scanning/attention difficulties and intact letter and number sequencing skills. Thus, Christina's difficulties on this particular assessment appear to be attributable to cognitive shifting and visual scanning weaknesses.

The *D-KEFS Verbal Fluency Test* yielded the following scaled scores:

Primary measures	Scaled scores
Letter fluency: total correct	11
Category fluency: total correct	13
Category switching: total correct	9
Category switching: total switching accuracy	10

Primary contrast measures	Scaled scores
Letter fluency vs. category fluency	8
Category switching vs. category fluency	6

Christina's Letter Fluency score of 11 is within the average range and suggests that she has strengths in several fundamental and executive function abilities, including verbal knowledge; rapid, systematic retrieval of lexical items; and simultaneous processing and monitoring. Christina earned a score of 13 on the Category Fluency task, which is within the above average range. This task requires similar skills to those required by the Letter Fluency condition, but typically requires less effortful processing. Christina obtained a Category Switching score of 9, which is within the average range, and a Category Switching Accuracy score of 10, which is also within the average range. Christina's Category Switching contrast measure is within the below average range and suggests that while Christina has strengths in verbal fluency, a deficit in cognitive shifting affected her performance on the Category Switching task.

Christina also completed the *D-KEFS Design Fluency Test* and earned the following scores:

Primary measures	Scaled score
Condition 1: filled dots	8
Condition 2: empty dots only	9
Condition 3: switching	7
Design fluency total correct	8

Christina's performance on both the Filled Dots and Empty Dots Only conditions was within the average range. This suggests that Christina may exhibit a number of cognitive strengths from motor speed to nonverbal creativity and simultaneous processing. Christina earned a Switching score of 7, which is in the below average range, and slightly lower than her other scores, again indicating a weakness in cognitive shifting.

The D-KEFS Color-Word Interference Test resulted in the following scores:

Primary measure	Scaled scores
Condition 1: color naming	1
Condition 2: word reading	11
Condition 3: inhibition	5
Condition 4: inhibition/switching	7
Combined naming + reading	6

Contrast measures	Scaled scores
Inhibition vs. color naming	14
Inhibition/switching vs. combined naming + reading	11
Inhibition/switching vs. inhibition	12
Inhibition/switching vs. color naming	16
Inhibition/switching vs. word reading	6

Christina obtained a scaled score of 1 on the Color Naming task, which is within the extremely low range. Scores in this range may be due to a word-finding impairment, a developmental verbal learning disability (LD), or other neurostructural or nonneurostructural factors that might affect speed of mental processing. Based on Christina's contrast scores for Color Naming, she performed significantly better on the higher level Inhibition (borderline range) and Inhibition/Switching (below average range) tasks. This suggests that while Christina may have some difficulties with rapid naming and inhibition, this particular task is unable to reveal them due to a deficit in the baseline condition of color naming. It should be noted that during this task, Christina commented on the color page making her feel dizzy and her eyes hurt, thus visual difficulties may have contributed to her performance to some extent.

Christina earned an average score on the Word Reading condition, indicating intact ability to read high-frequency words quickly. Given the difference between her naming and reading performance, the Combined Naming+Reading score and associated contrast score are not useful. The Word Reading contrast score, however, again suggests that cognitive flexibility represents a weakness for Christina. Her profile of scores prevents drawing specific conclusions regarding her verbal inhibition.

The *D-KEFS Twenty Questions Test* resulted in the following scores:

Primary measures	Scaled score
Initial abstraction score	15
Total questions asked	13
Total weighted achievement score	13

The initial abstraction score is the scaled score equivalent for the minimum number of objects that can be eliminated by the first question regardless of the yes or no answer across the four trials. Christina earned an initial abstraction score of 15, which is within the superior range. It should be noted that the directions had to be read to Christina several times before she understood the task. Once she understood the concept, she tended to begin with mid-level or high-level category questions. Christina's Total Questions Asked and Total Weighted Achievement scores were both within the above average range. Christina's performance on this test indicates strengths in the executive functions of categorization and the ability to use feedback to guide her problem-solving behavior.

The *D-KEFS Tower Test* resulted in the following scores:

Measures	Scaled score
Total achievement score	9
Time-per-move-ratio	8

Christina's overall performance on the Tower Test was within the average range. A score in this range likely reflects cognitive strengths in multiple fundamental skills and executive functions, particularly in spatial planning, rule learning, and inhibition. Christina's average time to make each move was also within the average range. It should be noted that she was always quick to make the initial move and then would either deliberate for a long period of time before making her next more or impulsively continue moving the disks. This inconsistent performance suggests that Christina may not have a consistent strength in inhibition. Christina violated the rules a total of five times, which is equal to or more often than 34 % of same-age peers. This suggests that her ability to establish and maintain cognitive set, or to learn instruction and apply the rules, on performance tasks is within the average range.

Christina's mother and teacher also completed the BRIEF, a questionnaire designed to provide a better understanding of a child's self-control and problem-solving skills by measuring eight aspects of executive functioning. The executive functions are mental processes that direct a child's thought, action, and emotion, particularly during problem solving. Raw scores obtained on the BRIEF are converted to T-scores, which have a mean of 50 and a standard deviation of 10. T-scores between 60 and 64* are considered mildly elevated and T-scores at or above 65** indicate clinically significant difficulties.

Index/scale	Parent T-scores	Teacher T-scores
Inhibit	42	48
Shift	50	69**
Emotional control	38	47
Behavioral Regulation Index (BRI)	42	54
Initiate	55	82**
Working memory	55	67**
Plan/organize	65**	78**
Organization of materials	45	72**
Monitor	67**	63*
Metacognition Index (MI)	59	73**
Global Executive Composite (GEC)	53	68**

* Mildly elevated
** Clinically significant difficulties

Ms. Ward's and Ms. Bennett's responses were reasonably consistent and were not overly negative and are, therefore, considered valid. The overall index, the Global Executive Composite (GEC), and the Behavioral Regulation Index (BRI) and Metacognition Index (MI) were within the expected range for Ms. Ward's report. Ms. Bennett's report yielded an elevated MI and GEC. While Ms. Bennett's ratings resulted in an average BRI, the Shift scale, which measures the ability to adjust to changes in routine or task demands, was elevated due to Christina's difficulty adapting to new situations and occasional difficulty bouncing back from disappointments. Within the MI, Ms. Ward and Ms. Bennett both expressed concern with Christina's ability to plan and organize problem-solving approaches (Plan/Organize). Ms. Ward also endorsed that Christina has difficulty monitoring her own behavior (Monitor). At school, Ms. Bennett noted that Christina also has difficulty initiating problem solving or activity (Initiate), sustaining working memory (Working Memory), and organizing her environment (Organization of Materials). Based on Ms. Bennett's report, Christina's working memory, planning/organization, and initiation are significantly impaired compared to same-age peers, and problems with task-oriented monitoring were strongly endorsed. This profile suggests significant difficulties with general metacognitive problem solving. Christina is likely to have significant difficulty with independent problem solving due to problems with her ability to actively hold multiple pieces of information in mind and systematically construct a plan. As a result, this has a negative impact on her attempts to initiate these tasks. In addition, Christina is likely to have difficulty monitoring her performance during tasks.

The CTOPP is an instrument that is designed to measure the ability to use phonological information, especially the sound structure of one's oral language, in processing written language. A deficit in some aspect of phonological processing ability is viewed as a contributing factor of a reading disability. The CTOPP measures three kinds of phonological processing, which includes phonological awareness, phonological memory, and rapid naming. Standard scores obtained on the CTOPP composites are based upon a mean of 100 and a standard deviation of 15. Standard scores obtained on the subtests of the CTOPP are based upon a mean of 10 and a standard deviation of 3. The following scores were obtained on the CTOPP.

Subtest/composite	Composite score	Percentile
Elision	8	25
Blending	8	25
Phonological awareness	*88*	*21*
Memory for digits	7	16
Nonword repetition	10	50
Phonological memory	*91*	*27*
Rapid digit naming	10	50
Rapid letter naming	9	37
Rapid naming	*97*	*42*
Rapid color naming	5	5
Rapid object naming	9	37
Alternate rapid naming	*82*	*12*
Phoneme reversal	5	5
Segmenting words	14	91

Phonological awareness refers to the awareness of and ability to use the basic phonological or sound structure of oral language. Difficulties in this area may affect a student's ability to identify and separate discrete sound "chunks," as well as to synthesize or blend sounds together to form words. Christina's Phonological Awareness Composite Score (PACS) was within the below average range, which indicates that she has a weakness in her ability to identify and manipulate the sound structure of oral language. The PACS is composed of two subtests, Elision and Blending Words. The Elision subtest measures the ability to remove phonological segments from spoken words to form other words. The Blending Words subtest measures the ability to synthesize and form words.

The Phonological Memory Composite Score (PMCS) consists of the Memory for Digits and Nonword Repetition subtests. Memory for Digits measures the ability to store and recall a series of numbers. Christina stated that she had difficulty remembering words, especially when there are several to be remembered. Her score on this subtest was one standard deviation below the mean, suggesting some difficulty. Nonword Repetition measures the ability to accurately repeat nonsense words. The PMCS represents an individual's ability to phonologically code information into working memory and may affect reading fluency. Christina's PMCS was within the average range.

The Rapid Naming Composite Score (RNCS) is comprised of the Rapid Digit Naming and Rapid Letter Naming subtests. The RNCS measures the efficiency of retrieval of phonological information from long-term memory and the ability to execute a series of operations quickly and repeatedly. Efficient retrieval of phonological information and execution of sequences of operations are required for decoding unfamiliar words. Christina's performance on the RNCS was within the average range. Christina's Alternate Rapid Naming Composite Score (ARNCS) was within the below average range. The ARNCS consists of the Rapid Color Naming and Rapid Object Naming subtests. Christina had significantly greater difficulty efficiently naming colors compared to letters, numbers, and objects. It should be noted that during the administration of the D-KEFS Color-Word Interference test, Christina stated that looking at the page of colors hurt her eyes and made her feel dizzy. Thus, Christina's poorer performance on the color rapid naming may be due to a visual issue. During all subtests, however, she had a tendency to add an "uh" that resembled an extra syllable to the end of words.

The *Test of Auditory Processing Skills, Third Edition (TAPS-3)* is an instrument designed to measure the ability of the brain to understand and interpret what the ears hear. The TAPS-3 is an individually administered assessment of auditory skills necessary for the development, use, and understanding of language commonly utilized in academic and everyday activities. The tasks on the TAPS-3 were designed to provide information for four areas: auditory attention, basic phonological skills, auditory memory, and auditory cohesion. Christina was administered the auditory cohesion subtests in order to assess her ability to understand and interpret spoken language. Scaled scores on the TAPS-3 subtests range in value from 1 to 19 and are based on a mean of 10 and a standard deviation of 3. Standard scores that are obtained are based upon a mean of 100 and a standard deviation of 15. The following scores were obtained:

Subtest	Standard score	Percentile
Auditory comprehension	10	50
Auditory reasoning	11	63

Composite	Standard score	Percentile
Cohesion	103	58

The Auditory Comprehension subtest is designed to show how well the student understands spoken information. On this subtest, Christina had difficulty remembering names of characters presented in target sentences and sometimes supplied answers that were logical, but were not drawn from the sentences. The Auditory Reasoning subtest measures the ability to understand higher order linguistic processing related to understanding jokes, riddles, inferences, and abstractions. It is designed to determine if the student can understand implied meanings, make inferences, or come to logical conclusions given the information in the sentence(s) presented. Christina primarily inferred the meaning from the information presented, but on some items seemed to base her response on her logic rather than the information. These subtests are combined to yield the Cohesion composite, which summarizes higher order linguistic skills that require the student to understand exactly what is said and to be able to make inferences, deductions, and abstractions. Christina's Cohesion composite score was within the average range, which suggests that her processing of auditory information is commensurate with her overall cognitive ability.

Summary of Cognitive Processing: Overall, based on the processing and language assessments detailed above, Christina appears to have several areas of strengths, weaknesses, and typical functioning. Weaknesses include the following: attention/concentration, the executive function of cognitive flexibility, phonological awareness, color naming, and long-term retrieval of symbols, which likely relate to a deficit in orthographic processing. Christina's ability was within the average or above average range in the following areas: verbal ability, auditory processing, fluid reasoning, processing speed, working memory, visual-spatial processing, and the executive functions of categorization and maintenance of cognitive set.

Christina was administered selected subtests of the WIAT-II to determine current levels of academic achievement. These tests are individually administered, norm-referenced tests that assess performance in the essential academic areas of reading, mathematics, and written language. Standard scores are based upon a mean of 100 and a standard deviation of 15. Scores that fall between 85 and 115 are considered to be within the average range.

Subtest/composite	Standard score	Percentile
Word reading	88	21
Reading comprehension	92	30
Pseudoword decoding	85	16
Reading composite	86	18
Numerical operations	98	45
Math reasoning	99	47
Mathematics composite	97	42
Spelling	93	32
Written expression	66	1
Written language	78	7

Christina obtained a Reading Composite score of 86 (18th percentile), which is in the below average range of functioning. This composite included three subtests—Word Reading, Reading Comprehension, and Pseudoword Decoding. Christina performed similarly across subtests, indicating some difficulty in decoding words, although she seemed to accommodate through strategies allowing her to perform slightly better on reading comprehension.

In the area of mathematics skills, Christina obtained a Math Composite score of 97 (42nd percentile), which is in the average range of functioning. This composite included two subtests—Numerical Operations and Math Reasoning. Christina occasionally made careless errors, but demonstrated expected levels of mathematics calculation and reasoning abilities.

Within the area of written language, Christina obtained a Written Language composite standard score of 78 (7th percentile) which is within the borderline range of functioning. This composite included two subtests—Spelling and Written Expression. On the Spelling subtest, Christina earned a standard score of 93, which is in the average range. On the Written Expression subtest, Christina earned a standard score of 66, which is within the borderline range. This score is considered a low estimate of Christina's writing ability, because she did not follow directions on some of the tasks.

In order to obtain a more accurate estimate of Christina's written expression, she was also administered the Written Expression subtest of the *Kaufman Test of Educational Achievement, Second Edition (KTEA-II)*, which is a standardized norm-referenced measure of achievement yielding scores on the same scale as the WIAT-II. On the KTEA-II Written Expression subtest, Christina earned a standard score of 109, which is within the average range. This result suggests that Christina's writing ability is commensurate with her cognitive ability. On the writing tasks, Christina used simple vocabulary with infrequent use of descriptive words, adjectives, and adverbs. She also used numerous misspellings and tended to reverse letters, mainly writing "b" for "d" and vice versa. She also exhibited difficulty combining sentences.

The *Test of Word Reading Efficiency (TOWRE)* is a measure of an individual's ability to pronounce printed words accurately and fluently. Reading is assessed for accuracy and fluency to understand proficiency in decoding and sight word recognition, which are necessary for comprehending written language. Scores on the TOWRE are scaled to a mean of 100 and a standard deviation of 15. Composite scores that fall between 90 and 109 are considered average. Christina earned the following scores:

Subtest/composite	Standard score	Percentile
Word reading efficiency	82	12
Phonemic decoding	84	14
Total word reading efficiency	83	13

Christina's overall word reading efficiency was within the below average range, as indicated by her score of 83 (13th percentile). The Word Efficiency subtest assesses fluent sight word recognition. Christina earned a standard score within the below average range. The Phonemic Decoding subtest requires sounding out pronounceable printed nonwords. Christina's score on this subtest was also within the below average range.

The GORT-IV is a measure of reading skills and oral reading comprehension for students 7–18 years of age. Reading ability is assessed for speed, accuracy, fluency (a combination of rate and accuracy), and comprehension through asking the student to orally read short passages of increasing length and complexity. The fluency and comprehension scores are combined to form an overall Oral Reading Quotient. The Oral Reading Quotient is represented by a standard score having a mean of 100 and a standard deviation of 15. Scores between 85 and 115, which include 68 % of the population, are considered to be within the average range. Christina earned an Oral Reading Quotient of 94, which equals or exceeds the performance of 34 % of her same-age peers.

The individual areas assessed yield standard scores having a mean of 10 and a standard deviation of 3.

Area	Standard score	Percentile
Rate	6	9
Accuracy	7	16
Fluency	6	9
Comprehension	12	75

Christina exhibited somewhat labored reading on longer passages containing more complex words and concepts. She would sometimes substitute orthographically similar words for irregular and uncommon words and was unable to sound out unfamiliar words. She also interchanged short common words such as "in" for "an" and "out" for "into." These tendencies affected her accuracy score and also impacted her reading rate, as attempting to identify and stopping to correct mistakes slowed her oral reading. Additionally, across reading tasks, she tended to add syllables (i.e., uh or eh) to the end of some words, regardless of familiarity. This contributed to slow choppy reading mixed within fluent reading. Together, Christina's reading rate and accuracy yielded a below average fluency score. Christina's comprehension ability was within the above average range and higher than would have been expected given her fluency. Across reading comprehension tasks, Christina tended to use prior knowledge and common sense rather than context clues to arrive at answers. On the GORT-IV, she was unable to look back at the reading passage when answering comprehension questions, but on other instruments in which the text remained available, she usually looked back at the passage to answer questions. On this and other measures, Christina sometimes lost her place, particularly when passages became longer and more difficult.

Christina's pattern of cognitive processing and reading and writing performance suggests that she has weaknesses in orthographic and phonological processing, which affect her performance on tasks involving symbols and language. Additionally, Christina's difficulties with concentration and cognitive flexibility appear to impact her ability to remember and use verbal information, even when provided with written directions to which she can refer. This difficulty affects her learning and performance across academic subjects, with particularly difficulty in reading.

Christina's mother, Ms. Ward, and teacher, Ms. Bennett, completed the BASC-2, a measure that evaluates levels of behavioral, emotional, and social competencies relative to other children their age and gender. On the Clinical scales and Composite scores of the BASC-2, T-scores of 70 and above** are considered clinically significant, scores between 60 and 69* are in the at-risk range, and scores of 41 through 59 are in the average range. Adaptive scale scores of 30 or less** are considered clinically significant, scores of 31–40* are at risk, and scores between 41 and 59 are average.

Skill area	T-score (mother)	T-score (teacher)
Hyperactivity	39	49
Aggression	46	46
Conduct problems	37	45
Externalizing problems	40	46
Anxiety	47	65*
Depression	45	66*
Somatization	36	47
Internalizing problems	41	62*
Attention problems	–	62*
Learning problems	–	78**
School problems	–	72**
Atypicality	41	59
Withdrawal	47	66*
Attention problems	51	–
Behavioral symptoms index	43	60*
Adaptability	55	45
Social skills	50	42
Leadership	46	42
Activities of daily living	49	–
Study skills	–	38*
Functional communication	50	41
Adaptive skills	50	40

* At risk

** Clinically significant/high level of maladjustment

Ms. Ward's and Ms. Bennett's F, Response Pattern, and Consistency indexes were within the acceptable range. Ms. Ward indicated that Christina is well adapted behaviorally, socially, and emotionally within the home environment. Ms. Bennett's ratings resulted in a significant School Problems composite, which reflect academic difficulties, including problems of motivation, attention, and learning and cognition. The Attention Problems scale was in the at-risk range due to a short attention span and some distractibility. The Learning Problems scale was significantly elevated due to Christina's difficulty with reading, spelling, mathematics, and handwriting. Ms. Bennett also reported that Christina demonstrates an at-risk level of

Internalizing Problems due to worrying and nervousness regarding tests (Anxiety) and saying that she does not have any friends (Depression). The Withdrawal scale was also in the at-risk range because Ms. Bennett endorsed that Christina often plays alone and has difficulty making new friends. The Behavioral Symptoms Index, which is composed of the Hyperactivity, Aggression, Depression, Attention Problems, Atypicality, and Withdrawal scales and reflects overall level of problem behavior, was also in the at-risk range.

Christina also completed the *Behavior Assessment System for Children-Second Edition Self-Report of Personality (BASC-2-SRP)* to provide her perception of her social and emotional functioning. As with the parent and teacher forms, the Clinical scales and Composite T-scores of 70 and above** are considered clinically significant, scores between 60 and 69* are in the at-risk range, and scores of 41–59 are in the average range. Adaptive scale scores of 30 or less** are considered clinically significant, scores of 31–40* are at risk, and scores between 41 and 59 are average. Specific T-scores obtained on the BASC-2-SRP are listed below:

Skill area	T-score
Attitude to school	68*
Attitude to teachers	40
School problems	55
Atypicality	47
Locus of control	42
Social stress	46
Anxiety	58
Depression	46
Sense of inadequacy	77**
Internalizing problems	53
Attention problems	53
Hyperactivity	40
Inattention/hyperactivity	46
Emotional symptoms index	55
Relations with parents	60
Interpersonal relations	59
Self-esteem	58
Self-reliance	47
Personal adjustment	58

* At risk
** Clinically significant/high level of maladjustment

Christina's F, Response Pattern, V, L, and Consistency indexes were within the acceptable range. On this self-report, Christina indicated that she experiences a significant Sense of Inadequacy. The Sense of Inadequacy scale assesses perceptions of low achievement expectations, a tendency to not persevere, and a perception of being unsuccessful, particularly in academic endeavors. Specifically, Christina expressed her perception that she should be able to do better, but regardless of her effort, she cannot do so. Christina's ratings also resulted in an at-risk Attitude to School scale due to her negative feelings related to her academic experiences. Despite these difficulties, Christina expressed satisfaction with her relationships as well as a positive self-concept.

Christina also completed a clinical interview. When asked what she would want if granted three wishes, Christina replied that she would want a laptop, be smart, and have a "good life." She described a good life as not getting in trouble a lot. When asked which three people she would take with her if she were on a deserted island, she responded that she would choose her friend, Andy, her mom, and her dad. When asked about a person she likes, she stated that she had liked a boy in her class last year because he was cute. When asked about a person she does not like, she reported that there is a girl in her class who never listens, whispers secrets, and "shoos" her away when she and her friend try to talk to her or her peer group. Christina reported that her favorite things to do are karate and skateboarding. She stated that there are three television channels that she likes to watch, but she does not have a favorite show. Christina disclosed that she would like to be a taekwondo artist after she finishes school.

Christina endorsed reading as her favorite subject, because it helps her get smarter. She stated that mathematics is her least favorite subject, because she is not good at it and gets bad grades. When asked what she would change about herself, Christina replied that she would be smart, not get bad grades, and be proud of herself. She reported that she knew she could do better, but felt she was trying to do her best. She also noted that there is too much talking in the classroom that prevents her from concentrating. Christina also reported that she was held back in kindergarten, because the first year she wanted to play instead of study since she did not understand the importance of jobs. When asked what she would change about her teacher, Christina wished that her mathematics teacher would be nicer, help the class "better," and be less worried about the time. She reported that if her mother could change anything about her, it would likely be her grades. Christina stated that she would not change anything about her parents because they are perfect and her father always forgives her. Christina reported that she would not change anything about her family. She noted that she and her 13-year-old sister, Kayla, get along at times and that she enjoys being Kayla's model when she is taking pictures.

Christina reported that getting to do something special, such as visiting family in Texas, makes her happy. She stated that she was sad when her mother gave away her bunny. Christina endorsed getting angry when someone says bad things about her, but she just ignores the person and controls herself.

Summary and Diagnostic Impressions

Christina is an 8-year-old, second grade student who was referred for a comprehensive evaluation to assist in determining eligibility for special education services. Current test results suggest that Christina is functioning intellectually in the average range. She displayed average abilities associated with language development and acquired knowledge, as well as nonverbal and fluid reasoning. Academically, Christina's performance in mathematics was in the average range, while her reading and writing abilities were below expectations. Her writing appeared to be rather low on the administration on one instrument in which she had difficulty following directions, but was within the normal range on the written expression subtest of another instrument. On both administrations, she demonstrated writing difficulties.

In terms of processing, Christina's weaknesses included long-term retrieval of symbols/language, concentration, cognitive flexibility, and phonological and orthographic processing. Christina demonstrated average or above average verbal knowledge, fluid reasoning, processing speed, working memory, visual-spatial thinking, categorization, and maintenance of cognitive set.

Christina's mother and her teacher completed behavioral rating scales. Ms. Ward's ratings indicated that Christina is a well-adjusted, typically behaving young girl. Ms. Bennett's ratings indicated that Christina has difficulties with learning tasks and exhibits some at-risk internalizing symptoms related to these difficulties. Christina's self-report through a rating scale and interview revealed that she is basically satisfied with her relationships and overall functioning, but perceives that she should be able to do better on academic tasks, although she applies herself to the best of her ability and continues to fail.

Current assessment results indicate that Christina is demonstrating significant learning difficulties associated with cognitive processing deficits, particularly in the areas of reading and writing. Based upon these findings, the following diagnostic impressions are offered: Reading Disorder [315.00] and Disorder of Written Expression [315.2].

NAME: Katherine Jenkins	REFERRED BY: IEP Team
BIRTH DATE: 03/12/1990	SCHOOL: Salem High School
AGE: 18 years, 3 months	GRADE: 12
SEX: Female	VISION: 03/11/2008
PARENT/GUARDIAN: Angela Jenkins	HEARING: 03/11/2008

TELEPHONE: 678–493-4742
DATES EVALUATED: 03/12/2008, 03/16/2008, 03/22/2008
ASSESSMENT TOOLS:
Wechsler Adult Intelligence Scale, Third Edition (WAIS-III)
Wechsler Individual Achievement Test, Second Edition (WIAT-II)
Gray Oral Reading Test, Fourth Edition (GORT-IV)
Writing Task
Comprehensive Test of Phonological Processing (CTOPP)
Woodcock Johnson III Tests of Cognitive Development (WJ-III COG)
Beery-Buktenica Developmental Test of Visual-Motor Integration (VMI)
Rey Complex Figure Test and Recognition Trial (RCFT)
Behavior Rating Inventory of Executive Function (BRIEF)
- Parent Form
- Teacher Form
- Self-Report Version

The Behavior Assessment System for Children, Second Edition (BASC-2)
Parent Rating Scales (PRS)
Self-Report of Personality (SRP)
Teacher Rating Scales (TRS)
Clinical Interview
Record Review

Following is a psychoeducational evaluation of Katherine Jenkins. Access to this report should be restricted in accordance with state special education regulations and procedures.

Referral and Background Information

Reason for Referral

Katherine was referred for a comprehensive psychoeducational evaluation in order to provide further documentation of the presence of a learning disability (LD) and to identify services and accommodations necessary for her to achieve postsecondary success. Katherine has been serving under the Learning Disabilities program since the third grade.

Educational History

According to a Callaway County eligibility team report, Katherine was originally referred to extra academic support in the fall of 1997, but did not make progress after interventions were implemented. An evaluation for special education was completed in the spring of 1998. Katherine earned average intelligence scores with below average achievement across areas, with written expression and mathematics calculation representing significant deficits. A neuropsychological report completed by a private practitioner in the summer of 1998 concluded that Katherine demonstrated difficulties with sequential processing that impacted her phonological awareness and paired association memory; decreased attention and concentration skills, particularly maintaining and shifting attention; and, impaired decision-making skills, such as producing a strategy and consistently using learned strategies. While Katherine has a well-documented history of LD impacting literacy skills, she is a highly motivated student who has been able to compensate for her disabilities through hard work and extra support (e.g., extra time for assignments and exams, lecture notes, audio books).

Background Information

Katherine's mother, Ms. Angela Jenkins, completed a phone interview. According to Ms. Jenkins, Katherine was the product of an uncomplicated, full-term pregnancy and was delivered through cesarean section, as were her two older siblings. Ms. Jenkins reported that Katherine reached all developmental milestones within normal limits. She had no health difficulties with the exception of having her tonsils removed before 3 years of age due to severe sleep apnea. Ms. Jenkins noted that Katherine began having academic difficulties in second grade, but in hindsight realized that she did things differently in prekindergarten and kindergarten and that her teachers had made comments about her learning style. Ms. Jenkins reported that Katherine's first grade teacher really worked with her, so she was able to make some progress. Reportedly, Katherine could correctly identify letters by pointing; however, she was unable to match sounds to letters. Ms. Jenkins stated that Katherine's grades were always average and above except in reading. Ms. Jenkins reported no family history of learning difficulties, although she believed that her oldest son has similar difficulties but was better able to memorize sight words than Katherine.

Ms. Jenkins reported that Katherine lives at home with her mother and father. She also noted that Katherine has belonged to the volleyball, basketball, and track teams and gets along well with her family and classmates. Ms. Jenkins noted that her only concern regarding Katherine was that she may have difficulty functioning without support in college.

General Observations and Impressions

Katherine is an 18-year-old high school senior who presented as well groomed and neatly dressed. She was tested at Salem High School over three sessions. Katherine entered the testing situation willingly, and rapport was easily established and maintained. She expressed her interest in completing the evaluation as soon as possible and was motivated to do well. Her affect was appropriate to the testing situation, and her mood was pleasant and cooperative. Katherine was alert and appeared oriented throughout the evaluative sessions. She approached tasks in an organized and logical manner. She frequently asked for items to be repeated, particularly early in the evaluation sessions. Her eye contact was appropriate and no disturbances in her thought processes were observed. This assessment is believed to be an accurate and reliable estimate of Katherine's potential and current level of functioning.

Test Results and Interpretations

Intellectual Functioning

Katherine was administered the WAIS-III in order to provide an estimate of her cognitive ability. The WAIS-III is an individually administered test designed to provide 14 subtest, 4 index, and 3 IQ scores that represent intellectual functioning in specific cognitive domains. Katherine's performance on this test was compared to that of similar-aged individuals in a standardization sample.

The following scores reflect Katherine's performance on the WAIS-III. Each subtest score is scaled to a mean of 10 and a standard deviation of 3. The various composite scores are scaled to a mean of 100 and a standard deviation of 15. Composite scores that fall between 90 and 109 are considered average.

Verbal scale		Performance scale	
Verbal comprehension		*Perceptual organization*	
Vocabulary	9	Picture completion	13
Similarities	8	Block design	10
Information	8	Matrix reasoning	10
Comprehension**	9	Picture arrangement**	11
Working memory		*Processing speed*	
Arithmetic	9	Digit symbol-coding	11
Digit span	6	Symbol search*	9
Letter-number sequencing**	6		

* Does not contribute to IQ score
** Does not contribute to index score

Index scores	Composite score
Verbal Comprehension Index (VCI)	91
Perceptual Reasoning Index (PRI)	105
Working Memory Index (WMI)	82
Processing Speed Index (PSI)	99
IQ scores	
Verbal IQ (VIQ)	88
Performance IQ (PIQ)	106
Full Scale IQ (FSIQ)	*95*

Katherine was administered 13 subtests of the WAIS-III from which her composite scores are derived. The Full Scale IQ (FSIQ) is derived from a combination of 11 subtest scores and is considered the most representative estimate of global intellectual functioning. Katherine's general cognitive ability is within the average range of intellectual functioning as measured by the FSIQ. Based on this score, her overall thinking and reasoning abilities equal or exceed those of approximately 37% of children her age. There is a 95% probability that her true score would be found within the score range of 91–99. It should be noted that there is a statistically significant difference between her performance on verbal and performance composites, thus her full-scale IQ score is not considered an accurate estimate of her intellectual functioning, and it is the examiner's opinion that the Perceptual Reasoning Index (PRI) more closely represents Katherine's actual intellectual ability.

Katherine's verbal reasoning abilities as measured by the Verbal Comprehension Index (VCI) are within the average range and equal or exceed those of approximately 27% of her peers. The VCI is designed to measure verbal reasoning and concept formation. Katherine performed comparably on the verbal subtests contributing to the VCI, suggesting that these verbal cognitive abilities are similarly developed.

Katherine's nonverbal reasoning abilities as measured by the PRI are within the Average range and equal or exceed those of 63 % of her peers. The PRI is designed to measure fluid reasoning in the perceptual domain with tasks that assess nonverbal concept formation, visual perception and organization, simultaneous processing, visual-motor coordination, learning, and the ability to separate figure ground and visual stimuli. Katherine performed comparably on the perceptual reasoning subtests contributing to the PRI, suggesting that her visual-spatial reasoning and perceptual-organizational skills are similarly developed.

Katherine's ability to sustain attention, concentrate, and exert mental control is in the low average range. She performed equal to or better than approximately 12 % of her age mates in the area of Working Memory.

Katherine's ability in processing simple or routine visual material without making error is in the average range when compared to her peers. She performed better than or equal to approximately 47 % of her peers on the processing speed tasks.

Overall, Katherine's intellectual functioning appears to be within the average range. She did, however, demonstrate a significant discrepancy between her Verbal IQ and Performance IQ. A difference of this magnitude occurred in only 10.7 % of the standardization sample. Additionally, the difference in her performance on the Perceptual Organization Index and the Working Memory Index occurred in only 9 % of the standardization sample. In other words, based on the WAIS-III results, Katherine appears to have a strength in nonverbal processing, and weaknesses in verbal processing and working memory.

Academic Achievement

Katherine was administered selected subtests of the WIAT-II to determine current levels of academic achievement. These tests are individually administered, norm-referenced tests that assess performance in the essential academic areas of reading and mathematics. Standard scores are based upon a mean of 100 and a standard deviation of 15. Scores that fall between 85 and 115 are considered to be within the average range.

	Standard score	Percentile
Word reading	87	19
Reading comprehension	109	73
Pseudoword decoding	86	18
Reading composite	*92*	*30*
Numerical operations	112	79
Math reasoning	108	70
Mathematics composite	*111*	*77*
Spelling	88	21
Written expression	106	66
Written language	*96*	*39*
Listening comprehension	88	21
Oral expression	109	73
Oral language	*97*	*42*

Katherine obtained a Reading Composite score of 92 (30th percentile), which is in the average range of functioning. This composite included three subtests—Word Reading, Reading Comprehension, and Pseudoword Decoding. On the Word Reading subtest, she obtained a standard score of 87, which is in the low average range. Katherine was able to read several words without difficulty but had a tendency to pronounce longer, unfamiliar words as if they included letters that were not present in the word. Additionally, she sometimes confused long and short vowels. On the Reading Comprehension subtest, Katherine obtained a standard score of 109, which is in the average range. The Reading Comprehension subtest also yields a reading rate descriptor that is determined by a combination of comprehension and speed. Katherine's comprehension was described as average to above average, while her speed was described as far below average to below average resulting in a reading rate that was below average to average. Finally, on the Pseudoword Decoding subtest, Katherine obtained a standard score of 86, which is in the low average range. Again, the majority of Katherine's mistakes were the result of pronouncing the incorrect vowel sound and adding, less frequently, adding or moving consonants.

In the area of mathematics skills, Katherine obtained a Math Composite score of 111 (77th percentile), which is in the high average range of functioning. This composite included two subtests—Numerical Operations and Math Reasoning. On the Numerical Operations subtest, she obtained a standard score of 112, which is in the high average range. On the Math Reasoning subtest, she obtained a standard score of 108, which is in the average range.

Within the area of written language, Katherine obtained a Written Language Composite score of 96 (39th percentile), which is in the average range. This composite included two subtests—Spelling and Written Expression. On the Spelling subtest, Katherine obtained a standard score of 88, which is in the low average range. Upon beginning the test, Katherine stated, "Oh no, I am horrible at spelling." Katherine's errors included not changing "y" to "i" when adding "er," omitting silent letters (e.g., "w" instead of "wh"), using spelling conventions incorrectly ("ought" for "oubt"), and substituting homonyms for five out of nine words with possible alternate spellings.

Katherine earned an Oral Language Composite score of 96 (39th percentile), which is within the average range. The Oral Language composite is composed of two subtests—Listening Comprehension and Oral Expression. Katherine's Listening Comprehension standard score was 88, which is in the low average range. Katherine has some difficulty identifying the picture that illustrated a word spoken from the examiner when given an array of four illustrations to choose from (receptive vocabulary) and also had some difficulty generating a word that represented a short description spoken by the examiner and pictured (expressive vocabulary). Katherine's Oral Expression subtest score was a 109, which is in the average range.

The GORT-IV is a measure of reading skills and oral reading comprehension for students 7–18 years of age. Reading ability is assessed for speed, accuracy, fluency (a combination of rate and accuracy), and comprehension through asking the student to orally read short passages of increasing length and complexity. The fluency and comprehension scores are combined to form an overall Oral Reading Quotient.

The Oral Reading Quotient is represented by a standard score having a mean of 100 and a standard deviation of 15. Scores between 85 and 115, which include 68% of the population, are considered to be within the average range. Katherine earned an Oral Reading Quotient of 76, which equals or exceeds the performance of 5% of her same-age peers.

The individual areas assessed yield standard scores having a mean of 10 and a standard deviation of 3.

Area	Standard score	Percentile
Rate	5	5
Accuracy	7	16
Fluency	4	2
Comprehension	8	25

Katherine exhibited somewhat labored reading on longer passages containing more complex words and concepts. She would sometimes substitute orthographically similar words for irregular and uncommon words and also tended to self-correct minor mistakes. These tendencies affected her accuracy score and also impacted her reading rate, as attempting to identify and stopping to correct mistakes slowed her oral reading. Additionally, her reading rate was slightly slower than would have been expected even taking self-corrections into consideration. Together, Katherine's reading rate and accuracy yielded a significantly below average fluency score. Katherine's comprehension ability was just within the average range and higher than would have been expected given her fluency. It appeared that Katherine was able to compensate for her fluency difficulties and obtain meaning from the passages she read. She was unable to compensate in this way, however, when reading a passage composed solely of irony.

Overall, based on the achievement results presented above, Katherine appears to have weaknesses in basic reading, reading fluency, spelling, and listening comprehension. Katherine's strengths include her ability to comprehend what she has read, her mathematics skills, and her ability to express her ideas in written and oral language.

Work Samples

Katherine was also asked to write an essay after choosing from a list of possible topics developed for use at the state university's testing center. She chose to write about how a friend had been affected by a particular physical characteristic. Katherine appeared motivated to do well on the task and produced a two-and-a-half-page essay consisting of 272 words after 29 min of writing. She started to use a schematic prewriting strategy for a different topic and then appeared to begin writing based on her chosen topic with no overt planning. Katherine's essay clearly focused on one topic, but was loosely organized, particularly in terms of informing the reader of what to expect. She inconsistently used informative topic sentences, and the lack of sophisticated cohesive devices resulted in choppy sentences that limited flow. She demonstrated average syntax and minor difficulties with semantics, such as incorrectly using certain words ("put a damper on her money," "health problems were at risk"). In terms of morphology, she used an incorrect pronoun ("she" for "her"), incorrectly used the singular form ("breast were"), and shifted from past to present tense within a paragraph. Katherine also exhibited below average spelling ability, providing similar spellings that were easily phonetically recognizable (e.g., sour for sore). Katherine's punctuation and handwriting were within acceptable levels.

Katherine's 12th grade English teacher, Ms. Schrake, also submitted an analyzed classroom work sample in which Katherine had written about choosing three wishes. Ms. Schrake identified Katherine's tendency to sometimes use fragmented sentences as being her main challenge. Katherine did use many fragmented sentences within the sample that interfered with the flow of her writing. Additionally, Katherine frequently included unnecessary commas and made several spelling mistakes. A rough draft was included with the final written product and showed that Katherine had made many revisions to spelling and word choice. Despite the errors noted above, Katherine's resultant essay was engaging and efficiently expressed her wishes.

Mr. Kendall, Katherine's advanced algebra and trigonometry teacher, also submitted an analyzed work sample. Katherine received a grade of 94 on the selected test and Mr. Kendall noted that the quality of Katherine's work was above average for the class.

Cognitive Processing

The CTOPP assesses phonological awareness, phonological memory, and rapid naming. A deficit in one or more of these kinds of phonological processing abilities is viewed as the most common cause of LD, particularly in reading. Good phonological processing abilities support development of mathematics calculation, listening comprehension, and reading comprehension skills.

Each of the composite scores has a mean of 100 and a standard deviation of 15. Approximately two thirds of the population obtain scores between 85 and 115 and about 95% obtain scores between 70 and 130. The subtests comprising each area are listed in parentheses. Each subtest standard score has a mean of 10 and a standard deviation of 3. Approximately two thirds of the population obtain scores between 7 and 13.

Subtest/composite	Composite score	Percentile
Elision	8	25
Blending	7	16
Phonological awareness	*85*	*16*
Memory for digits	7	16
Nonword repetition	6	9
Phonological memory	*79*	*8*
Rapid digit naming	4	2
Rapid letter naming	5	5
Rapid naming	*67*	*1*

Phonological awareness refers to the awareness of and ability to use the basic phonological or sound structure of oral language. Difficulties in this area may affect a student's ability to identify and separate discrete sound "chunks," as well as to synthesize or blend sounds together to form words. Katherine's Phonological Awareness Composite Score (PACS) was within the low average range, which indicates that she has difficulty identifying and manipulating the sound structure of oral language. The PACS is composed of two subtests, Elision and Blending Words. The Elision subtest measures the ability to remove phonological segments from spoken words to form other words. The Blending Words subtest measures the ability to synthesize and form words.

The Phonological Memory Composite Score (PMCS) consists of the Memory for Digits and Nonword Repetition subtests. Memory for Digits measures the ability to store and recall a series of numbers. Nonword Repetition measures the ability to accurately repeat nonsense words. The PMCS represents an individual's ability to phonologically code information into working memory and may affect reading fluency. Katherine's PMCS was within the borderline range, indicating that she has a deficit in phonological memory that likely impairs the decoding of new words, particularly longer words that require decoding in small segments.

The Rapid Naming Composite Score (RNCS) is comprised of the Rapid Digit Naming and Rapid Letter Naming subtests. The RNCS measures the efficiency of retrieval of phonological information from long-term memory and the ability to execute a series of operations quickly and repeatedly. Efficient retrieval of phonological information and execution of sequences of operations are required for decoding unfamiliar words. Katherine's performance on the RNCS was within the extremely low range. While she correctly identified the letters and numbers, her rate of identification indicated that she has limited efficiency in retrieving information from long-term memory when compared to same-age peers.

The WJ-III COG was administered to assess several aspects of Katherine's cognitive processing. Additional measures were also administered to supplement the results of the WJ-III COG and are summarized later in this chapter. The WJ-III COG consists of 20 subtests, each measuring a different aspect of cognitive ability. The tests are combined to form clusters for interpretative purposes. Typically, a select battery of tests is given to each child based on his or her individual needs. Composite scores on the WJ-III COG have a mean of 100 and a standard deviation of 15. Scores between 90 and 110 are considered average.

Subtest	Task demand	Standard score	Percentile rank
Visual-auditory learning (*Glr;* 2)	Learning, storage, and retrieval of visual-auditory associations	87	19
Spatial relations (*Gv*; 3)	Visual-spatial thinking to complete shape	104	61
Sound blending (*Ga*, 4)	Auditory processing to blend sounds	91	28
Concept formation (*Gf*; 5)	Categorical reasoning and flexibility to derive rules	104	61
Numbers reversed (*Gsm*; 7)	Short-term memory and reversal of sequence	91	27

Subtest	Task demand	Standard score	Percentile rank
Incomplete words (*Ga*; 8)	Auditory analysis and closure	90	25
Auditory working memory (*Ga*; 9)	Short-term memory and sequencing	96	40
Retrieval fluency (*Glr*; 12)	Fluency of retrieval from categories of stored knowledge	87	20
Picture recognition (*Gv*; 13)	Visual memory of objects or pictures	132	98
Auditory attention (*Ga*; 14)	Selective attention for words	100	49
Decision speed (*Gs*; 16)	Cognitive efficiency of simple concept processing	85	15
Memory for words (*Gsm*; 17)	Short-term memory for unrelated words	75	5
Rapid picture naming (*Gs*; 18)	Cognitive fluency for knowledge recall	90	26
Planning (19)	Determining, selecting, applying solution with forethought	105	64
Pair cancellation (20)	Interference control, sustained attention, processing speed	74	4

Cluster	Standard score	Percentile rank
Broad attention (7, 9, 14, 20)	84	14
Phonemic awareness (4, 8)	91	27
Cognitive fluency (12, 16)	86	18
Working memory (7, 9)	92	29
Long-term retrieval (*Glr*; 2, 12)	85	16
Short-term memory (*Gsm*; 7, 17)	79	8
Executive processes (5, 19, 20)	88	21
Visual–spatial thinking (*Gv*; 3, 13)	123	94

Katherine's performance on the WJ-III COG suggests that her thinking ability (intentional cognitive processing) is in the average range when compared to others her same age. When compared to same-age peers, her performance was superior in visual-spatial thinking; average in auditory processing, phonemic awareness, and working memory; low average in long-term retrieval; and low in short-term memory, particularly memory for words. During testing, Katherine's ability to focus her attention on relevant stimuli was very limited to average. While her working memory and speech-sound discrimination appeared to be within the average range, her attention and concentration were within the low range of ability. Her overall ability to plan, monitor, and arrive at solutions to problems was limited to average. It should be noted that while Katherine performed within the average range on the Planning subtest, she repeatedly traced designs in the air above the paper, resulting in an administration time of approximately 1 h. It is likely that if the subtest were administered under time constraints, Katherine's performance would be much lower. Finally, Katherine's speed in performing cognitive tasks was limited.

It should be noted that the result of the WJ-III COG Phonemic Awareness cluster suggests that Katherine is able to process speech sounds, or in other words, has some age-appropriate phonological abilities, which contradicts the results of the CTOPP presented above. On both instruments, Katherine demonstrated much greater difficulty blending words that were composed of many different phonemes and correctly pronouncing words with central phonemes omitted. She also experienced some difficulty with a CTOPP task that required her to repeat nonsense words after hearing them on a tape recorder. It seems likely that there is some variability in Katherine's ability to identify and manipulate phonemes, and the results of the CTOPP should be considered an accurate representation of her phonological abilities, particularly her ability to identify novel phonemic arrangements, phoneme deletion, and phoneme blending.

The Beery-Buktenica Developmental Test of VMI is an evaluation tool, which was designed to assess the extent to which individuals can integrate their visual and motor abilities. The VMI is a developmental sequence of geometric forms to be copied with paper and pencil. Standard scores from 83 to 117 are considered average.

Katherine obtained a standard score of 85 on the VMI, which is within the average range of functioning. This score placed her at the 16th percentile when comparing her performance to other individuals her same age. Results of the VMI suggest that Katherine's visual/perceptual-motor skills are consistent with expectations given her chronological age, but somewhat lower than what would be expected given her intellectual ability.

The RCFT is a measure of visuospatial constructional ability and visuospatial memory. The administration of the RCFT involves a copy trial, a 3-minute immediate recall trial, a 30-minute delayed recall trial, and a recognition trial. The recognition trial measures the respondent's recognition memory for different elements of the complex figure and ability to use cues to retrieve information. Thus, the RCFT measures the encoding, storage, and retrieval aspects of memory in addition to visual-motor ability. The recall and recognition trials are reported in terms of *T*-scores with a mean of 50 and a standard deviation of 10. Scores between 45 and 54 are considered to be average. The copy trial and analysis of the recognition trial yield percentile rank ranges, with percentile ranks above the 16th percentile indicating optimal performance.

Trial	T-score	Percentile rank
Immediate recall	57	76
Delayed recall	53	62
Recognition	67	96

Trial	Raw score	Percentile rank
Copy	35	>16
Time to copy	212 s	>16
Recognition		>16
True positives	12	>16
False positives	0	>16
True negatives	12	>16
False negatives	0	>16

The results of the RCFT indicated that Katherine's visuospatial constructional ability is within the average range. Her visuospatial memory was also within the average range. She demonstrated a strength in visual recognition memory. She correctly identified all aspects of the design without mistakenly identifying figures that were not a part of the original figure.

Katherine, her mother, and her literature teacher, Ms. Brake, also completed the BRIEF, a questionnaire designed to provide a better understanding of a child's self-control and problem-solving skills by measuring eight aspects of executive functioning. The executive functions are mental processes that direct a child's thought, action, and emotion, particularly during problem solving. Raw scores obtained on the BRIEF are converted to T-scores, which have a mean of 50 and a standard deviation of 10. T-scores between 60 and 64* are considered mildly elevated and T-scores at or above 65** indicate clinically significant difficulties.

Index/scale	Parent T-scores	Teacher T-scores	Student T-scores
Inhibit	41	46	42
Shift	38	45	40
Shift subscales	–	–	*41*
	–	–	*41*
Emotional control	42	46	44
Monitor	–	–	37
Behavioral regulation index (BRI)	*39*	*46*	*39*
Initiate	53	44	–
Working memory	48	45	56
Plan/organize	54	46	63
Organization of materials	53	46	42
Monitor	40	44	–
Task completion	–	–	57
Metacognition index (MI)	*50*	*44*	*57*
Global executive composite (GEC)	*45*	*44*	*49*

All raters' Negativity and Inconsistency scales were within the acceptable range so the results are considered valid. The overall index, the Global Executive Composites (GEC), was within the expected range and the Behavioral Regulation Index (BRI) and Metacognition Index (MI) were within normal limits. None of the individual scales was elevated, suggesting that Katherine exhibits appropriate ability to inhibit impulsive responses (Inhibit), adjust to changes in routine or task demands (Shift), and modulate emotions (Emotional Control). Within the metacognitive domain, Katherine is described as appropriately able to initiate problem solving or activity (Initiate), sustain working memory (Working Memory), plan and organize problem-solving approaches (Plan/Organize), organize her environment and materials (Organization of Materials), and monitor her own behavior (Monitor). Additionally, Katherine described herself as being able to appropriately finish tasks, such as homework or projects (Task Completion).

Summary of Cognitive Processes

Process	Sources of information	Strength/weakness
Attention	WJ-III broad attention	Weakness
Oral language	WIAT-II	----
Phonological/orthographic processing	WJ-III phonemic awareness CTOPP	Weakness
Fluency/automaticity	WJ-III cognitive fluency	Weakness
Memory/learning	WJ-III LTM, STM, WM RCFT CTOPP	Weakness
Executive functions	WJ-III executive processes BRIEF	Weakness
Visual-perceptual/visual-spatial	WJ-III visual-spatial Thinking RCFT	Strength
Visual-motor	VMI RCFT	Weakness

Katherine demonstrated a strength in visual-spatial and visual-perceptual processing. Her oral language skills were average in comparison to her intellectual ability and same-age peers. She did, however, perform in the low average range on the Listening Comprehension subtest on the WIAT-II. It seems likely that Katherine's verbal abilities have been impacted by her phonological and orthographic processing weaknesses. In other words, Katherine's difficulty in fluently decoding words hinders her ability to gain access to many types of verbal knowledge, which may then depress her receptive vocabulary and verbal reasoning ability in general. Katherine also displayed a weakness in cognitive fluency and automaticity. This weakness appeared to affect her performance on several timed tasks throughout the evaluation. As seen above, Katherine also appeared to have difficulty with attention and executive functioning. Both domains were depressed primarily to a particular subtest that required her to scan pictures and circle two pictures each time they appeared in a certain order within a time limit. Thus, while she may have some difficulties in these areas, she appears to perform more poorly when given time constraints. Katherine also displayed an overall weakness in memory and learning, but her performance varied across the different memory requirements. She had the most difficulty remembering orally presented words and nonsense words, while her ability to remember visually presented stimuli with no verbal demands was within the average range. Finally, Katherine also had a slight weakness in visual-motor integration as measured by the VMI, but her ability to complete the copy and recall tasks of the RCFT suggests that this processing weakness likely does not have a great impact on her academic functioning.

The processing deficits discussed above result in underachievement in reading decoding (WIAT-II Word Reading 19th percentile, WIAT-II Pseudoword 18th percentile, GORT-IV Accuracy 16th percentile), functional reading rate (GORT-IV Rate 5th percentile, Fluency 2nd percentile), spelling (21st percentile), and spelling and word usage within spontaneous writing (writing samples).

Social/Emotional/Behavioral Rating Scales

Katherine's mother and physics teacher, Ms. Raisig, completed the BASC-2, a measure that evaluates levels of behavioral, emotional, and social competencies relative to other children their age and gender. On the Clinical scales and Composite scores of the BASC-2, T-scores of 70 and above** are considered clinically significant, scores between 60 and 69* are in the at-risk range, and scores of 41–59 are in the average range. Adaptive scale scores of 30 or less** are considered clinically significant, scores of 31–40* are at risk, and scores between 41 and 59 are average.

Skill area	T-score (mother)	T-score (teacher)
Hyperactivity	50	42
Aggression	40	43
Conduct problems	42	43
Externalizing problems	*43*	*42*
Anxiety	50	46
Depression	43	45
Somatization	47	43
Internalizing problems	*46*	*44*
Attention problems	–	38
Learning problems	–	43
School problems	–	*40*
Atypicality	45	44
Withdrawal	38	44
Attention problems	47	–
Behavioral symptoms index	*42*	*41*
Adaptability	61	62
Social skills	56	64
Leadership	53	49
Activities of daily living	58	–
Study skills	–	61
Functional communication	59	65
Adaptive skills	*59*	*61*

* At risk
** Clinically significant/high level of maladjustment

The F, Response Pattern, and Consistency indexes were within the acceptable range for Ms. Bridge's and Ms. Raisig's ratings. Both raters indicated that Katherine appears to be well adjusted, both socially and emotionally. It is noteworthy that while Katherine has experienced difficulty with some school tasks, this difficulty does not affect her ability to function within the academic environment as perceived by Ms. Raisig.

Katherine completed the *Behavior Assessment System for Children, Second Edition—Self-Report Form (BASC-2-SRP)* to share her perception of her behavioral, emotional, and social competence. Her F, Response Pattern, V, L, and Consistency indexes were within the acceptable range. Specific T-scores obtained on the BASC are listed below:

Skill area	T-Score
Attitude to school	60*
Attitude to teachers	39
Sensation seeking	60*
School problems	*54*
Atypicality	42
Locus of control	44
Social stress	40
Anxiety	53
Depression	41
Sense of inadequacy	47
Somatization	47
Internalizing problems	*43*
Attention problems	54
Hyperactivity	51
Inattention/hyperactivity	*53*
Emotional symptoms index	*45*
Relations with parents	57
Interpersonal relations	55
Self-esteem	57
Self-reliance	47
Personal adjustment	*56*

* At risk

** Clinically significant/high level of maladjustment

Katherine's responses resulted in Attitude to School and Sensation Seeking scores within the at-risk range. She endorsed being bored at school and preferring not to think about school. Katherine's mildly negative attitude toward school is not unexpected given her past difficulties completing reading assignments and the stress she reported experiencing. She also reported that she likes exciting activities, such as taking chances, experimenting, and playing rough sports. Overall, the BASC-SRP results indicate that Katherine is well adjusted and satisfied with herself and her relationships.

Clinical Interview

In a separate interview, Katherine stated that she has two older brothers, aged 22 and 26 years, who live outside the home. She reported playing basketball and volleyball and enjoying ceramics. When asked about her future goals, Katherine stated that she wants to go to college in order to get a better job, but that she has no idea what she wants to study. Katherine described her general mood as good and said that she only feels frustrated when she has too many things to do for school at once. She stated that she deals with this by prioritizing and completing tasks in order of importance.

Katherine endorsed liking mathematics and disliking literature. She said that spelling was her weakest skill. She reported having problems with reading for as long as she could remember and being worried about having a lot of reading in college. She described her reading difficulties as being due to not knowing what some of the words are and/or what they mean, as well as feeling rushed when reading. She endorsed being able to sound out some words and determine their meaning, mainly if they do not have silent letters and there are enough clues in the passage. When asked how she currently copes with reading assignments, she replied that she does not have to do reading in any of her classes because they do not even have books to take home and that her mom usually helps when she does have a reading assignment. She stated that she is also able to take notes without problems because they are presented on an overhead projector, but she worries that this would not be the case in college. Katherine reported that her grades were quite poor when she was younger and that she still has to work hard on her assignments. She reported that her current grades consist primarily of As, with two Bs.

IDEA Disability Criteria

[Specific learning disability]
The child with a specific learning disability (SLD) has one or more serious academic deficiencies and does not achieve adequately according to age, to meet grade level standards. These achievement deficiencies must be directly related to a pervasive processing deficit and to the child's response to scientific, research-based interventions. The nature of the deficit(s) is such that classroom performance is not correctable without specialized techniques that are fundamentally different from those available in the general education classroom, basic remedial/tutorial approaches, or other compensatory programs.

Summary

Katherine is an 18-year-old senior in high school who was referred for a comprehensive evaluation to identify academic and cognitive strengths and weaknesses and assist in determining what services she may benefit from in a postsecondary setting. Current test results suggest that Katherine is functioning intellectually in the average range. While her verbal and perceptual reasoning abilities are both within the average range, her perceptual reasoning ability was significantly better than her verbal reasoning ability. She displayed cognitive processing weaknesses in phonological/orthographic processing, cognitive fluency, and verbal memory. Her attention and executive functioning were also weaknesses when given time constraints. Katherine's oral language ability was within the average range and her visual-spatial processing constituted a strength. Katherine's processing deficits resulted in academic underachievement in reading decoding, functional reading rate, spelling, and spontaneous written expression requiring correct spelling and word usage. She displayed strengths in reading comprehension, mathematics, oral language, and expressive aspects of writing. Behavioral rating scales and student and parent interviews indicated that Katherine is a well-adjusted, motivated young woman who does not demonstrate behavioral or emotional difficulties.

Based on the results of this evaluation, Katherine appears to continue to meet criteria for an SLD. More specifically, she demonstrates significant deficits in functional reading rate, reading decoding (DSM-IV Reading Disorder [315.00]), and written expression (DSM-IV Disorder of Written Expression [315.2]) that impact her ability to achieve at expected levels without extra support.

Summary of Key Points

- Psychological, or cognitive, processes have been posited to underlie LD, but no clear agreed-upon conception of what a process is exists.
- Processes originated with the Greek philosophers and continued intermittently until present day.
- In the past century, processes known as "faculties" were emphasized with exercise believed to improve learning to strengthen them. Lack of evidence for this led to a decline in focus on processes except in special education.
- Examples of processing approaches/instruments include: Dehn's (2006) *Essentials of Processing Assessment,* WJ-III COG based upon the Cattell-Horn-Carroll (CHC) theory, and the CAS PASS model.
- Processing assessment typically involves comparing various factors and/or subtests of instrument(s) to determine strengths and weaknesses.
- Proponents of processing assessment argue that its advantages include identifying strengths and weaknesses that provide assistance in designing interventions and accommodations and early identification.
- Disadvantages of processing assessment to identify LD have been argued to include lack of evidence for treatment validity, the frequent occurrence of profile variability in the general population, the ability of achievement data to provide more useful information, and the lack of research linking different processes to certain types of LD.

Questions and Answers with the Expert: Jack Naglieri

Meet the expert: Jack Naglieri, Ph.D., is an Emeritus Professor of Psychology at George Mason University and Senior Research Scientist at the Devereux Foundation's Center for Resilient Children. He has authored numerous research publications, books including *Helping Children Learn Second Edition,* and tests such as the Cognitive Assessment System (CAS), Wechsler Nonverbal Scale of Ability, Naglieri Nonverbal Ability Tests, Devereux Elementary Student Strength Assessment, and Autism Spectrum Rating Scales. His areas of interest include cognitive assessment and intervention, specific learning disability (SLD) and attention-deficit hyperactivity disorder (ADHD) eligibility determination, and measurement of intelligence, psychopathology, and resilience.

Question 1: How does processing assessment differ from ability assessment?

Answer 1: In order to answer this question, the terms process and ability need to be operationally defined. Naglieri (2010) defined a "cognitive process" as a neuropsychologically identified function that provides the means by which an individual meets the demands of this world. A specific cognitive process provides a unique ability but a group of cognitive processes is needed to meet the multidimensional demands of our complex environment. Having several cognitive processes affords us the capability of completing the same task using different types or various combinations of processes. This has important implications for learning and educational remediation. In Naglieri's definition, a process is used as a modern term for the concept of ability. The essential aspect of a process test is that the tasks should have been identified based upon how the question is solved rather than the content of the question. That is, does the task require sequencing? If so, it does not matter if the test content is words, numbers, or hand movements as long as the order of events influences the score.

The term "ability" has been associated with and operationalized by traditional group and individually administered IQ tests. These tests use questions categorized into verbal, quantitative, and nonverbal scales based on the content of the items. It is common to talk about verbal and nonverbal abilities, for example, even though this conceptualization is inconsistent with the views of, for example, Wechsler (see Wechsler and Naglieri 2008). This use of the term ability is not the same as a process view of ability. The two differ on the point that a test used to measure a process should be: (a) defined by a theory of cognition and (b) built on the basis of the intellectual demand of the task rather than the content of the test.

Question 2: What are the benefits of identifying learning disabilities (LD) through processing assessment?

Answer 2: Although the traditional view of ability measured by verbal, quantitative, and nonverbal test questions is well entrenched in psychology and education (Matarazzo 1992), researchers and theoreticians have recently argued that intelligence is better conceptualized as cognitive processes (Ceci 2000; Das 2002; Fagan 2000; Naglieri 2008; Sternberg 1988). Using a processing approach offers several important advantages. First, processing tests avoid achievement-like verbal and quantitative test questions found on traditional IQ tests making them more appropriate for assessment of culturally and linguistically diverse populations (Fagan 2000; Naglieri and Conway 2009; Suzuki and Valencia 1997). Second, a processing approach could allow for early detection of disabilities in advance of academic failure, have better diagnostic accuracy, and provide a way to better understand children's disabilities (Ceci 2000). Third, a cognitive processing approach has instructional relevance (Naglieri and Pickering 2010; Naglieri and Conway 2009). Fourth, a multidimensional theory of psychological processes could provide a more comprehensive view of ability (Naglieri 2005; Sternberg 1988).

Question 3: What instruments do you consider optimal for assessing processing strengths and weaknesses? Why?

Answer 3: In order to adequately assess strengths and weakness in a specific cognitive process related to LD, clinicians should ensure that the test they use is designed to measure a group of important theoretically defined cognitive processes. One test has been developed and standardized using this approach is the CAS (Naglieri and Das 1997). The test was developed to measure ability within a cognitive process approach referred to as the Planning, Attention, Simultaneous, Successive (PASS) theory. The PASS theory was used as the foundation of the CAS, so the content of the test was determined by the theory and the intellectual demands, rather than the content, of the tasks. The PASS theory merges cognitive and neuropsychological constructs like executive function (Planning and Attention), selective attention (Attention), visual-spatial ability (Simultaneous), and the serial nature of language and memory (Successive) under the concept of ability, or intelligence. Most importantly, there is considerable evidence that the PASS theory as measured by the CAS: (a) is effective for evaluation of minority populations, (b) yields PASS profiles that can help with diagnosis, and (c) is related to instruction and intervention (see Naglieri and Conway (2009) for a recent summary).

Question 4: How do the results of processing assessment influence diagnosis and intervention in the field of LD?

Answer 4: There is considerable amount of evidence that the PASS theory as operationalized by the CAS is effective for assessment of individuals with LD. First, Naglieri and Rojahn (2004) found that the CAS was highly correlated with achievement for a large representative sample of 1,559 students aged 5–17 years. This study illustrated that each PASS process is important for academic success. Second, researchers have found that groups of children with different exceptionalities have specific profiles of PASS processing scores (Naglieri 2005). English-speaking children as well as English language learners with specific reading decoding failure obtain low scores relative to their average PASS score and the normative mean on the Successive scale of the CAS (Naglieri 1999; Naglieri et al. 2007). In contrast, children diagnosed with ADHD Hyperactive/Impulsive type earned low standard scores in Planning (Naglieri et al. 2004) and those with an autism spectrum disorder had low standard scores on the Attention scale (Goldstein and Naglieri 2009). These findings support the view that PASS processes have utility for differential diagnosis and, as other research has suggested, intervention.

There is a line of research demonstrating how instruction based on the PASS theory can improve reading decoding skills (Carlson and Das 1997; Das et al. 1995); Boden and Kirby 1995; Parrila et al. 1999, Das et al. 2000). Haddad et al. (2003) showed that a PASS theory-based intervention improved the reading comprehension skills. PASS-based instruction has also been found to improve classroom performance in mathematics calculation for individuals with SLD and attention deficit disorder (Iseman and Naglieri in press; Naglieri and Gottling 1995, 1997; Naglieri and Johnson 2000). These findings suggest that children can be taught to better utilize PASS processes and improvements in academic performance have resulted.

Question 5: What processing areas do you recommend as essential to the identification of an LD?

Answer 5: Reading decoding is the predominant area of failure for students with SLD. Successive processing underlies reading decoding because of the highly serial nature of the task including the perception of stimuli in sequence and the linear execution of sounds and movements (Naglieri and Das 2005). For this reason, successive processing is involved with phonological analysis and the syntax of language and has been experimentally related to the concept of phonological skills and reading decoding failure (Das et al. 1994). Successive ability is similar to the concept of sequential processing included in the K-ABC-2 (Kaufman and Kaufman 2004) and tests that require recall of serial information such as Digit Span Forward. For these reasons, in order to determine if a child's reading decoding failure is the result of inadequate instruction or a disability in the successive process from PASS, a comprehensive evaluation should be conducted.

Question 6: What do you consider best practice for LD identification?

Answer 6: There are many reasons why children experience academic failure. This includes poor instruction, lack of motivation, visual problems, lack of exposure to books and reading, methods of instruction that are not best for a child's particular style of learning, overall limited intellectual ability, an SLD, or a deficit in cognitive process(es). Identification of an SLD should be based on evidence of the "identification of a core cognitive deficit, or a disorder in one or more psychological processes, that is predictive of an imperfect ability to learn, is a marker for a specific learning disability" (U.S. Department of Education Roundtable, American Institutes for Research 2002, p. 5). In order to utilize a cognitive processing approach in SLD identification that is consistent with this position, three main findings are needed. First, the child must have significant intraindividual differences among the basic psychological processes such that the lowest processing score is substantially below the child's average ability level. Second, there needs to be a significant difference between some high processing and low achievement scores. Third, there needs to be consistency between low processing and academic scores, indicating a disorder in processing and deficit in achievement (Hale and Fiorello 2004; Naglieri 1999, 2005). This was referred to as a discrepancy/consistency model by Naglieri (1999). In order to determine if a child meets the dimensions of the discrepancy/consistency model, a comprehensive evaluation by a qualified professional is required (see Naglieri 2008 for more details).

Chapter 4
Response to Intervention

With the reauthorization of the Individuals with Disabilities Educational Improvement Act (2004) and the final regulations that were published on April 14, 2006, response to intervention (RTI) became a hot topic in the field of learning disabilities (LD). The new regulations specified that the use of a severe discrepancy could no longer be required, the use of a process based on a student's response to "scientific, research-based intervention" must be permitted, and the use of other research-based procedures for identifying a student as having an LD may also be permitted. If RTI is used, the federal regulations require documentation of the instructional strategies used and the data collected.

RTI has been the primary focus of most educators and researchers in the discussions and debates generated by the latest regulations. Prior to the reauthorization of the Individuals with Disabilities Education Act (IDEA), RTI had been touted by many researchers as an alternative approach to identifying individuals with specific LD that can overcome the diagnostic shortfalls of other methods. Indeed, in a survey prior to the reauthorization, over two thirds of respondents indicated that treatment validity, or an RTI approach, should be included in the definitional criteria for LD (Speece and Shekitka 2002). While there are many factors that can vary within an RTI model, the general framework involves providing appropriate instruction that is varied depending on the performance and associated needs of groups and/or individuals.

RTI is a multitiered approach to education in which schools provide increasing intensity of services to students based upon need. While there are various RTI models, the most common and basic consists of three steps. First, classwide assessment is conducted using locally developed curriculum-based measurement (CBM) to determine the average reading level and growth for the class as a whole. If most students are achieving at a prespecified level, then poor instruction can be ruled out as the cause for individual students' low achievement. Next, students are identified as unresponsive to general instruction based on a comparison of their performance and rate of improvement to those of their normally achieving peers. Finally, the identified students receive continued assessments with adaptations and referral for special education services if they do not achieve a certain level or amount of growth (Vaughn and Fuchs 2003).

A. E. B. Taylor, *Diagnostic Assessment of Learning Disabilities in Childhood,*
Contemporary Issues in Psychological Assessment, DOI 10.1007/978-1-4939-0335-1_4,

© Springer Science+Business Media New York 2014

Fuchs and Fuchs (2009) recommended a unified model of RTI, rather than varying models to make implementation easier and more effective. Their model is typically referred to as the standard treatment protocol (Fuchs et al. 2004; Fuchs et al. 2002). This consists of the first step, which is referred to as primary prevention, of regular education, determining the overall rate of responding within the classroom and making changes that allow all students access to the primary prevention program. In secondary prevention, students identified as performing and improving at a rate below those of classmates receive time-limited small-group instruction. Additional assessment guides instructional modifications to determine if better growth can be attained in the classroom for those individuals. Finally, tertiary prevention involves continuing assessment to document effective interventions through the development of an Individualized Education Program (IEP) or continue aiding in the development of an intervention plan. It is recommended that special education resources be utilized at this level.

Another model that focuses on individualized remediation throughout the RTI process, typically through a team-based approach, is often referred to as the problem-solving model. The problem-solving model typically begins with pre-referral intervention teams when a student has begun evidencing difficulties, rather than encompassing all of general education. A combination of the standard protocol and problem-solving methods is typically the approach referred to in discussions of RTI rather than the general education approach originally referred to by Fuchs and colleagues (see Fuchs and Fuchs 1998).

Curriculum-Based Measurement in an RTI Framework

CBM is typically the assessment of choice in RTI models. It should be noted that CBM falls under the broader umbrella of curriculum-based assessment (CBA), which includes several different methods for gathering information and making decisions (see Fig. 4.1). These methods differ in the manner of curricular sampling in order to assess a broad or more specific range of skills (Hintze et al. 2006). For a more in-depth discussion of the various types of CBA, the reader is referred to Hintze et al. (2006).

CBM originated with Stan Deno and colleagues (see Deno 1985) at the University of Minnesota Institute for Research on Learning Disabilities (IRLD) around the time that the original IDEA law, PL 94–142, was developed (Stecker et al. 2005). The goal of CBM was to create a measurement system that could be efficiently used by teachers, provide information about relative performance and growth, assess the effectiveness of academic programs in producing growth, and help teachers plan more effective instruction (Deno et al. 2001). Use of CBM involves identifying a pool of items or content either from within or outside the curriculum that reflects the general, long-term goal of instruction rather than the content that is currently being taught. Students are assessed using equivalent forms at least once a week and results are graphed to assist in determining how the student is performing compared

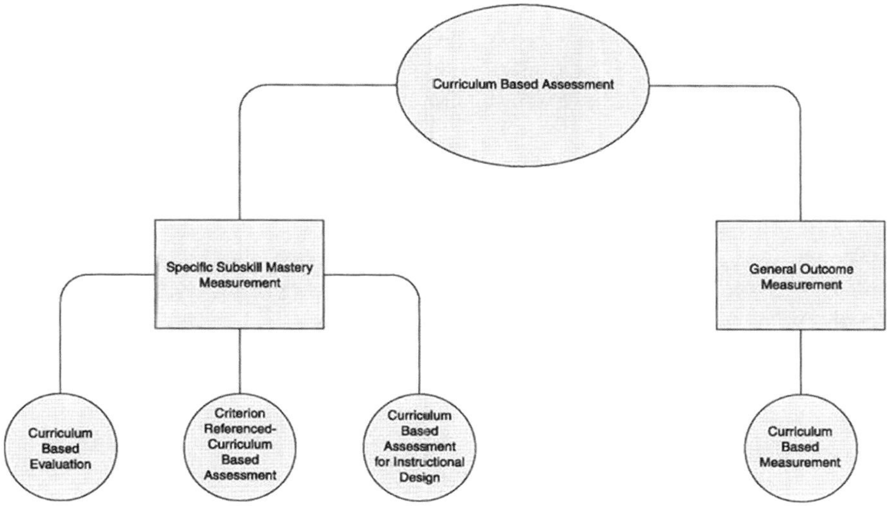

Fig. 4.1 Organization chart of different models of curriculum-based assessments. (Source: Hintze et al. 2006. Copyright 2006 by John Wiley & Sons, Inc. Reprinted with permission)

to classmates and whether the student is progressing with the current instruction (Stecker et al. 2005).

Stecker et al. (2005) conducted a review of the CBM research with a focus on how CBM is implemented most effectively to result in growth in student achievement. CBM tasks are typically straightforward timed tests. The most common use of CBM in reading involves oral reading fluency, which counts the number of words in a passage read aloud correctly in 1 min, and maze, which requires the student to choose from three word choices to complete blanks within a reading passage. In mathematics, a similar process is used with computational or conceptual and applied problems. The researchers determined that within special education, students make gains when teachers use CBM data to tailor instruction, comply with a data-decision framework for modifying instruction when gains are greater or less than expected, and use skills analysis to identify areas of strength and weakness. All of these things were more likely to happen when teachers were provided with computer software and ongoing consultation. Within the general education, students of teachers who used classwide CBM demonstrated greater growth; however, the classrooms studied used Peer-Assisted Learning Strategies (PALS; see McMaster et al. 2007).

One of the earliest pilot tests of CBM for determining special education eligibility was conducted by Marston et al. (1984) using procedures developed at the University of Minnesota IRLD. These researchers determined that as compared to the teacher-referred group of students, the group of students that was identified using repeated evaluation performed similarly on standardized tests of aptitude and achievement, contained a more balanced distribution of males and females, was less influenced by teacher perceptions of behavioral difficulties, and resulted in less bias in the eligibility decision-making process.

Fuchs et al. (2002) proposed a treatment validity model of LD identification in which the first step is to determine whether the overall rate of responding within the classroom indicates that an appropriate instructional environment is provided. Next, students are assessed to identify those whose performance and growth rate are below those of classmates. Additional assessment guides instructional modifications to determine if better growth can be attained in the classroom for those individuals. Finally, a diagnostic trial of special education services with continuing assessment is continued to document effective interventions through the development of an IEP or continue aiding in the development of an intervention plan. A similar but more intensive model has also been used with the third step reformulated to focus on remediation of at-risk students' deficits, which has been called the standard treatment protocol (Fuchs et al. 2004). Another model that focuses on individualized remediation throughout the RTI process is often referred to as the problem-solving model. A combination of the standard protocol and problem-solving methods is typically the approach referred to in discussions of RTI rather than the general education approach originally referred to by Fuchs and colleagues (see Fuchs and Fuchs 1998).

Deno et al. (2001) identified normative oral reading fluency growth rates using an existing database to provide a reference for determining adequate growth. The growth rate for typical students was higher in the early grades with 1.8 words per week in the first grade and 1.66 words per week in the second grade with a decrease to about 0.60 words per week in the fifth and sixth grades. For students in special education, the growth rates for the first grade was 0.83 words per week, then the growth rate decreased to about 0.58 for the second through sixth grades. The growth rate for students with LDs who were participating in a validated treatment in second through sixth grades was 1.39 words per week. These results demonstrate the significant differences that can be expected when using different types of instruction and different normative groups.

Support for Response to Intervention

Proponents support RTI because it allows for early intervention, does not use intelligence quotient (IQ) as a determinant, and it has the ability to discriminate between poor instruction and individual learning (Fuchs et al. 2002), and more specifically, between students who demonstrate achievement growth with intervention versus those who do not, which is often interpreted as identifying students who truly have an inability to learn.

Fuchs et al. (2002) indicated that RTI models allow students access to interventions prior to being placed in special education. Students who are later identified as being nonresponders who participated in well-designed interventions within general education have been shown to have better outcomes than nonresponders who did not participate (Speece et al. 2003). Additionally, all students may benefit from broad application of RTI through its contributions to instructional planning through a problem-solving model. Additionally, within a general education framework, RTI allows easier access to special education while the standard treatment or intensive approach may prevent more serious learning difficulties from developing (Fuchs et al. 2004).

As has been argued regarding methods of identification requiring intelligence tests, RTI approaches that use a dual-discrepancy method to determine which students have responded and which require additional support do not appear to demonstrate a gender or ethnic bias (Burns and Senesac 2005; Speece et al. 2003). Additionally, RTI does not require discriminating between children with learning difficulties who do and do not demonstrate discrepancies between achievement and intelligence, who have been shown to require similar instruction (Fletcher et al. 1998), and instead provides instruction for all struggling students regardless of IQ.

RTI provides the ability to discriminate between poor learning outcomes due to ineffective instruction and poor learning outcomes due to genuine inability or difficulty to learn. When the first explanation is indicated, all students benefit from improved instruction. When the latter is the case, and overall results indicate that most students do in fact demonstrate academic growth, those students who have not responded similarly to their peers are provided with additional intervention and, if they continue to show deficits in growth and/or performance, are considered to have an LD. These identified students demonstrate meaningful differences from other low-achieving and typically achieving students in terms of academic and behavioral outcomes (Speece et al. 2003). Fuchs and colleagues (2002) determined that the estimated prevalence of nonresponders is 7.7 %, which approximates the generally agreed upon incidence of LDs. When RTI procedures continue throughout the special education process, as is typically suggested, the data gathered also provide an indication of when students' services can be scaled back to the point of return to the general education environment. Perhaps most importantly, the ability to assess a lack of response to quality instruction represents the ability to measure an inclusionary clause, i.e., nonresponse to adequate education, rather than the typical exclusionary clause, i.e., lack of quality instruction (Fletcher and Vaughn 2009).

A Model under Construction

While RTI certainly has the benefit of providing early intervention, there are several problems with the methodology, beyond the obvious amount of time and effort required. The majority of these problems relate to the lack of a common definition and operationalization of what RTI actually is. The first example of this lack of consensus is the varying descriptions of instruction within RTI models. Some researchers conduct studies based on general education as in Fuchs' treatment validity approach (e.g., Fuchs et al. 2002), while some employ intensive intervention (e.g., Vellutino et al. 1996) described as the standard treatment protocol. The resources required for implementing these different interventions, rather than the appropriateness for the situation, may determine which are used and may lead to unreliability in who is identified. It is possible that some students will respond to changes in the regular classroom, while others may require more intensive interventions that would be available through a different approach.

It has been pointed out that more intensive forms of education may allow struggling students to make progress while being served through special interventions, but the progress they demonstrated in the second or third tier of an intensive system will likely not be maintained once returned to general education (Fuchs et al. 2004). In fact, one third of students' gains have been shown to deteriorate upon return to the regular classroom (Vaughn et al. 2003). Thus, students are assumed to not have an LD and are returned to the general education classroom where they cannot make progress, leading to another "wait to fail" situation that was deemed unacceptable within a discrepancy framework. Fuchs et al. (2004) aptly compared returning students from intensive intervention to regular instruction after showing progress to "concluding that a patient never had cancer because surgery restored her to health" (p. 218). Issues of intensity are particularly complex when considering the size of the group receiving the instruction, the duration of each individual session, and the frequency and duration of the sessions across time.

Wanzek and Vaugh (2008) compared the effects of varying amounts of intervention, including a single 30-minute daily session over 13 weeks versus no intervention and two 30-minute daily sessions over 13 weeks versus no intervention, for students who had previously demonstrated a low RTI. The results indicated that students in the treatment group demonstrated greater growth than those in the control group; however, students participating in once-daily and twice-daily interventions performed similarly. Students in all conditions made negligible gains in oral reading fluency. These results suggest that providing specialized instruction may be more critical than the duration of instruction provided. This also highlights the importance of using data from RTI to determine when it is time to modify an existing intervention and/or implement a new intervention altogether.

In addition to different types of instruction, there are various methods for distinguishing responders from nonresponders because responsiveness can be assessed at various times and frequencies and compared to several standards. For instance, responsiveness can be measured by the child's final status or status at a given point, their growth throughout the intervention, or a combination of the two, i.e., dual discrepancy. Some research has supported a dual-discrepancy approach over individual criteria (Burns and Senesac 2005; Fuchs et al. 2002).

Once the type of data to be used to determine responsiveness has been selected, determining whether a child has responded may be based on comparison to the full distribution of student performance, only other tutored students, or a benchmark associated with a desired outcome. Once method and comparison groups have been chosen, a required outcome level for determining which children have responded must also be decided upon. The use of each of these different methods results in different prevalence rates and different children being identified (Fuchs et al. 2004; Fuchs 2003). Furthermore, the entire model may rest on the collection of local norms and comparisons to those norms, rather than national norms based upon a large normative sample, thus making the diagnosis ungeneralizable across municipalities.

An analogous situation would be to adjust the attention deficit/hyperactivity disorder (ADHD) diagnostic criteria based on local factors.

Some evidence suggests that children can be predicted to be nonresponders to intervention who will eventually be labeled as having an LD prior to going through the entire RTI process. More specifically, evidence has suggested that the group of children identified as having LDs is the one with the greatest cognitive risk, that is, the children with the lowest academic achievement and intelligence test scores at the outset of schooling. In a 3-year longitudinal mixed methods investigation of first and second grade children, the group with the lowest reading, intelligence, and phonological processing test scores at the outset of the study were the ones that continued to lag behind their classroom peers, making them the most likely to need involvement in special education (Case et al. 2003). This failure to respond to intervention group had mean intelligence test scores, word attack, and letter–word identification scores in the low to mid-80s (using a standard score scale where mean = 100 and standard deviation = 15) for the duration of the study. These results suggest that a group of children with very low, but clearly outside the mental retardation range, academic achievement and other cognitive test scores may need more intensive academic interventions earlier in development, such as those that may be offered in special education or a similar environment.

It may be more beneficial and fair to identify this group of children with persistent reading problems earlier using standardized academic achievement test results and providing intensive interventions without requiring progress through a multi-tiered system. Further, several characteristics of nonresponders have been explored in the literature with only phonological awareness identified as a clear correlate of lack of response to literacy interventions (Al Otaiba and Fuchs 2002). Other possible characteristics lacking sufficient research included phonological memory, rapid naming, intelligence, attention or behavior, orthographic processing, and demographics. This also points to the possibility that students may fail to respond to interventions for reasons other than an LD or lack of adequate instruction, such as behavioral problems or an impoverished home environment.

In addition to possessing a “wait to fail” component, there is concern that RTI will transform LD into a general learning problem, potentially including all children with below average achievement, thus making the LD category untenable (Kavale et al. 2005). Even in the best-case scenario, RTI may cause the LD field to remain stagnant because its implementation has not been carefully controlled across states and school districts. Consider, for example, that students whose response is slower than expected will be considered learning disabled (Vaughn et al. 2003). The expected response is based on other students’ level and growth, boiling down to another version of a discrepancy formula with all of the problems of its predecessor.

Given all of these issues and the lack of available research addressing promising practices (Burns and Senesac 2005), it is readily apparent that more research is necessary before employing RTI as a diagnostic method. Considering the trend in educational intervention research toward fewer and briefer intervention studies, with fewer still focused on children (Hseih, P. et al. 2005), it is not certain that the much-needed research database will be established quickly enough for widespread implementation of quality, research-based RTI models in order to identify students as having LDs. While many studies have been conducted with more under way, additional work remains to be done (see Fuchs and Vaughn 2012 for an overview). It is recommended that those states, districts, and individual schools that choose to establish RTI systems remain continuously immersed in the emerging RTI research and be willing to make changes as necessary.

Below are two sample written reports. The first report presents RTI data as well as some additional formal assessment. The second report uses RTI as well as historical data without individual standardized evaluation.

Case Examples

ST. CLAIR COUNTY SCHOOL DISTRICT
CONFIDENTIAL
PSYCHOEDUCATIONAL REPORT

NAME: Cooper Davis
Birth date: 01/22/2002
AGE: 7 years
SEX: Male
SCHOOL: Harmony Elementary School
GRADE: 1st
REPORT DATE: 02/25/2009
DATES OF DATA COLLECTION: 10/02/2009–01/09/2009
PROCEDURES:
Progress monitoring
Review of records
Parent interview
Reynolds Intellectual Assessment Scales (RIAS)
The Behavior Assessment System for Children, Second Edition (BASC-2)

Parent Rating Scales (PRS)
Teacher Rating Scales (TRS)
Self-Report Interview (SRP-I)

Clinical Interview
Classroom Observation

REASON FOR REFERRAL:
Cooper was initially referred to the response to intervention (RTI) team due to difficulties with letter learning in kindergarten. He made some progress in identifying letter names and sounds but has demonstrated significant difficulty applying letter and sound knowledge to reading. As a result, the RTI team continued interventions during his first grade year. Currently, Cooper has transitioned to the third, and final, tier of interventions. The RTI team requested intelligence and social–emotional assessment in addition to background information and progress-monitoring data to determine if other factors may account for Cooper's learning difficulties.

BACKGROUND INFORMATION:

Cooper was initially referred to RTI on August 20, 2007, due to his teacher's concerns with Cooper's ability to transfer knowledge and follow through on directions. At that time, his kindergarten teacher implemented interventions and Cooper was considered to have met the criteria for adequate progress. A second RTI meeting was convened on September 18, 2007. While Cooper's ability to follow instructions had improved, he continued having difficulty following directions and learning academic concepts, particularly letters of the alphabet. Ms. Gilreath again developed an intervention plan, this time using the letter machine in her classroom, zoo phonics with another teacher, and the use of Leap Frog at home. After approximately 6 weeks of intervention, Cooper exhibited uneven performance, learning new letters and then forgetting them in the subsequent weeks.

Cooper continued receiving RTI services with additional reading instruction provided in and out of the classroom. According to the RTI team notes from the beginning of his first grade year, Cooper knew his letters and individual sounds, but struggled with blending letters to create actual words and transitioning from one word family to another. The committee also expressed concern with Cooper's understanding of the connection between written and spoken language. Cooper's goals for tier 3 intervention included increasing his reading fluency and sight words. Interventions included participating in PALS for 30 min per day as well as small-group and individual instruction focusing on word families with the reading specialist in addition to classroom reading instruction.

PROGRESS-MONITORING DATA

Oral Reading Fluency

Goal: Increase oral reading fluency at a rate of 1.8 words read correct per minute each week (ultimate goal of 39.8 WRC)

Intervention: Peer-assisted learning strategies (PALS), repeated reading

As can be seen from the words read correct per minute data, Cooper demonstrated variable gains during tier 3 interventions with an average weekly growth rate of 0.91 words per minute. Thus, he failed to meet the growth and benchmark criteria for reading fluency.

Sight Word Recognition

Goal: Increase sight word recognition of words containing consonant blends from 4 to 12

Intervention: Small-group instruction three times weekly and individual instruction two times weekly with reading specialist

While Cooper has increased his sight word recognition, he continues to struggle with consonant blends and did not meet the criteria for progress.

FAMILY AND HEALTH HISTORY:

Mr. Davis noted that Cooper is an only child and lives at home with his mother, Ms. Jeannette Davis. According to Mr. Davis, Cooper was born in Chicago, Illinois, at full term weighing 5 pounds, 1 ounce, through a cesarean section. There was no evidence of injury at birth. Cooper met most developmental milestones within normal limits, speaking at 12 months and walking at 14 months. He completely achieved toilet training at 5 years of age, which is somewhat late. Mr. Davis reported that Cooper underwent surgery twice in infancy, due to a hernia. Cooper also had surgery to have tubes put in his ears at the age of 2 years. He noted that Cooper's frequent illnesses include allergies, for which he previously took Zyrtec, and earaches. He described Cooper's current health as generally healthy, as well as underweight and overly active. Cooper passed a vision and hearing screening on September 12, 2008, as part of the RTI process.

EDUCATIONAL HISTORY

According to Mr. Davis, Cooper was cared for by his great grandmother until 7 months, at which time he began attending day care. He continues to go to day care for after-school care. Mr. Davis reported that Cooper struggled in kindergarten and that his most difficult subject is reading. He stated that Cooper studies for 30–40 min with a parent present, but he will not do so independently.

SOCIAL AND EMOTIONAL HISTORY

Mr. Davis described Cooper as feeling happy with himself, playing well with others, being trustworthy, and relating well to adults. Additionally, he disclosed that Cooper has few close friends, has difficulty listening, tries to control others, is loud, acts younger than same-age peers, and is restless. He reported that Cooper rarely gets in trouble. Mr. Davis reported that Cooper relates very well to family members and talks openly to them. He also reported that Cooper is very friendly with classmate and socializes well, although he has very few friends. He listed Cooper's major interests as including basketball and soccer. Mr. Davis endorsed most enjoying Cooper's sense of humor, his sense of reality, and how he describes things he sees.

GENERAL DESCRIPTION AND TESTING BEHAVIOR:

Cooper is a 7-year-old first grade student who appeared somewhat small for his chronological age. He was tested at Bascomb Elementary School in a single session. Cooper entered the testing situation willingly, and rapport was easily established and maintained. Cooper's affect was very upbeat and his mood was pleasant and cooperative. He attempted all tasks and put forth adequate effort. He often engaged in spontaneous conversation that tended to be unrelated to the task at hand. He had difficulty following directions when presented orally and required repetition. Cooper was alert and appeared oriented throughout the evaluative sessions. His eye contact was appropriate, except when he became restless and was moving about the room. Overall test results appear to be a valid estimate of Cooper's current level of functioning.

TEST RESULTS AND INTERPRETATION:

Cooper was administered the Reynolds Intellectual Assessment Scales (RIAS) in order to provide an estimate of his cognitive ability. The RIAS is an individually administered test designed to provide subtest and composite scores that represent intellectual functioning in specific cognitive domains.

The following scores reflect Cooper's performance on individual subtests. Each subtest score is scaled to a mean of 50 and a standard deviation of 10. Subtest scores that fall between 45 and 54 are considered average. The various indexes are scaled to a mean of 100 and a standard deviation of 15. Composite scores that fall between 90 and 109 are considered average.

Index score	Standard score	Percentile
Verbal Intelligence Index (VIX)	87	19
Nonverbal Intelligence Index (NIX)	81	10
Composite Intelligence Index (CIX)	81	10
Composite Memory Index (CMX)	83	13

Verbal subtest	*T-Score*
Guess What (GWH)	42
Verbal Reasoning (VRZ)	37
Nonverbal subtest	*T-Score*
Odd-Item Out (OIO)	36
What's Missing (WHM)	38
Memory subtest	*T-Score*
Verbal Memory (VRM)	38
Nonverbal Memory (NVM)	42

Cooper's Composite Intelligence Index (CIX) score was a standard score of 81, which corresponds to the 10th percentile, indicating that Cooper is functioning equal to or better than 10 % of children his same age. The chance that the range of scores from 77 to 87 includes Cooper's true IQ is 95 out of 100.

In the area of verbal skills, Cooper obtained a Verbal Intelligence Index (VIX) composite score of 87 (19th percentile), which is in the low average range of functioning. This composite included two subtests—Guess What and Verbal Reasoning. The Guess What subtest assesses verbal reasoning in combination with vocabulary, language development, and overall fund of available information. Tasks on this subtest involve deducing the object or concept being described when given a set of two to four clues. On the Guess What subtest, Cooper obtained a T-score of 42, which is in the low average range. The Verbal Reasoning subtest assesses verbal-analytical reasoning ability, but with fewer vocabulary and general knowledge demands than the Guess What subtest. Tasks on the Verbal Reasoning subtest involve listening to a propositional statement that essentially forms a verbal analogy. The child is asked to respond with one or two words that complete the idea or proposition. On the Verbal Reasoning subtest, Cooper obtained a T-score of 37, which is in the below average range.

In the area of nonverbal skills, Cooper obtained a Nonverbal Intelligence Index (NIX) composite score of 81 (10th percentile), which is in the below average range of functioning. This composite included two subtests—Odd-Item Out and What's Missing. The Odd-Item Out subtest assesses nonverbal reasoning skills but also requires the use of spatial ability, visual imagery, and other nonverbal skills on various items. It is a form of reverse nonverbal analogy. On the Odd-Item Out subtest, the child is presented with a picture card containing from five to seven pictures or drawings and is asked to designate which one does not belong or go with the others. On the Odd-Item Out subtest, Cooper obtained a T-score of 36, which is in the borderline range. The What's Missing subtest assesses nonverbal reasoning wherein the examinee must conceptualize the picture, analyze its gestalt, and deduce what essential element is missing. On this subtest, the child is shown a picture with some key element or logically consistent component missing and is asked to identify the missing essential element. On the What's Missing subtest, Cooper obtained a T-score of 38, which is in the below average range.

In the area of memory, Cooper obtained a Composite Memory Index (CMX) composite score of 83 (13th percentile), which is in the below average range. This composite included two subtests—Verbal Memory and Nonverbal Memory. The Verbal Memory subtest assesses the ability to encode, briefly store, and recall verbal material in a meaningful context where associations are clear and evident. On this subtest, on the basis of the child's age, a series of sentences or brief stories are read aloud by the examiner and then recalled by the child. On the Verbal Memory subtest, Cooper obtained a T-score of 38, which is in the below average range. The Nonverbal Memory subtest assesses the ability to encode, store, and recognize pictorial stimuli that are both concrete and abstract without meaningful referents. On this subtest, the child is presented with a stimulus picture, which is presented for 5 s, followed by the presentation of an array of pictures from which the child must identify the target picture. On the Nonverbal Memory subtest, Cooper obtained a T-score of 81, which is in the below average range.

Cooper's VIX and NIX are consistent with his CIX and this indicated that his verbal and nonverbal abilities are similarly developed. When compared to his overall intelligence, Cooper's memory score (CMX) indicates commensurate working memory skills in both the verbal and nonverbal areas.

SOCIAL/EMOTIONAL/BEHAVIORAL RATING SCALES:
Cooper's mother and teacher completed the Behavior Assessment System for Children, Second Edition (BASC-2), a measure that evaluates levels of behavioral, emotional, and social competencies relative to other children their age and gender. On the Clinical scales and Composite scores of the BASC-2, T-scores of 70 and above** are considered clinically significant, scores between 60 and 69* are in the at-risk range, and scores of 41 through 59 are in the average range. Adaptive scale scores of 30 or less** are considered clinically significant, scores of 31 through 40* are at risk, and scores between 41 and 59 are average.

Skill area	T-Score (mother)	T-Score (teacher)
Hyperactivity	47	52
Aggression	51	44
Conduct Problems	64*	43
Externalizing Problems	*54*	*46*
Anxiety	34	59
Depression	45	53
Somatization	44	43
Internalizing Problems	*39*	*52*
Attention Problems	–	56

Skill area	T-Score (mother)	T-Score (teacher)
Learning Problems	–	64*
School Problems	–	*61**
Atypicality	41	44
Withdrawal	46	52
Attention Problems	43	–
Behavioral Symptoms Index	*44*	*50*
Adaptability	48	58
Social Skills	51	47
Leadership	53	49
Activities of Daily Living	56	–
Study Skills	–	53
Functional Communication	58	51
Adaptive Skills	*54*	*52*

*At risk
**Clinically significant/high level of maladjustment

Both raters' F, Response Pattern, and Consistency indexes were within the acceptable range. No clinically significant scores were reported across the composites and scales. Cooper's mother endorsed observing some Conduct Problems at home, such as disobeying at times. Mr. Baugh indicated that Cooper displays at-risk Learning Problems at school, including difficulties with reading and poor grades.

Cooper also completed the Behavior Assessment System for Children, Second Edition Self-Report Interview (BASC-2-SRP-I) to provide his perception of his social and emotional functioning. As with the parent and teacher forms, the Clinical scales and Composite T-scores of 70 and above** are considered clinically significant, scores between 60 and 69* are in the at-risk range, and scores of 41–59 are in the average range. Adaptive scale scores of 30 or less** are considered clinically significant, scores of 31–40* are at risk, and scores between 41 and 59 are average. Specific T-scores obtained on the BASC-2-SRP are listed below:

Skill area	T-Score
Attitude to school	43
Attitude to teachers	49
Atypicality	47
Social stress	49
Anxiety	45
Depression	41
Emotional Symptoms Index	*44*
Interpersonal relations	55

*At-Risk
**Clinically Significant/High Level of Maladjustment

Cooper's Response Pattern and Consistency indexes were within the acceptable range. On this self-report, Cooper indicated that he perceives himself as being well adjusted and satisfied with his relationships.

A structured interview was also completed with Cooper. When asked if he had three wishes, what they would be, he responded that he would: (1) get a new game, (2) get a Nintendo DS, and (3) buy a new DS game. If he were on a deserted island and could only choose three people to join him, he endorsed wanting his Uncle Eric, Cousin Sydney, and his mother to be there. When asked what he would change about individuals in his life, he reported that he would get his mom a new gift for Mother's Day, his dad would get a new shooting game for him, and his teacher would be nice to him and always let him play his favorite computer game. If he could change something about the school, Cooper would want his friends to pretend to be ninja turtles. He also noted that he would get all As on his report card.

Cooper disclosed that his best friend is Dave and described him as being skinny. He reported that he and Dave enjoy playing ninja turtles together. He stated that he also enjoys playing soccer, playing baseball, playing football, and riding on jet skis. He said that his favorite subject is science and that he also likes reading. He endorsed disliking mathematics and the fish pools in art. Cooper stated that the thing he is best at and likes most about school is going home.

Classroom Observation

Cooper was observed from 11:15 a.m. to 12:00 p.m. on March 11, 2008. For 20 min of the observation, Cooper's behavior was recorded as being on task or off task after 1-minute intervals. Cooper was on task 96 % of the time versus 94 % for a randomly selected comparison student. Within the 4 % of time spent off task, Cooper was fidgeting and out of his seat one time each, and primarily tended to look around the room or at other students' activities. At the beginning of the observation, Cooper was sitting at a table with another group of students completing a phonics assignment. He initially was flipping his paper over and looking around, but he completed the task. During the transition time, he and another child were putting their heads under the desk and were redirected by the teaching assistant. The class then went to the computer laboratory and Cooper appropriately walked with his classmates. Once in the computer laboratory, Cooper proceeded directly to his computer and began working. He was mainly engaged in his task but often counted out loud and occasionally gazed around the room or at his neighbor's monitor, at which time he would comment, "I'm not on that one."

The teaching assistants who accompanied the class to the computer room described Cooper's behavior as being typical during the 45-minute session. They described him as being more fidgety during reading assignments than at other times.

SUMMARY:

Cooper is a 7-year-old kindergarten student who was referred for RTI services for remediation of reading difficulties and additional evaluation to determine eligibility for special education services. Current test results suggest that Cooper is functioning intellectually in the below average range. He displayed below average abilities associated with language development and acquired knowledge, as well as nonverbal reasoning. While Cooper's intelligence is not within the average range, he is well above the range of mental retardation and considered able to learn academic concepts. Cooper was provided with intensive tier 3 interventions and he did not achieve the expected growth or benchmark levels.

Cooper passed his hearing and vision screenings and behavioral ratings indicated that he is not demonstrating emotional or behavioral difficulties that may interfere with his learning. Additionally, educational history indicates that he has received a consistent and quality education throughout which he has demonstrated reading and phonics difficulties requiring extra support. Based upon all available information, it appears that the most likely explanation for Cooper's reading difficulties is the presence of a specific learning disability in the area of reading.

RESPONSE TO INTERVENTION REPORT
BARNARD COUNTY SCHOOLS

Name: Danielle Bagoda	Parent/Guardian: Mother Bagoda
School: Barnard Elementary	Age: 8
Grade: 2	Report date: February 12, 2009

INFORMATION SOURCES

Educational record
Progress-monitoring data
Observation
Parent, teacher, and student interview

REFERRAL REASON

Danielle was referred to the problem-solving team at Barnard Elementary due to low test grades in reading, writing, and mathematics. In particular, Danielle has struggled with word recognition and comprehension. Previous interventions within the classroom have included one-on-one instruction with the teacher, consult with the reading specialist, and small-group instruction with little progress in academic performance.

BACKGROUND INFORMATION

Danielle is an 8-year-old second grader at Barnard Elementary. Danielle was the product of an uncomplicated pregnancy and delivery. The available medical history indicates that no significant problems exist. Developmental history suggests that milestones were met within normal time limits. Danielle lives with her mother, stepfather, 10-year-old sister, and 5-year-old brother. She reported that she sometimes stays with her father for 2 days at a time. The family relationship is described as loving and caring. Her mother describes Danielle as well adjusted, happy, and "bubbly." Danielle expressed affection for her stepfather and stepsiblings as well as a tendency to miss her father after visits. She reported otherwise being happy and rarely feeling sad or anxious. Danielle enjoys playing outside and drawing. She also enjoys spending time with other individuals regardless of their age. Her mother describes her as a caring "people pleaser" who would do anything for others.

Danielle's educational history includes prekindergarten at Exceptional Learning Center and kindergarten and first grade at Barnard Elementary. According to the parent report, Danielle experienced learning problems beginning in kindergarten, specifically with reading, which has caused Danielle to feel frustrated. The family reportedly sought tutoring at an outside institution as well as reading with Danielle at home. Despite difficulty reading and understanding, Danielle reports that reading is her favorite part of school while mathematics is her least favorite subject, and her mother reports that Danielle still enjoys the social aspects of school. Danielle shared that she likes to make her teacher and classmates happy and tries to be good. She noted she sometimes "acts silly" so she will not "mess up" on an assignment.

Danielle's teacher reports that Danielle attempts to avoid work that is difficult and seeks attention when completing assignments. The teacher also said that Danielle struggles to do work when she is not given directions and when Danielle is required to read the directions herself, she does not know how to proceed when she reaches the problems to be completed. According to the teacher, Danielle often requests permission to go to the bathroom or the clinic when she is in a situation with which she is uncomfortable or unsure of her performance. Records indicate that Danielle has visited the clinic many times for complaints such as a hurt finger, an elbow bumped with a friend's, and chapped lips, just to name a few. The reading specialist with whom Danielle has received consult services for 2 years reports similar behavior when she is working with Danielle. For example, Danielle often runs into things and then asks for permission to go to the clinic and she regularly loses her place when reading and asks where she was.

CLASSROOM AND STANDARDIZED ACHIEVEMENT SCORES

Danielle's grades for the first semester of her second grade year are as follows: 87 in social studies, 85 in science, 72 in reading, 69 in spelling, 69 in writing, and 68 in mathematics. Danielle is being considered for retention due to her low grades. Danielle participated in the Cognitive Abilities Test (CogAT), a group-administered intelligence test, in September 2008. The following standard scores were reported: Verbal 98, Quantitative 103, Nonverbal 111, and Composite 104. She also took the Iowa Tests of Basic Skills (ITBS), a group-administered standardized achievement test, in Fall 2008 and obtained the following percentile ranks: Reading 10th, Language 20th, Mathematics 16th, Social Studies 25th, and Science 27th.

INTERVENTIONS AND PROGRESS MONITORING

READING:

Intervention(s):

Paired repeated reading for reading fluency (three times weekly, 30 min each)
Individual direct instruction with reading specialist (four times weekly, 30 min each)
Reciprocal teaching for reading comprehension (two times weekly, 60 min each)
General classroom instruction

Criteria for progress:

Reading fluency: Weekly growth rate of 1.6 words read correct per minute (benchmark target of 61 words read correct per minute (WPM))

Week 1	Week 2	Week 3	Week 4	Week 5	Week 6	Week 7	Week 8
41	40	41	43	44	42	45	45
Week 9	**Week 10**	**Week 11**	**Week 12**	**Week 13**	**Week 14**	**Week 15**	**Week 16**
46	48	50	49	49	53	51	51

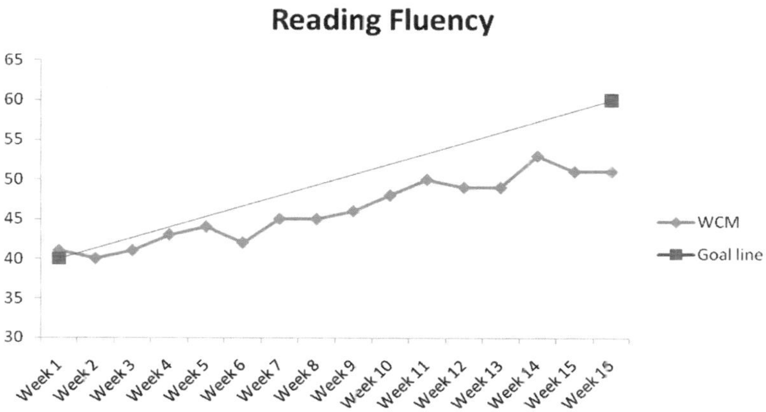

Reading comprehension: Increase in multiple-choice reading comprehension score from 3 out of 12 correct to 8 out of 12 correct

Week 1	Week 2	Week 3	Week 4	Week 5	Week 6	Week 7	Week 8
3	3	4	5	4	4	5	6
Week 9	**Week 10**	**Week 11**	**Week 12**	**Week 13**	**Week 14**	**Week 15**	**Week 16**
5	5	5	6	4	6	6	5

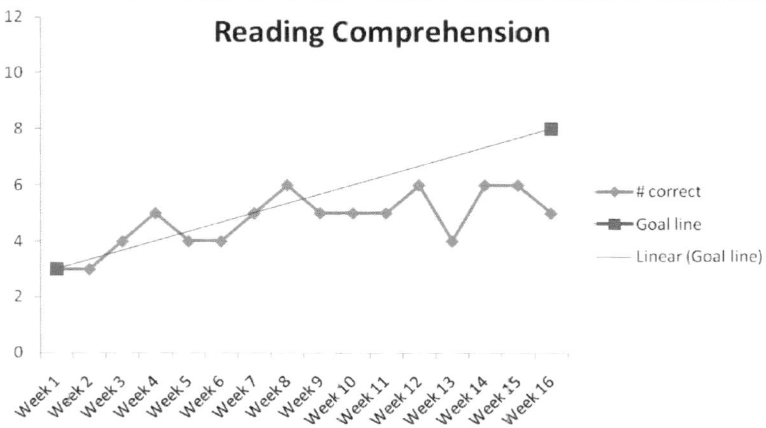

WRITING:
Intervention(s):

Integrated writing instruction (five times weekly, 30 min each)
General classroom instruction

Criteria for progress: 20 words written in 3 minutes

Week 1	Week 2	Week 3	Week 4	Week 5	Week 6	Week 7	Week 8
13	12	14	14	15	18	17	18
Week 9	**Week 10**	**Week 11**	**Week 12**	**Week 13**	**Week 14**	**Week 15**	**Week 16**
17	19	19	18	20	21	20	22

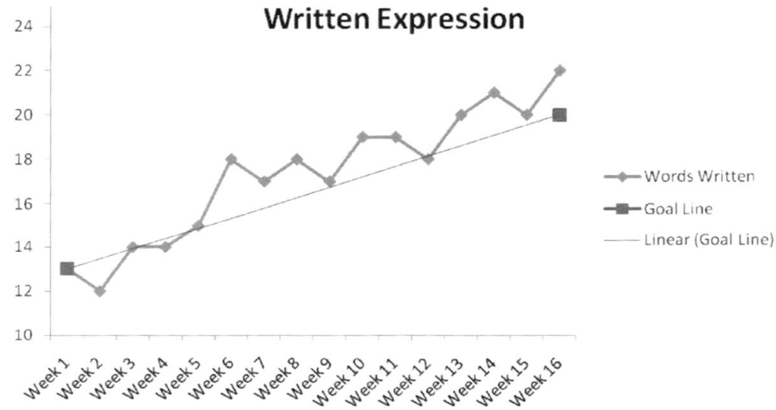

MATHEMATICS:
Intervention(s):

Cover–copy–compare (five times weekly, 30 min each)
Individual direct instruction with teacher (three times weekly, 30 min each)
General classroom instruction

Criteria for progress: Mathematics calculation digits correct increase from 40 to 65 %

Week 1	Week 2	Week 3	Week 4	Week 5	Week 6	Week 7	Week 8
40%	39%	40%	44%	45%	43%	45%	46%
Week 9	**Week 10**	**Week 11**	**Week 12**	**Week 13**	**Week 14**	**Week 15**	**Week 16**
48%	45%	42%	44%	49%	47%	45%	49%

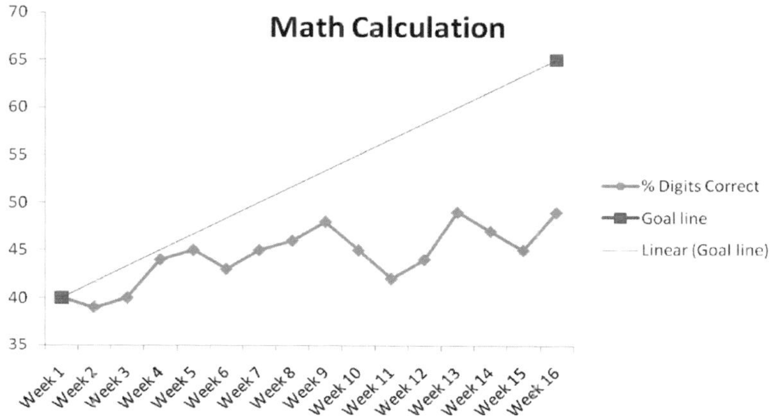

OBSERVATION

Danielle was observed in her classroom on two occasions. The first observation session was conducted from 10:10 to 10:40 a.m. During this time, the class was finishing a mathematics work sheet and then transitioned to independent work. While the class was completing the mathematics work sheet, Danielle volunteered answers and corrected any answers that he had gotten incorrect. During the independent work time, Danielle was asked to complete paired repeated reading with a teacher assistant. She was easily distracted by her peers using the computers and moved to another area of the room at the teacher's request. While she chose a quiet area, she still tended to look away from her book often and watch other students for short periods of time. The second observation was conducted after lunch at 11:40 a.m. At this time the class was reading aloud from a book about science and answering questions from a work sheet. Danielle slowly struggled through her first turn reading aloud and asked if she could skip her turn to read aloud the second time.

FACTORS CONSIDERED

Quality of previous instruction: Danielle was provided with quality classroom instruction and has received intensive individualized interventions through the problem-solving team's RTI process.

Visual or hearing deficits: Danielle passed vision and hearing screening.

Motor disability: Teacher observations and parent interviews indicated that Danielle's motor development is typical.

Intellectual functioning: Danielle demonstrated average or better intelligence on the CogAT and teacher and parent observations indicate that she is bright and intuitive.

Emotional disturbance: Interviews with Danielle, her parents, and her teacher indicated that she displays some anxiety, inattention, and attention seeking that are demonstrated during difficult academic tasks only and never observed at home. It seems likely that these mild behavioral symptoms are due to academic frustration rather than an emotional or behavioral disability.

Environmental, cultural, or economic disadvantage: Danielle's background history and interview with parents indicated that she has experienced an enriched environment.

SUMMARY

Danielle exhibits significant difficulties with reading and mathematics. She has received intensive interventions, which did not result in the expected progress in terms of growth and outcome. Based upon the available information, no exclusionary factors appear to contribute to Danielle's academic struggles. It is the problem-solving team's opinion that Danielle is a child who exhibits characteristics of a child with a specific LD and it is recommended that she be allowed to receive interventions through the special education program.

Summary of Key Points

- The 2004 reauthorization of the Individuals with Disabilities Education Act (IDEA) specified that the use of an RTI process must be allowed.
- RTI generally consists of three tiers:
  - Tier 1: Classroom-wide instruction and assessment of progress is carried out.
  - Tier 2: Students who do not respond to general instruction receive additional intervention and progress monitoring.
  - Tier 3: Students who continue to show inadequate response receive more intensive differentiated instruction and possible special education referral.
- The problem-solving approach uses more intensive interventions, while the treatment validity approach and standard protocol approaches focus more on quality instruction in a general education environment.
- Curriculum-based measurement, which is developed based upon objectives of a specific curriculum, is typically used within an RTI process to measure student progress over time.
- RTI benefits include early access to interventions for all struggling students, ability to distinguish between poor instruction and learning difficulties, and less gender and racial bias in identification.
- The use of different norm groups within CBM across locations, different response indicators, and differing treatment approaches lead to variability in the identification of nonresponders, or students ultimately classified as having an LD.
- Gains made in intensive interventions common within the standard treatment protocol are unlikely to be maintained upon return to a regular education environment.
- Research has identified few similarities between nonresponders with the exception of phonological awareness and very low achievement and cognitive scores.

Questions and Answers with the Expert: Scott Ardoin

Meet the expert: Scott Ardoin, Ph.D., is a tenured associate professor of the school psychology program at the University of Georgia. His research interests include application of applied behavior analysis principles in classrooms. He has many publications, including journal articles and book chapters, as well as serving as an associate editor and reviewer for journals. He has most recently been working on Institute of Education Sciences-funded grants within local school districts.

Question 1: What are the benefits of response to intervention (RTI) as a tool to identify students with learning disabilities (LD)? Answer 1: There are many benefits that should result from schools employing an RTI model, but I think the one benefit that I have observed across all of the schools in which I have worked is the early identification of students who are in need of supplemental intervention. Providing supplemental instruction to students early in their academic career is not only beneficial for the students but also beneficial for the school and society. We know how to help students to be successful in school, but if we wait to provide that assistance, the task can seem overwhelming and result in abundant frustration for all involved. There have been far too many individuals that the educational system has failed because they were not given the type of instruction needed to develop adequate reading and mathematics skills. Some of these students were identified with LD, but that disability diagnosis did not provide direction regarding how to best instruct those students. Many others were not provided with the instruction that they needed because the tests they were administered suggested that they were simply low achieving students as opposed to students with an LD. The benefit of employing an RTI model as the model for identifying which students need intervention and the level of intervention that they need is that all students who need intervention theoretically should get that intervention. If RTI is used simply as a pre-referral process and ultimately the resources provided to a student are based upon the results of a battery of tests, then we are going to continue to fail many students. LD designation should not determine whether a child receives special education or other services; a child's educational needs should determine the services that a child receives.

Question 2: What are the disadvantages of using RTI to diagnose LD? Answer 2: The disadvantages of using an RTI model stem from poor implementation. If implemented as intended, the right students will receive intervention and they will receive effective intervention that maximizes their academic growth. The complication is that schools generally do not have the resources and expertise to properly implement an RTI model. In my experience, schools seem most concerned with whether they have the resources to implement effective supplemental interventions, but even with the implementation of effective interventions, RTI models can fail horribly. They will fail students when supplemental interventions are not supplementing quality core instruction. RTI models will also fail students when schools lack personnel with the skills necessary to properly interpret screening and progress-monitoring data. Unfortunately, the extent of training provided to school personnel regarding data interpretation is often limited to identifying which students have failed to meet a prespecified level of performance and how to employ decision rules with CBM progress-monitoring data. School personnel are not generally trained in other necessary skills for which there are no clearly stated rules that can be applied to data. For instance, school personnel often lack the skills necessary to use the screening and progress-monitoring data collected in order to evaluate (a) the quality of a school's curriculum for the larger student body; (b) the quality of a school's curriculum for specific groups of students (e.g., English as a second language (ESL), gifted); (c) whether individual student progress-monitoring data are reliable and thus are appropriate for use in making educational decisions; or (d) whether the assessment instrument employed to measure student improvement is appropriate for the intervention being implemented. These are not generally skills that are taught to teachers and administrators when they are earning their degrees and for this reason, school psychologists and others trained in the assessment, measurement, statistics, and implementation of interventions with integrity need to be involved across the RTI decision-making process.

Question 3: Describe how you believe RTI best fits into LD identification/intervention. Answer 3: I am unaware of a standardized test or set of tests that tells us specifically why a student is not achieving as might be expected or a test that tells us specifically what type of instruction should be provided to a student in order to maximize his/her achievement. There also does not exist an LD diagnosis that is associated with a curriculum or instructional practice known to maximize the achievement of students with that specific disability. Knowing that an individual has an LD provides us with little information except to say that the student is going to need substantial modifications. Until a test or diagnosis can be rendered that has treatment utility, there is little need to identify a student as having a specific LD. Instead, we need to identify what instructional practices need to be in place for students to maximize their achievement. For the large majority of students, this should be the general education curriculum, but other students will need slight modifications to the curriculum to maximize their achievement and still others will require significant modifications. Proper implementation of an RTI model allows for the determination of what level of modification is needed and allows for the continual evaluation of whether the modifications are resulting in sufficient changes.

If RTI is implemented correctly, it does not fit into an LD identification system, but rather it is the system. It must start early and it must continue through students' educational careers.

Question 4: What do you consider the best practice for LD identification? Answer 4: When psychoeducational evaluations are necessary to determine special education eligibility, regardless of their comprehensiveness, the ultimate determination of eligibility is based upon the results of the battery of tests administered. Likewise, the instructional accommodations provided to students are based upon those tests' results. Eligibility and instructional modifications should be based upon data that reflect what instructional modifications help a student to maximize their achievement. Instead of administering a battery of tests and using those results to recommend treatments that are not directly linked to the results, we should develop hypotheses regarding what is causing a student not to succeed academically, then empirically test those hypotheses. Thus, the best practices of LD identification are the effective implementation of an RTI model.

Question 5: What outcome do you predict for RTI as an identification process for LD? Answer 5: Despite being an advocate of RTI, I fear that it was adopted too soon by too many schools. Schools adopted it early because they realized that they were failing too many students by waiting too long to provide the services that the student needed. Early adoption of RTI has resulted in schools having to employ both an RTI model and an IQ-achievement discrepancy model. In such cases, students' eligibility for special education remains based largely upon the results of psychoeducational evaluations, and thus the funding sources for providing special education services remain based upon results of psychoeducational evaluations. As a result, the administrative support and personnel training necessary to effectively implement an RTI model are not provided and RTI models are often not properly implemented. This is problematic because RTI is being judged not truly based upon the implementation of RTI. Proponents of RTI need to realize the training necessary for its effective implementation and provide the appropriate ongoing training to schools. It is not sufficient to only provide schools with a day or even a week's worth of training in the RTI process; training must be ongoing. Furthermore, proponents of RTI must recognize the limitations and challenges of RTI along with its many benefits. Failure to do so will lead not only to the demise of RTI but also to many students not receiving the instruction they need to succeed in the core academic areas.

Chapter 5
Low Achievement

More than two decades ago the eminent measurement scientist Lori Shepard concluded that the most effective assessment strategy for learning disabilities (LDs) is to start with the evidence of inadequate learning and then test for other explanations of the problem (Shepard 1989, p. 559). In other words, it is most important to determine that a child has difficulty learning and then attempt to identify the cause of the learning difficulty, such as poor instruction, low general intelligence, hearing difficulties, etc. Shepard (1989) highlighted the difficulty in identifying underlying causes of mild disabilities, including LDs, and the need to focus on the signs and symptoms. As discussed in the introduction to this book, it is important to classify individuals as having a disorder based on their common characteristics so that research may be conducted. Before LDs can be diagnosed based upon their etiology or underlying brain functioning, we must first be able to identify a group of individuals who have common observable characteristics of LDs so that quality research can be conducted in order to move toward a better understanding of etiology.

Well-respected researchers such as Linda Siegel and Keith Stanovich have similarly argued for many years that children should be identified as having LDs based on their achievement scores, which are objective and observable. Kavale and Forness (1985) recommended a dual criteria definition similar to mental retardation (MR) that included significant subaverage academic impairment and intelligence quotient (IQ) in the average range. Numerous investigations began to use Shepard's and others' simple model of below-average reading scores to "diagnose" children in need of reading intervention (Swanson 1999; Vellutino et al. 1996). One study conducted in Europe demonstrated that children could be accurately identified as having reading disabilities using word recognition and reading comprehension achievement tests (Rispens et al. 1991).

In the Rispens et al. (1991) study, the researchers examined the effect of comparing only word recognition and/or reading comprehension achievements test scores to the average score for the age group. Those scores that were 1.65 z score points or more below the mean, which is roughly equivalent to a standard score of 75.25, were considered to be evidence of significantly low achievement representative of a LD. They concluded that not using IQ in identification had a very limited effect on the number of children who were classified as having a reading disability. Such

A. E. B. Taylor, *Diagnostic Assessment of Learning Disabilities in Childhood*, Contemporary Issues in Psychological Assessment, DOI 10.1007/978-1-4939-0335-1_5,

© Springer Science+Business Media New York 2014

a low achievement approach to LD diagnosis holds great promise and warrants further analysis.

Low achievement methods for identifying students as learning disabled typically require that students score below a certain cut-point (e.g., 25th percentile) on an academic achievement measure and have cognitive scores somewhere above the MR range (i.e., IQ > 70). The actual cut scores are arbitrarily chosen by independent researchers or are based on social policy issues, such as resource allocation. Several researchers support this type of method for LD diagnosis because it is parsimonious and reliable across locations. More salient, though, are findings that groups identified using low achievement and IQ-discrepant definitions do not significantly differ on cognitive characteristics, response to intervention, and other outcomes (Shaywitz et al. 1992; Steubing et al. 2002; Stanovich 1991). In fact, those differences that were found were primarily related to differences in IQ, with IQ-discrepant children performing better than low achievement children on some measures as would be expected given the correlation between intelligence and academic achievement scores (Shaywitz et al. 1992).

Ysseldyke et al. (1982) are often credited as being the first researchers to explore the differences and similarities between low achieving students and those with LDs. They determined that students identified as having LDs were not reliably distinguishable from low achieving students. Based on their findings, these researchers asserted that LD was not a useful construct. Later, other researchers (Kavale et al. 1994) reanalyzed the data from Ysseldyke and colleague's study and concluded that the majority of the students with LDs were distinguishable from low achieving students due to lower achievement scores. Shaywitz et al. (1992), on the other hand, found similar results to the Ysseldyke study and suggested that both groups of students should receive special education services.

As has been demonstrated across approaches to LD identification, once again the definitions used to establish samples also have to be taken into consideration. In yet another study comparing low achieving students and students labeled as having an LD, the authors pointed out that their sample likely differed from those in other studies and even included students with average achievement scores in the low achieving sample (Gresham et al. 1996). These studies also highlight that while varying definitions of LDs based upon low achievement have been considered useful within a research context, the approach requires a clear operationalized definition of what constitutes low achievement in order to be used for identification in daily practice.

Concerns Regarding Use of Low Achievement

Opponents of low achievement test score use argue that the use of a cut-point for determining LD lacks research support for the decision that children achieving at certain levels should be included or excluded from eligibility for the diagnosis (Stuebing et al. 2002). A major reason for the arbitrary nature of cut-points used for LD diagnosis is that achievement is normally distributed, despite Rutter and Yule's

(1975) well-known conclusion that there is a "hump" at the lower end of the reading distribution representing children with specific reading retardation. Because there is no natural breaking point in the achievement distribution, setting a cut-point to distinguish between underachievers and individuals with LD is not a straightforward matter (Francis et al. 2005). Thus, LD is distributed along an unobservable dimension and it seems unlikely that a single test score can accurately determine how much of a latent construct, LD, an individual actually possesses (Fletcher et al. 2005).

Additionally, the concern about the ability of a low achievement method to capture the "unexpected" nature of LDs has been cited as a drawback (Fletcher et al. 2005). Relatedly, it has been argued that the approach is also atheoretical (Speece et al. 2003), whereas the intra-individual approach assumes underlying psychological processes and response to intervention assumes non-optimal instruction. Instead, a low achievement model is based upon observable behavior and data, which some may argue is a strength.

Francis et al. (2005) have raised concerns about the use of a low achievement definition for diagnosing LD beyond the argument that cut-points are not inherently related to the construct. They argued that cut-points are not meaningful due to error in measurement and used both real and simulated data to demonstrate that groups formed by cut-points are unstable over time. In this study, LD was defined as scores below the 25th percentile, and 32 % of children classified as disabled using this criterion at time 1 were classified as nondisabled at time 2.

It is similarly asserted that a low achievement definition of LD is questionable because it depends on a single indicator, i.e., an achievement score. This argument holds that a single test score cannot "capture perfectly a student's ability on an imperfectly measured latent variable" (Fletcher et al. 2005, p. 510). This is partly due to measurement error because a score will fluctuate around a cut-point on repeated testing. It is also because LD is a latent construct that must be inferred based on observable data, with more information available for making an inference allowing the inference to be more valid (Fletcher et al. 2005). Furthermore, it is believed that academic achievement is influenced by several factors that may be cognitive, behavioral, and social (Francis et al. 2005), and a single test of academic achievement cannot assess all of these factors.

Support for Low Achievement Approaches

Despite these problems, there is evidence for the validity of low achievement markers for identifying students as having an LD. As noted previously, studies have shown that IQ-discrepant and low achieving poor readers do not differ from one another on many outcomes of interest. This finding suggests that the "unexpected" underachievement thought to be captured by the discrepancy approach is not actually a useful concept, since students identified with significant LDs based on a low achievement model respond similarly to treatment and evidence difficulties with learning similar to those of children who are considered to demonstrate "unexpected" learning delays. Therefore, there is no need to reject a low achievement model of identification because it does not capture the "unexpected" aspect of LDs, the concept of which has been argued against elsewhere (see Stanovich 1999). In addition, the low achievement method does not discriminate against individuals whose ability level is below the mean, and are therefore less likely to be identified by other approaches. A low achievement definition of LDs, in fact, does not require any comparison within individuals, but simply bases decision-making on comparison to national norms and evidence of impairment.

Other research has demonstrated that groups formed based on the mental retardation exclusion and achievement scores below the 25th percentile result in subgroups of underachievers that can be validly differentiated from typical achievers based on neurological markers and other external variables (Fletcher et al. 2005; Lyon et al. 2003). For instance, studies by Vellutino et al. (1996, 2000) have demonstrated that level of reading achievement predicts response to intervention, with those children who are lowest achieving being the slowest responders. Results were interpreted to indicate that measures of reading achievement, rather than intelligence, more closely estimate the constructs underlying reading ability, are more time efficient, and more predictive of response to reading intervention (Gresham and Vellutino 2010). It logically follows that students who have received adequate instructions yet remain well below average academically are the students with the greatest learning difficulties, and thus the most in need of special services. These students would be quickly and reliably identified through the implementation of low achievement criteria.

A recent review of various diagnostic methods also concluded that the low achievement model is more reliable and valid than aptitude–achievement and intra-individual difference models. The authors suggested that through a combination of response to intervention (RTI) to rule out poor instruction or curricular causes and low achievement criteria, a reliable and unique group of underachievers could be identified (Fletcher et al. 2005; Fletcher et al. 2005).

Cut Scores

Another issue in the use of a low achievement definition of LD retaining the exclusionary clause is whether the cut-point for IQ should simply be the level at which MR is identified or if it should be some higher value. Rispens et al. (1991) found that the IQ cut-point chosen for inclusion in the category made a greater difference in prevalence than not using IQ in identifying students as learning disabled. For example, with a lower limit of a standard score equal to 85, 3.8 % of students were diagnosed as learning disabled versus 5 % for a lower limit of 80 and 6.5–7.0 % for a lower limit of 70. Stanovich (1999) argued that intelligence should play no role in the diagnosis of LD, but it seems rational to assume that students classified as MR suffer from general inability to learn, not a "specific" LD and based upon the study cited above, the numbers of students identified using an IQ lower limit of 70 would not be burdensome. Not only does the IQ cut-point influence the prevalence of LDs, but it also determines the amount of confounding with mental retardation

Study	Subtest	Responsiveness Description and Standard Score			
Vellutino, Scanlon, & Lyon (2000)		Very Low	Low	Good	Very Good
Grade 1	Word Attack	74.58	77.5	76.89	80.05
	Word Identification	80.89	86.22	93.17	93.74
Vellutino, Scanlon, Small, & Fanuele (2006)		Difficult to Remediate	Less Difficult to Remediate	No Longer at Risk	
Grade 1	Word Attack	93.32	102.23	102.15	
	Word Identification	94.63	105.73	109.24	
Grade 2	Word Attack	84.68	101.54	102.26	
	Word Identification	83.94	102.73	107.47	
Berninger, et al (2002)		Slower	Faster		
Grade 1	Word Attack	80.8	86.3		
	Word Identification	75.9	85.8		

Fig. 5.1 Mean standard scores of students identified as at-risk and grouped by responsiveness to intervention

that would occur (Kavale 2001). Again, this highlights the importance of considering specific versus general learning difficulties.

Stanovich (1999) agreed that there is no "magic" point where one does or does not have a disability since most disorders, including LD, appear to be normally distributed. He suggested that a cut-point reflecting social policy issues, such as the allocation of scarce resources, could prove useful. Vellutino et al. (2000) work revealed that standard scores below 80–85 were associated with the lowest rates of reading growth for students receiving intensive intervention. This work and others (Case et al. 2003), as shown in Fig. 5.1, indicates that a cutoff score at approximately the 15th percentile can be expected to reliably and validly identify students with LD.

The use of the cut-point does not necessarily mean that students scoring near but above that point should not receive services. Instead, it may be more reasonable for schools to provide accommodations on a continuum, so that students do not have to be identified as having a LD to receive assistance. Regardless, the fact that LD exists on a continuum should not prevent the field from providing a means for educators and clinicians to identify which students should receive the diagnosis, just as has always been the case for MR and other diagnoses.

Choosing a Cut-Point in Practice

Stanovich (1999) has pointed out that the concept of "unexplained" underachievement is unfounded, since students with LDs have deficits, such as poor phonological awareness, that do, in fact, explain their academic performance. Based on this logic, academic underachievement must be the unifying distinction in LDs. However, as with most constructs, achievement exists on a continuum. Therefore, it is necessary to distinguish low achievement from severe underachievement that is indicative of disorder.

In the field of psychiatry, the presence of functional impairment has traditionally been a requirement for an individual to meet criteria for any type of disorder. Functional impairment has been defined as specific deficits in multiple domains of functioning developing subsequent to a disorder and includes the concept of adaptive functioning or adjustment to life's demands across multiple domains (Winters et al. 2005). In fact, the most commonly accepted measures of functional impairment assess adaptive skills such as interpersonal relations, academic progress, and participation in leisure and other activities (Fabiano et al. 2006; Lewandowski et al. 2006). It is important to note that functional impairment is not analogous to severity, which is the number of symptoms manifested or the seriousness of the disorder itself. This distinction is best illustrated by the Diagnostic and Statistical Manual's (American Psychiatric Association 2000) inclusion of distress or impairment as well as the Global Assessment of Functioning in addition to requiring that a certain number of symptoms, i.e., severity, be present for diagnosis.

Another example of functional impairment is the *Diagnostic and Statistical Manual of Mental Disorders*, Fourth Edition (DSM-IV) and the American Association on Mental Retardation (AAMR) criteria for mental retardation (MR; now known as Intellectual Disability in the DSM, Fifth Edition (DSM-5)) requirements of subaverage intellectual functioning (IQ below 70) with concurrent deficits in adaptive functioning (AAMR Ad Hoc Committee on Terminology and Classification 2002, p. 1; American Psychiatric Association 2000). Studies of individuals with MR have demonstrated high rates of comorbid emotional and behavioral disorders (Hodapp and Dykens 2003) indicating that the cut score does identify individuals for whom the disorder is associated with significant impairment. It would be expected that the use of a cut score based on meaningful level of low achievement for LD diagnosis would also result in identification of individuals who experience functional impairment associated with their LD.

By assessing for "the essence of" LD, i.e., a level of underachievement that causes marked impairment, "absolute" poor achievers would be identified rather than "relative" poor achievers, thus allowing educators and clinicians to conserve limited resources while still identifying the students who are most in need of services (Gordon et al. 1999). In addition, LD diagnosis would meet the requirements of the Americans with Disabilities Act by complying with the "average person" standard, i.e., individuals are only disabled if their functional impairment limits them relative to most people. Thus, LD would no longer be the only disorder that questionably allows "average" persons to have a disability (Stanovich 1999).

In the next chapter, original research attempting to identify the achievement score range associated with substantial functional impairment using the method of latent class analysis (Taylor and Kamphaus 2008) will be presented along with recommendations for incorporating low achievement into diagnostic practices. This approach would capture the essence of the LD construct while allowing LD to meet the requirements of disorder. Thus, the cut score used would represent both poor academic achievement and problems functioning in the school and other environments. This approach holds the potential to help guarantee that special services are available to those students who are most in need.

Case Examples

Below are two sample written reports using a low achievement approach. The first report uses academic achievement tests alone to assess an adolescent with a suspected reading disability. Social and emotional ratings provide further evidence that this student's learning difficulties are impacting his functioning. The second report not only employs academic achievement measures but also includes intellectual assessment as requested by the child's parents. It is noteworthy that this child would likely have been identified as having a LD using an aptitude achievement discrepancy model, but was not identified when using an absolute low achievement approach.

Psychological Associates, INC.
Name: Trent Banner
Birth Date: 05/29/1995
Age: 14 years, 5 months
Sex: Male
Parent/Guardian: Jared and Tracy Banner
Dates Evaluated: 11/23/2009
Methods of Evaluation:
Wechsler Individual Achievement Test, Second Edition (WIAT-II)
Woodcock-Johnson III Tests of Achievement (WJ III ACH)
Behavior Assessment System for Children, Second Edition (BASC-2)
Parent Rating Scales (PRS)
Teacher Rating Scales (TRS)
Self-Report of Personality (SRP)
Clinical Interview
Classroom Observation
Records Review

Referral and Background Information

Trent, a 14-year-old eighth grade student currently enrolled at Puget Middle School, was referred for a psychological evaluation at the request of his parents. Despite appearing to be bright and previously achieving primarily good grades, Mr. and Mrs. Banner expressed concerns that Trent may have a LD in the area of reading.

Trent's mother, Ms. Tracy Banner, completed an interview on November 22, 2009, and reported that Trent lives at home with her, his father, and his 11-year-old brother. Ms. Banner endorsed receiving regular prenatal care during her pregnancy with Trent, although she noted that she drank during the first month of pregnancy prior to learning that she was pregnant. Trent was reportedly delivered at full term through a normal and uncomplicated pregnancy at a weight of 7 pounds, 12 ounces. No health problems were reported during infancy and early childhood. Ms. Banner was unable to recall when Trent met developmental milestones. She noted that she provided Trent's childhood care in the home.

Ms. Banner reported that Trent was not excited to start school, although he did not have any difficulties separating. She indicated that he had more difficulty than other children learning his letters in kindergarten and continued to be behind his peers in reading skills in later grades, although he performed typically in other subjects. She reported that his elementary teachers tended to normalize his reading difficulties stating that boys tended to "take off" in reading later than girls. She noted that they continued waiting for improvement, but Trent has increasingly struggled in middle school across subjects as more reading has become necessary in all of his classes. Ms. Banner described Trent as completing his homework without coercion and asking for help and support when needed. She indicated that he does not have any difficulties at home other than "typical teenage behaviors."

She endorsed that he displays numerous positive behaviors, with the only negatives including arguing with her and his brother, having a negative body image, and rare fits of temper. Trent's mother reported that he gets along very well with all of his family members. She endorsed that he enjoys music, computers, games, TV, talking on the phone, and hanging out with friends. She reported most enjoying Trent's kind, loving, and caring disposition.

Trent's homeroom teacher, Mr. Cochran, reported that Trent is pleasant in the classroom and has many friends, although he has noticed some difficulties due to what he described as a low frustration tolerance. He noted that Trent sometimes made negative statements about his own intellectual ability when completing homework assignments.

Trent's classroom grades for the first quarter of the 2009–2010 school year were as follows: Physical education (PE) 99, Reading 76, Language Arts 88, History 85, Physical Science 89, and Math 95.

Classroom Observation

Trent was observed on November 21, 2009 from 9:50 a.m. until 10:20 a.m. while in Mr. Cochran's classroom. The class was completing centers and Trent was assigned the task of independently completing a physical science assignment during the first 20-minute center. He worked quietly and waited patiently while Mr. Cochran graded his assignment during the beginning of the next center. He appeared somewhat frustrated and groaned when asked to complete corrections for approximately five problems, but did so without arguing. He was observed during his reading class the following period. Trent appeared to follow along as the class read aloud from a short novel. It was notable that Trent asked to use the restroom shortly before it was his turn to read and thereby avoided reading aloud.

Trent's teachers indicated that this behavior was typical of Trent. They reported that while Trent is not always motivated to put much effort into his work, he does what is required of him. His behavior was described as typical of a middle school student with no problems occurring since he had been in their class.

General Testing Observations

Trent is a 14-year-old male who is noted to be of average height and weight for his chronological age. He was tested at the offices of Psychological Associates. Trent entered the testing situation willingly and rapport was easily established and maintained. He displayed an appropriate range of affect and his mood was pleasant and polite. He was very cooperative, attempted all tasks, and put forth adequate effort. On several occasions, Trent became frustrated and called himself stupid. Despite this, he appeared motivated and continued to complete all assigned tasks. The quality of Trent's expressive language was considered to be within the average range. He was alert and appeared oriented throughout the evaluative sessions. He approached tasks in an organized and logical manner. Trent's eye contact was appropriate and no disturbances in his thought processes were observed. Overall test results appear to be a valid estimate of Trent's current level of functioning.

Test Results and Interpretation:

Academic Achievement

The WJ III ACH and WIAT-II were administered to determine Trent's current level of academic ability. Both are individually administered achievement tests containing various subtests that yield standard scores with a mean of 100 and a standard deviation of 15. Standard scores between 85 and 115, which include 68 % of the general population, are considered to be within the average range.

Area	Subtest	Standard score	Percentile rank
Oral Expression	Story Recall (WJ III ACH)	99	48
	Picture Vocabulary (WJ III ACH)	98	46
Listening Comprehension	Understanding Directions (WJ III ACH)	125	95
	Oral Comprehension (WJ III ACH)	101	54
Written Expression	Writing Samples (WJ III ACH)	104	60
	Spelling (WJ III ACH)	84	15
	Writing Fluency (WJ III ACH)	97	42
Basic Reading Skills	Letter-Word Identification (WJ III ACH)	73	4
	Word Attack (WJ III ACH)	68	2
	Word Reading (WIAT-II)	72	3
	Pseudoword Decoding (WIAT-II)	70	2

Area	Subtest	Standard score	Percentile rank
Reading Comprehension	Passage Comprehension (WJ III ACH)	80	9
	Reading Fluency (WJ III ACH)	82	12
Mathematics Calculation	Calculation (WJ III ACH)	97	42
	Math Fluency (WJ III ACH)	95	37
Mathematics Reasoning	Applied Problems (WJ III ACH)	92	29

Oral Expression: These skills involve the ability to use spoken language to communicate ideas. Trent's performance on both Oral Expression subtests was within the average range. Story Recall required Trent to listen to and repeat paragraphs of increasing length. Picture Vocabulary required Trent to identify pictured objects that became increasingly difficult in order to measure his word knowledge.

Listening Comprehension: These skills involve the ability to understand spoken language. Trent's performance on the Listening Comprehension subtests indicated that he is functioning at or above the average range. Trent demonstrated a strength in his ability to listen to and remember a sequence of direction and then follow the directions by pointing to various objects in a picture. Oral Comprehension required Trent to comprehend a short passage and then supply the missing words as a measure of his language understanding.

Written Expression: These skills involve the ability to communicate ideas effectively in writing with appropriate language rather than simply considering mechanical aspects of writing. Trent's writing skills were average, although he demonstrated below-average spelling ability.

Basic Reading Skills: These skills involve the ability to decode written symbols. Trent's performance on the subtests measuring basic reading skills was within the very low to low range suggesting that reading decoding is a significant weakness for him. While Trent was able to read the simpler words presented, he appeared to guess when reading unfamiliar words by using only the first few letters. Trent's ability to phonetically decode words as measures by a nonsense word task provided further confirmation of basic reading difficulties.

Reading Comprehension: These skills involve the ability to decode and understand the meaning of written language. Trent's scores indicated that he is performing within the low average range, which is somewhat better than his reading–decoding skills but still a weakness.

Mathematics Calculation: These skills involve an individual's ability to process numerical symbols and perform basic computations as well as higher order mathematics problems. Trent's ability to solve simple mathematics facts as well as those requiring regrouping, division, and decimals was within the average range.

Mathematics Reasoning: These skills involve a student's ability to analyze and solve practical problems in mathematics. Trent's scores were within the average range. He was able to solve problems involving money, time, and measurement.

Social/Emotional/Behavioral Rating Scales

Trent's mother and teacher completed BASC-2 in order to provide information about Trent's social, emotional, and behavioral functioning.

The following chart is provided as a guide to T-score interpretation:

Clinical scales		Adaptive scales	
70+	**Clinically significant	70+	Very high
60–69	*At risk	60–69	High
41–59	Average	41–59	Average
31–40	Low	31–40	*At risk
30 and below	Very low	30 and below	**Clinically significant

Skill area	T-score (mother)	T-score (teacher)
Hyperactivity	47	52
Aggression	51	44
Conduct Problems	64*	43
Externalizing Problems	*54*	*46*
Anxiety	34	59
Depression	45	53
Somatization	44	43
Internalizing Problems	*39*	*52*
Attention Problems	–	56
Learning Problems	–	64*
School Problems	–	*61**
Atypicality	41	44
Withdrawal	46	52
Attention Problems	43	–
Behavioral Symptoms Index	*44*	*50*
Adaptability	39*	35*
Social Skills	42	48
Leadership	49	44
Activities of Daily Living	38*	–
Study Skills	–	40*
Functional Communication	58	52
Adaptive Skills	*44*	*43*

*At risk

** Clinically significant/high level of maladjustment

Ms. Banner's and Mr. Cochran's F, Response Pattern, and Consistency indexes were within the acceptable range. No clinically significant scores were reported across the composites and scales. Ms. Banner endorsed observing some Conduct Problems at home, such as using foul language and disobeying at times. Mr. Baugh indicated that Trent displays at-risk Learning Problems at school, including difficulties with reading and mathematics and poor grades. Within the Adaptive Skills composite, mild difficulties were noted with adaptability, activities of daily living, and study skills.

Trent also completed the Behavior Assessment System for Children, Second Edition Self-Report of Personality (BASC-2-SRP) to provide his perception of his social and emotional functioning. As with the parent and teacher forms, the Clinical scales and Composite T-scores of 70 and above** are considered clinically significant, scores between 60 and 69* are in the at-risk range, and scores of 41 through 59 are in the average range. Personal Adjustment scale scores of 30 or less** are considered clinically significant, scores of 31 through 40* are at-risk, and scores between 41 and 59 are average. Specific T-scores obtained on the BASC-2-SRP are listed below:

Skill area	T-score
Attitude to School	45
Attitude to Teachers	41
Sensation Seeking	59
School Problems	*48*
Atypicality	43
Locus of Control	50
Social Stress	47
Anxiety	39
Depression	43
Sense of Inadequacy	67*
Somatization	40
Internalizing Problems	*52*
Attention Problems	54
Hyperactivity	44
Inattention/Hyperactivity	*49*
Emotional Symptoms Index	*47*
Relations with Parents	39*
Interpersonal Relations	48
Self-Esteem	50
Self-Reliance	40*
Personal Adjustment	*42*

*At risk
**Clinically significant/high level of maladjustment

Trent's F, Response Pattern, V, and L Indexes were within the acceptable range. His Consistency Index was just within the caution range due to answering similar items differently. Examination of these items indicated that his responses were plausible and that the results should be considered valid. Trent did not report experiencing school problems, symptoms of internalizing disorders, or troubling attention problems and hyperactivity. The very low score on the Anxiety scale may, however, represent an inflated sense of well-being. Trent did indicate at-risk levels of Sense of Inadequacy, which is likely related to his perceptions that he does not perform as well academically as others his age. Trent's responses resulted in a Personal Adjustment composite that suggests overall positive interpersonal relationships and self-acceptance.

He did indicate some relational problems with his parents as well as some lack of confidence in his ability to make decisions and solve problems independently.

Clinical Interview

In a separate interview, Trent reported that he is 14 years old and in the eighth grade. He was oriented to person, place, time, situation, and objects. Trent disclosed that he lives at home with his mom, dad, 12-year-old brother, and puppy. He endorsed getting along "OK" with his mom, "great" with his dad, and "kinda OK" with his brother. He described his dad as being strict and noted that he gets grounded when he is in trouble, which means he loses everything for a month or two. Trent described things at home as being OK and noted that he, his dad, and his brother all participate in karate.

Trent shared that he was born in Oregon, moved to New Jersey when he was 1 or 2 years old, and then moved to New York when he was about 6 years old. He reported that he lived in New York for a couple of years, which is where he started school, and it was his favorite place, because it was "cool" and there were "cool people." He thought that he had always been. He shared that his favorite subject is science and his least favorite is mathematics even though he does "OK" in it.

Trent described his current mood as happy and rated it as a 6 on a scale from 1 to 10, where 1 is the worst he has ever felt and 10 is the best. He rated his usual mood as a 5. He stated that his mood was last really good when he got his black belt last year. He endorsed being happiest when he is sitting around by himself watching YouTube videos. He denied crying in the past month or ever feeling that he could not control his feelings. He stated that he never feels depressed and when he does feel sad it only lasts for a couple of hours. He reported last feeling down when he lost computer privileges as a consequence. Trent endorsed previously having some problems with impulse control, but no current difficulties. He shared that he usually isolates himself when he feels angry. Trent denied experiencing obsessions, compulsions, delusions, dissociation, hallucinations, illusions, mania, and paranoia. He denied current and previous thoughts of self-harm or of hurting others.

Trent described his current health as being good, with no appetite or weight changes. He endorsed sleeping well with no difficulties falling or staying asleep. Trent reported that he does not and never has used substances such as alcohol, drugs, and tobacco.

Trent reported having some friends at home and at school. He noted that he had just spent time with friends the previous day. Trent was uncertain about whether he had a best friend and described a boy who he had been friends with at his previous school. He stated that his friend "tried to be like a gangster," which he described as acting tough. He noted that they were friends because he was "kinda cool" and that they talked while they were running in PE. He reported going to his other friends' houses and playing video games with them.

When asked to describe himself with three words, Trent said that he is independent, quiet, and weird. He endorsed that his greatest strength as a person is playing the drums. He stated that the most important thing to happen in his life was getting his black belt in karate. He noted that he goes to karate classes twice weekly, training in the adult classes, and instructing in the child classes. Trent shared that he enjoys listening to music, playing the drums, and watching and making YouTube videos. He stated that he would also like to start a band. When asked about his plans after high school, Trent stated that he was unsure because he was afraid he could not handle all of the reading in college. He noted that he would like to be some sort of scientist, though.

Conclusion and Diagnosis

Trent is a 14-year-old eighth grade student who was referred for evaluation due to reading difficulties. Trent's performance in oral expression, listening comprehension, writing, and mathematics was within the average range indicating that he is able to complete academic tasks at expected levels for his age. His basic reading ability, however, represented a significant weakness with scores primarily within the low range. His reading comprehension ability was somewhat higher but still within the low average range. Behavioral ratings indicated that Trent is not experiencing significant social or emotional problems. Some mild problems were noted in areas related to his academics, e.g., Learning Problems, Study Skills, as well as some problems with social skills. Given Trent's consistently low reading achievement scores, corresponding deficits in some aspects of school functioning, and average performance in other areas, Trent appears to have a reading disability.

CONFIDENTIAL
PSYCHOEDUCATIONAL REPORT
NAME: Scott Fischer PARENT/GUARDIAN: Crystal and William Fischer
BIRTH DATE: 09/07/1998 AGE: 11 years
SEX: Male SCHOOL: Walker Elementary School
GRADE: 5
DATES OF EVALUATION: 09/11/2009, 09/12/2009
EVALUATION INSTRUMENTS:
Reynolds Intellectual Assessment Scales (RIAS)
Wechsler Individual Achievement Test, Second Edition (WIAT-II)
KeyMath—3 Diagnostic Assessment (KeyMath-3 DA)
BASC-2
PRS
TRS
SRP
Piers–Harris Children's Self-Concept Scale (Piers– Harris)
Structured Clinical Interview
Review of Records

Referral Reason

Scott was referred by his parents for an initial evaluation to assist in determining eligibility for special education services due to difficulties in mathematics that they feel have led to emotionality and apparent lack of motivation.

Background Information

Scott was initially referred for pre-referral intervention on April 29, 2006 while in second grade at Walker Elementary School in order to discuss Scott's attention issues in relation to third grade. The committee described Scott as being bright with much potential, but struggling due to inattention that caused him to miss instruction. The committee met again on November 15, 2005 due to Scott's difficulty completing activities and a low computation score on the Iowa Tests of Basic Skills (ITBSs). It was noted that Scott went to "Characters in Action" and the team suggested that he also go to "friendship group." Additionally, the team recommended the use of a timer for work completion. Another pre-referral intervention meeting was held on January 30, 2007 due to continuing statements about being "dumb" and "retarded." It was noted that Scott was able to focus on some tasks without difficulty, but appeared unwilling to attend to others, which was described as a lack of motivation. The team recommended a student conference, continuing friendship group and character education with a counselor, and moving on to additional interventions with a focus on mathematics.

On August 31, 2008, Scott was dismissed from pre-referral interventions due to passing standardized statewide reading and mathematics tests, adequate end-of-year grades, and adequate benchmark scores. Scott's parents were concerned when his mathematics grades continued to be lower than those he received in other classes. The Special Education Referral Form indicated that Scott's strengths include his avid reading and high level of intelligence, while his weaknesses include his low motivation and not turning in homework in all subjects. He was reported to be performing at grade level for reading, mathematics, and English and to have received gifted services since February 2008. He was noted to have three absences and 12 tardies for the year.

Scott's third quarter grades for the 2008–2009 school year were as follows: Art 100, Language Arts 89, Math 73, Music 100, PE 100, Reading 90, Science 85, and Social Studies 92. Scott was administered the Cognitive Abilities Test (CogAT), a group administered intelligence test, during his fourth grade year and earned a verbal standard score of 122, quantitative standard score of 100, nonverbal standard score of 104, and composite standard score of 109. Scott also participated in statewide standardized a group administered achievement test, and earned the following standard scores in Spring 2008 during his fourth grade year: Reading 854, English/LA 870, Mathematics 330, Science 871, and Social Studies 350. He met expectations for all subject areas. During his fifth grade year, Scott earned scores corresponding to the following percentile ranks on the ITBS, another group administered norm-referenced achievement test: reading 82 %, language 39 %, mathematics 43 %, and composite 95 %.

Social History

Scott's mother, Ms. Crystal Fischer, completed a social history information form on August 14, 2009. Ms. Fischer noted that Scott lives at home with his mother, father, 8-year-old brother, and uncle. In a brief interview on September 12, 2009, Ms. Fischer reported that her husband had been working in South Africa for the past 6 weeks for the second time in the past year. She also stated that the rest of the family would be visiting South Africa in July and possibly relocating there temporarily at some time in the future.

According to Ms. Fischer, Scott was the product of a full-term uncomplicated pregnancy and was delivered weighing 8 pounds, 12 ounces after 17 hours of labor. Ms. Fischer reported that Scott met all developmental milestones within normal limits, saying his first words at 12 months, walking at 14 months, speaking clearly at 24 months, dressing himself at 36 months, and achieving toilet training at 38 months. Scott's early care included staying with his mother and grandmother from birth to 6 months of age, 4 days per week of daycare from 6 months to 2 years of age, staying with his mother from 2 to 3 years of age, and preschool from 3 to 5 years of age. Ms. Fischer described Scott as appearing to be in good health, although he tires easily and lacks energy. Frequent minor illnesses experienced by Scott were noted to include colds or allergies and stomachaches that appear to be stress related. Scott wears glasses for vision correction.

Ms. Fischer described Scott as playing well with other students, relating well with adults, being trustworthy, following directions, being a daydreamer, having difficulty adjusting to changes, and being easily frustrated. She noted that Scott is rarely disciplined, but discipline methods used on those occasions include rewards, talking, and deprivation of privileges. Scott was reported to respond to discipline with sulking and pouting as well as behavior change. Ms. Fischer described Scott as usually enjoying with his parents, but being harsh with his brother. She indicated that he plays well with and gets along with his friends. She reported that Scott enjoys cartooning and taking classes at the community arts center, as well as computer games and flash animation. Ms. Fischer disclosed that Scott may continue to be adversely affected by the deaths of his grandmother and great-grandmothers because he continues to talk about them. In relation to school, Ms. Fischer endorsed being concerned about Scott's insistence that he is stupid and everyone dislikes him, while at home she is concerned with his negative comments about himself. Ms. Fischer endorsed most enjoying Scott's creativity and willingness to begin and finish creative projects, as well as his sense of humor. She noted that she treasures Scott's uniqueness although she understands that it is this quality that often makes it difficult for him to fit in with peers at school.

General Description/Testing Observations

Scott is an 11-year-old male who is noted to be tall and thin for his chronological age. He was tested at Walker Elementary School over two sessions. Scott was somewhat resistant to accompanying the examiner initially, but once he entered the testing situation he willingly participated. Rapport was easily established and maintained and after a short time together Scott felt comfortable discussing personal information with the examiner. Scott's affect was appropriate to the testing situation. His mood was pleasant and cooperative. He attempted all tasks and put forth adequate effort. The quality of Scott's expressive language was considered to be within the above-average range. He claimed to be tired and yawned several times at the beginning of each session, but then became involved in the assessment activities and was alert and appeared oriented throughout the remainder of the evaluative sessions. He approached tasks in an organized and logical manner. His eye contact was appropriate and no disturbances in his thought processes were observed. Overall test results appear to be a valid estimate of Scott's current level of functioning.

Test Results and Interpretation

Intelligence

Scott was administered the RIAS in order to provide an estimate of his cognitive ability as requested by his parents. The RIAS is an individually administered test designed to provide subtest and composite scores that represent intellectual functioning in specific cognitive domains. The RIAS also yields a co-normed, supplemental measure of memory. The RIAS includes a two-subtest Verbal Intelligence Index (VIX) and a two-subtest Nonverbal Intelligence Index (NIX). The scaled sums of T-scores for the four subtests are combined to form the Composite Intelligence Index (CIX), which is a summary estimate of global intelligence.

The following scores reflect Scott's performance on individual subtests. Each subtest score is scaled to a mean of 50 and a standard deviation of 10. Subtest scores that fall between 45 and 54 are considered average. The various indexes are scaled to a mean of 100 and a standard deviation of 15. Composite scores that fall between 90 and 109 are considered average.

Index score	Standard score	Percentile
Verbal Intelligence Index (VIX)	121	92
Nonverbal Intelligence Index (NIX)	118	88
Composite Intelligence Index (CIX)	121	92

Verbal subtest	T-score
Guess What (GWH)	61
Verbal Reasoning (VRZ)	63
Nonverbal subtest	*T-score*
Odd-Item Out (OIO)	53
What's Missing (WHM)	66

Scott's score on the VIX suggested superior verbal reasoning ability and crystallized intellectual functioning. His performance on the NIX suggested above-average non-verbal reasoning ability and fluid intellectual functioning. The 13 point difference in Scott's performance on the NIX subtests is clinically significant at the 0.01 level, but is not considered meaningful as 26 % of the standardization sample displayed a discrepancy of this magnitude or greater. Scott's overall performance was within the superior range of intellectual functioning. His CIX score was a standard score of 121, which corresponds to the 92nd percentile, which means that he is functioning equal to or better than 92 % of children his same age. The chance that the range of scores from 115 to 126 includes Scott's true IQ is 95 out of 100. Scott's VIX and NIX are consistent with his CIX and indicated that his verbal and nonverbal abilities are similarly developed.

Academic Achievement

Scott was administered selected subtests of the WIAT-II to determine current levels of academic achievement. These tests are individually administered, norm-referenced tests that assess performance in the essential academic areas of reading and mathematics. Standard scores are based upon a mean of 100 and a standard deviation of 15. Scores that fall between 85 and 115 are considered to be within the average range.

Subtest/composite	Standard score	Percentile
Word Reading	115	84
Reading Comprehension	120	91
Pseudoword Decoding	113	81
Reading Composite	*119*	*90*
Numerical Operations	99	47
Mathematics Reasoning	91	27
Mathematics Composite	*93*	*32*
Spelling	105	63

Scott obtained a Reading Composite score of 119 (90th percentile), which is in the above-average range of functioning. This composite included three subtests—Word Reading, Reading Comprehension, and Pseudoword Decoding. On the Word Reading subtest, Scott obtained a standard score of 115, which is in the above-average range. On the Reading Comprehension subtest, Scott obtained a standard score of 120, which is also in the superior range, and finally, on the Pseudoword Decoding subtest, Scott obtained a standard score of 113, which is in the above-average range.

In the area of mathematics skills, Scott obtained a Math Composite score of 93 (32nd percentile), which is in the average range of functioning. This composite included two subtests—Numerical Operations and Math Reasoning. On the Numerical Operations subtest, Scott obtained a standard score of 99, which is in the average range. On the Math Reasoning subtest, obtained a standard score of 91, which is also in the average range.

In the area of written language, Scott earned a Spelling standard score of 105, which is in the average range.

Scott was also administered the KeyMath-3 DA, a comprehensive, norm-referenced measure of essential mathematical concepts and skills organized into three content areas: Basic Concept (conceptual knowledge), Operations (conceptual skills), and Applications (problem solving). It is designed to provide diagnostic information that can be sued to develop effective and individually tailored intervention programs. KeyMath-3 DA yields scale scores with a mean of 10 and standard deviation of 3 for subtests and standard score with a mean of 100 and standard deviation of 15 for content areas. Subtest scores from 8 to 12 and content area scores from 86 to 114 are considered average.

Subtest/area	Scale/standard score
Numeration	9
Algebra	13
Geometry	11
Measurement	8
Data Analysis and Probability	13
Basic Concepts	*102*
Mental Computation and Estimation	7
Addition and Subtraction	8
Multiplication and Division	11
Operations	*92*
Foundations of Problem Solving	13
Applied Problem Solving	7
Applications	*96*
Total Test	*97*

The Basic Concepts content area measures an individual's conceptual understanding with five subtests, including Numeration, Algebra, Geometry, Measurement, and Data Analysis and Probability. Scott earned a Basic Concepts standard score of 102 (55th percentile), which is within the average range. His performance on the Numeration subtest, which measures an individual's understanding of whole and rational numbers, was within the average range. The Algebra subtest measures understanding of pre-algebraic and algebraic concept. Scott earned an Algebra score within the above-average range. The Geometry subtest provided a measure of Scott's ability to analyze, describe, compare, and classify two- and three-dimensional shapes. He obtained a score within the average range. The Measurement subtest measures an individual's ability to compare objects on a variety of attributes and to use nonstandard and standard units to measure those attributes. Scott's performance on this subtest was within the average range. It should be noted that Scott was unable to tell time using analog clocks on this test and the WIAT-II. On the Data Analysis and Probability subtest, which measures the ability to collect, display, and interpret data as well as understanding of the concepts associated with chance and probability, Scott's score was within the above-average range.

The Operations content area includes three subtests that measure an individual's written and mental computation skills with respect to addition, subtraction, multiplication, and division of whole and rational numbers and variables. Scott earned an Operation standard score of 92 (30th percentile), which is within the average range. The Mental Computation and Estimation subtest measures the ability to mentally compute answers to given mathematics problems using the above-mentioned operations. Scott's score on this subtest was within the below-average range. The Addition and Subtraction subtest focused on written algorithmic procedures and concepts and measures an individual's ability to add and subtract whole and rational numbers, including two- and three-digit numbers, fractions, mixed numbers, decimal values, and integers. On this subtest, Scott obtained a score within the average range. The Multiplication and Division subtest is similar to Addition and Subtraction, but requires multiplication and division. Scott also earned an average score on this test.

The Applications content area includes two subtests that assess an individual's ability to apply conceptual knowledge and operational skills to solve mathematics problems. Scott earned an Applications standard score of 96 (39th percentile), which is within the average range. The Foundations of Problem-Solving subtest assesses "readiness" for applied problem solving and measures an individual's ability to identify the necessary elements, operations, and strategies required to solve mathematics problems. Scott's score on this subtest was within the above-average range. The Applied Problem-Solving subtest measures an individual's ability to interpret problems set in a context and to apply computational skills and conceptual knowledge to produce a solution. On this subtest, Scott earned a score within the below-average range. The difference in his performance on these subtests suggests that Scott understands strategies for problem solving, but has difficulty applying strategies and incorporating mathematical operations.

Scott's Total Test score of 97 (42nd percentile) was within the average range and was consistent with his performance across the content areas. Thus, Scott's overall mathematical ability is evenly developed and within the average range.

Social/Emotional/Behavioral Rating Scales

Scott's father and teachers also completed the BASC-2, a measure that evaluates levels of behavioral, emotional, and social competencies relative to other children, their age and gender. On the Clinical scales and Composite scores of the BASC-2, T-scores of 70 and above[**] are considered clinically significant, scores between 60 and 69[*] are in the at-risk range, and scores of 41 through 59 are in the average range. Adaptive scale scores of 30 or less[**] are considered clinically significant, scores of 31 through 40[*] are at-risk, and scores between 41 and 59 are average.

Skill area	T-score (father)	T-score (teacher)
Hyperactivity	45	50
Aggression	57	48
Conduct Problems	54	54
Externalizing Problems	*52*	*51*
Anxiety	57	48
Depression	72**	93**
Somatization	56	43
Internalizing Problems	*65**	*64**
Attention Problems	–	62*
Learning Problems	–	54
School Problems	–	*59*
Atypicality	52	95**
Withdrawal	60*	87**
Attention Problems	51	–
Behavioral Symptoms Index	*58*	*78***
Adaptability	44	31*
Social Skills	42	31*
Leadership	46	39*
Activities of Daily Living	49	–
Study Skills	–	32*
Functional Communication	55	44
Adaptive Skills	*47*	*33**

*At risk

** Clinically significant/high level of maladjustment

All validity indexes were within the acceptable range. Scott's teacher's ratings resulted in a clinically significant Behavioral Symptoms Index, which is an indicator of overall behavioral and emotional difficulties. Both raters endorsed that Scott displays significant depressive symptoms, particularly pessimism, sadness, loneliness, and negative statements. Scott's teacher also indicated that he displays significant Atypicality, such as talking to himself and saying things that may not make sense, and Withdrawal. Scott's teachers also indicated some difficulties maintaining attention and distractibility from classroom tasks. He also indicated at-risk and significant Adaptive Skills difficulties, such as not adjusting well to changes or setbacks (Adaptability), spontaneously and courteously interacting with others (Social Skills), displaying leadership qualities (Leadership), effectively preparing for class activities (Study Skills), and clearly communicating ideas on a daily basis (Functional Communication). Overall, these ratings suggest that Scott displays symptoms of depression across environments which is the only difficulty noted at home. Scott was reported to display a greater variety of emotional difficulties, including strange behaviors, withdrawal, and some adaptive deficits, at school.

Scott also completed the BASC-2-SRP to provide his perception of his social and emotional functioning. As with the parent and teacher forms, the Clinical scales and Composite T-scores of 70 and above** are considered clinically significant, scores between 60 and 69* are in the at-risk range, and scores of 41 through 59 are in the average range. Adaptive scale scores of 30 or less** are considered clinically significant, scores of 31 through 40* are at-risk, and scores between 41 and 59 are average. Specific T-scores obtained on the BASC-2-SRP are listed below:

Skill area	T-score
Attitude to School	79**
Attitude to Teachers	74**
School Problems	*80***
Atypicality	47
Locus of Control	62*
Social Stress	75**
Anxiety	57
Depression	70**
Sense of Inadequacy	68*
Internalizing Problems	*66***
Attention Problems	82**
Hyperactivity	74**
Inattention/Hyperactivity	*80***
Emotional Symptoms Index	*75***
Relations with Parents	46
Interpersonal Relations	20**
Self-Esteem	10**
Self-Reliance	43
Personal Adjustment	*23***

*At risk
** Clinically significant/high level of maladjustment

Scott's Response Pattern, V, L, and Consistency Indexes were within the acceptable range. His F Index was in the caution range due to endorsing several negative statements that he affirmed on several other instances during the evaluation. Scott's ratings resulted in significant School Problems, Inattention Hyperactivity, and Personal Adjustment composites and a significant Emotional Symptoms Index (ESI). The ESI is the most global indicator of serious emotional disturbance, particularly internalized disorders and is composed of four scales from the Internalizing Problems Composite (Social Stress, Anxiety, Depression, Sense of Inadequacy) and two scales from the Personal Adjustment composite (Self-Esteem, Self-Reliance). Elevated ESI scores such as Scott's typically signal the presence of serious emotional disturbance that is broad-based in its impact on the thoughts and feelings of the individual. Scott expressed negative perception of school (Attitude to School) and teachers (Attitude to Teachers) and indicated that he has difficulty paying attention (Attention Problems) as well as controlling his activity and volume levels (Hyperactivity). While the Internalizing Problems composite was within the at-risk range, Scott also endorsed significant sadness and hopelessness (Depression) and social isolation (Social Stress). The Personal Adjustment composite indicated that Scott is very satisfied with his relationship with his parents (Relations with Parents) and ability to work out his problems (Self-Reliance), but has significantly negative perceptions of how others' view him (Interpersonal Relations) and of himself (Self-Esteem).

The Piers–Harris was also administered. The Piers–Harris is a self-report questionnaire designed to assess how children and adolescents feel about themselves. The Piers–Harris measures an individual child's self-evaluative attitudes and behaviors which have a bearing on self-concept. The Piers–Harris yields six "cluster scales" and an overall assessment of self-concept. The cluster scales include: Behavioral Adjustment, Intellectual and School Status, Physical Appearance and Attributes, Freedom from Anxiety, Popularity, and Happiness and Satisfaction. Raw scores on the Piers–Harris are converted to T-scores with a mean of 50 and a standard deviation of 10. A T-score between 35 and 39* is considered to be below average, while a T-score below 35** is considered significantly low. High scores indicate favorable self-concept, whereas lower scores are associated with lower self-concept.

Scale	T-scores
Behavior	31**
Intellectual and School Status	30**
Physical Appearance and Attributes	26**
Anxiety	38*
Popularity	29**
Happiness and Satisfaction	20**
Total Score	31**

Scott indicated an overall low self-concept, which was reflected by significantly low scores on all scales, except for Anxiety, which was somewhat depressed. Low Total Scores on the Piers–Harris are characteristics of children with low self-worth, low self-confidence, and disturbances in mood and behavior that may require therapeutic intervention. The Behavior domain suggests that Scott feels he causes trouble for his family and teachers. The Intellectual and School status domain represents Scott's sense that he does not fit in at school and is not smart. Within the Physical Appearance and Attributes domain, Scott indicated poor self-esteem in relation to his body image and physical strength. The Popularity domain reflects Scott's unhappiness with his social functioning and feelings of being isolated and made fun of. The Happiness and Satisfaction domain reflects general unhappiness and dissatisfaction with himself.

Clinical Interview

A structured interview was also completed with Scott. When asked if he had three wishes, what they would be, he responded that he would: (1) be able to stick with things and never give up, (2) have a lot of money and (3) be the kind of guy people make friends with immediately. When asked to choose three people he would take on a deserted island, he thought for several minutes and chose his father, mother, and grandfather. Scott endorsed liking his friend, Marcus, because he is never afraid to do anything, knows a lot of the same "stuff" as Scott, and is very strong "like Superman." He disclosed that he and Marcus also have adventures together, like exploring the woods, and spend a lot of time together at home and school. Scott endorsed having a few friends and being happy with them. Scott reported not liking school due to the people there. When asked to describe why he did not like a particular person, he stated that a boy in his previous class always teased him, was mean, and had the classroom "thugs" as his "minions." He disclosed that this student and others do not like him because he is not good at sports and looks like the stereotype of nerds presented on television. When asked about other aspects of school, Scott reported that reading is his favorite subject and he particularly enjoyed the poetry section. He previously enjoyed reading nonfiction, but is currently reading the Percy Jackson series of books. He endorsed mathematics as his least favorite subject because he is not good at it and usually does not get it even when he works really hard. He did, however, share that he had put extraordinary effort into learning multiplication tables and now knew them very well.

Scott reported that his favorite activities are going outside, playing video games, and playing a game he and his friends made up that is similar to "World of Warcraft." He reported that he watches a lot of television, because there are no kids in his neighborhood "except for jerks." His enjoys watching Nickelodeon and Anime. Scott endorsed having many career aspirations that depend on his mood and said that he may be an inventor as he has already developed a few inventions. When asked what he would change about himself he said he would not look like a nerd. He reported that his mother would want him to stop lying and not be a picky eater. Scott was then asked what he would change about several other people. He reported that it is tough on his mom for his dad to be away because she is not used to being in control, so he wished she would not yell during those times. He stated that he would make his dad less stubborn, so he would come home immediately. He wanted his fifth grade homeroom teacher to be more attentive because he did not do anything about it when kids called him names or harassed him. He reported that he wanted his family members to be younger so they would live longer and they could spend more time together. Scott also stated that he does not get along well with his 8-year-old brother because he purposely annoys him. He noted that he would also give his school a bigger budget.

When asked what makes him happy, Scott was unable to answer. When asked to think of a time he had been happy and describe it, he said that when he was younger he was always happy because he was "clueless." When asked about what makes him sad or depressed, Scott replied "lots of things" and listed missing his dad, kids being mean and making him feel bad, and feeling frustrated because he cannot do something. He reported that he has lost a lot of people in his family because they tend to live to very old ages, but that the last time he was very little so he was not affected by it. Scott described his current mood as bored and said that he is usually bored, but endorsed feeling happy more than he feels sad. He stated that the only way he could feel happy at school is by being the only person there. Scott endorsed being less interested in previously enjoyable activities, feeling depressed daily due to school (particularly a few months ago), losing weight due to picky eating habits, having difficulty falling asleep at night and waking in the morning, feeling restless, and feeling tired. Scott denied thoughts of suicide or wanting to hurt himself or others. Scott endorsed having a very short temper and, therefore, being made angry by anything that is annoying. He endorsed trying to ignore annoying things, but sometimes hitting the person and telling them to stop after a while.

Summary

Scott is an 11-year-old fifth grade student whose parents referred him for a comprehensive evaluation to assist in determining eligibility for special education services. Current test results suggest that Scott is functioning intellectually in the superior range. He displayed superior abilities associated with language development and acquired knowledge and above-average abilities associated with fluid and nonverbal reasoning. Academically, Scott's performance in reading was in the above-average range, while his mathematics and spelling abilities were in the average range. While Scott's mathematics abilities were lower than may be expected given his level of intelligence, his mathematics scores were within the average range, and therefore not representative of a disability.

Scott, his father, and his teacher completed behavioral rating scales. Mr. Fischer's ratings indicated significant difficulties with depression. Scott's teachers indicated more severe depressive symptoms at school along with some inattention, withdrawal, atypical behaviors, and adaptive skills deficits. Results of Scott's self-reports indicated that he experiences depressive symptoms, low self-esteem, low overall self-concept, and significant interpersonal difficulties. It should be noted that Scott did indicate having a few close friends, which is an important protective factor in light of his social–emotional difficulties. Many of Scott's emotional problems appear to be related to poor peer relationships due to his intellect and unusual interests for a male his age. It is possible that some of Scott's difficulties completing class work and mastering some concepts are related to these difficulties. It is recommended that the pre-referral intervention team, eligibility team, and Scott's parents consider implementing interventions related to his depressed mood and interpersonal troubles.

Summary of Key Points

- Several researchers in the field have argued that the most accurate way to identify individuals as having LDs is based on observable and objective achievement score data.
- A low achievement method typically requires an achievement score below a certain cut-point and intelligence scores above the mental retardation range.
- Critics of a low achievement model of LD identification argue that cut-points are arbitrary, contain measurement error, and are unreliable due to the use of a single score. Additionally, a low achievement model does not capture the "unexpectedness" of LDs.
- The strengths of a low achievement approach include the following: individuals identified with a low achievement approach do not differ significantly from those identified with a discrepancy model, it does not discriminate against individuals with IQs below the mean, low achievers are distinguishable from typical

achievers, and a low achievement model is more reliable than aptitude-achievement discrepancy and intra-individual difference models.
- Further research is necessary to identify an appropriate cut-point and it is possible that inclusion of functional impairment criteria will allow a meaningful cut-point, or range, to be established.

Questions and Answers with the Expert: Linda Siegel

Meet the Expert: Linda Siegel, PhD, is a Professor of Educational and Counseling Psychology and the Dorothy Lam Chair in Special Education at the University of British Columbia. She has researched and published articles in the areas of the cognitive aspects of learning disabilities (LDs), early identification of individuals at risk for LDs, arithmetic, reading, and English language learning. Dr. Siegel was awarded the 2010 Canadian Psychological Association Gold Medal Award for Distinguished Lifetime Contributions for Canadian Psychology.

Question 1: What types of instruments do you recommend using to determine whether a child's achievement is indicative of an LD?

Answer 1:

- A word recognition test (isolated words).
- A pseudoword reading test (isolated pseudowords).
- A spelling dictation test.
- A reading comprehension test—with caution on the interpretation.
- A mathematics calculation test.
- A mathematics problem-solving test.
- A writing fluency test.
- A writing composition test (e.g., Writing Samples from the Woodcock Johnson).
- An interview to determine strengths.

Question 2: What level of low achievement do you consider necessary for an individual to be considered to have an LD?

Answer 2: One standard deviation or more below the mean on an achievement test.

Question 3: How does cognitive ability factor into a low achievement definition of LDs? For example, can an individual be within the mental retardation range?

Answer 3: Individuals in the mental retardation range are "not" learning disabled although they may have the same problems and benefit from remediation. See below for more information

Question 4: How is general low achievement, or being a "slow learner," differentiated from low achievement indicative of a disability?

Answer 4: By a score on the IQ test but see below.

Question 5: What do you consider best practice for LD identification?

Answer 5: Giving the achievement tests indicated above is essential. A low score on any of them is indicative of a problem. Only in cases where mental retardation is suspected should an IQ test be given and, even then, interpreted with caution.

Chapter 6
Promising Practices

This chapter first reviews a proposed academic impairment definition of learning disability (LD) that retains the exclusion of learning difficulties due to lack of educational opportunity or another disability. This type of approach has been advocated by Brueggemann et al. (2008), Dombrowski et al. (2004), Siegel (1999), and Stanovich (1999). Several of these authors have suggested different arbitrary cut points, which, as mentioned in the previous chapter, are the main argument against this method. Despite this criticism, an academic impairment approach to diagnosis has been demonstrated to work and the reviewed research attempts to determine an optimal cut point for clinical use. After reviewing this research, an integrated model of learning identification that may be considered a promising practice based on the best evidence currently available is introduced.

Functional Impairment

The proposed low achievement model takes into consideration the need to consider several areas before determining "caseness," or whether an individual has a particular disorder (Bird 1999). These considerations include criteria for classification, such as *Diagnostic and Statistical Manual of Mental Disorders Fifth Edition* (DSM-5; APA 2013) or Individuals with Disabilities Education Act (IDEA) requirements, distress associated with the condition, and the presence of impairment assessed independently of the core symptoms. The last requirement, functional impairment, has been defined as specific deficits in multiple domains of functioning developing subsequent to a disorder and includes the concept of adaptive functioning or adjustment to life's demands across multiple domains (Winters et al. 2005). Impairment may be conceptualized as the negative impact that results from the core symptoms of a disorder (Fabiano and Pelham 2009).

Functional impairment is a more global construct than severity and a characteristic of the individual (Bird 1999). Traditionally, LD diagnosis has not incorporated functional impairment, yet the field of psychiatry has placed increasing importance on its presence in determining psychopathology and on cut points for the number of

A. E. B. Taylor, *Diagnostic Assessment of Learning Disabilities in Childhood*, Contemporary Issues in Psychological Assessment, DOI 10.1007/978-1-4939-0335-1_6,

© Springer Science+Business Media New York 2014

symptoms to make a diagnosis. The growing interest in functional impairment has been a result of the emphasis given in the DSM, health-care providers' and parents' focus on improvement in functioning as a treatment outcome, and outcome research demonstrating that the resolution of symptoms does not always correlate with psychosocial improvement (Winters et al. 2005). The DSM's inclusion of distress or impairment and the Global Assessment of Functioning (GAF) is probably the most salient evidence of this trend distinguishing between symptom severity and level of functioning. The assessment of impairment is a better fit with clinicians' inclination to evaluate and make treatment decisions in a dimensional, rather than categorical, manner (Bird 1999). While the DSM-5 no longer includes the GAF due to subjectivity in determining the GAF score, the importance of determining a global measure of functioning is still highlighted through inclusion of the World Health Organization (WHO) Disability Assessment Schedule 2.0 (WHODAS 2.0).

The Children's Global Assessment Scale (CGAS; Shaffer et al. 1983) provides an example of how functional impairment can be determined. It is a "single unidimensional global measure" of severity of a disorder as well as social functioning (Shaffer et al. 1983). The use of the CGAS as a measure of functional impairment has been shown to improve the ability to determine whether a child has responded to treatment over traditional behavioral rating scales (Schaffer et al. 1983), illustrating the difference between core symptoms exhibited and the effect on daily functioning. It is reasonable to assume that a global indicator of functioning will result in a more accurate identification at initial evaluation as well as at reevaluation. Another example of functional impairment requirements for diagnosis is the DSM-IV and American Association on Mental Retardation (AAMR) criteria for mental retardation as discussed in the previous chapter.

The incorporation of functional impairment in diagnostic decisions may identify students who are most in need of services, thus conserving limited resources by not providing unnecessary services to students whose functioning is unimpaired. For example, there has been a growth in "relative" compared to "absolute" poor achievers receiving services, allowing high-functioning students with achievement discrepancies to gain more resources than lower functioning students (Gordon et al. 1999). Bird (1999) has found that including impairment in decision-making results in two to three times fewer cases being identified compared to diagnostic criteria alone. Additionally, Stanovich (1999) has pointed out the irrationality of individuals with average achievement and high IQ scores being identified as having an LD, so that LD is the only disorder that considers "average" persons to have a disability. By including functional impairment with low achievement test performance in the diagnostic criteria for LD, we would be ensuring that the average person standard of the Americans with Disabilities is met.

Defining Functional Impairment for Learning Disabilities

According to a review of studies investigating the social–emotional functioning of students with LD (Rourke and Fuerst 1991), there do appear to be distinct types of social–emotional and behavior disturbances found more frequently in students with

LD than among their average peers. Despite these disturbances, children with LD do achieve "adequate" psychosocial adaptation (Rourke and Fuerst 1991, p. 85). Reynolds and Kamphaus (2004) found LD cases to have T-scores that are at about a half standard deviation or higher on clinical scales from the normative mean in the deviant direction. McKinney (1989) found seven subtypes of children with LD using cluster analysis and concluded that LD children with attention and conduct problems had poorer academic outcomes than those in other groups. Based on this research, we would expect that students with LD would demonstrate more mild adaptive and behavioral difficulties than students classified as having a behavioral disorder or other disorders, yet slightly elevated levels of difficulties compared to normative samples that may be used as evidence of behavioral or emotional functional impairment that could be associated with possessing an LD.

While the above conceptualization of LD may prove useful, it is to be interpreted as presuming that all students with LD demonstrate social and emotional disturbances. It is the case though that an individual must have some functional impairment in order to be considered to have a disorder. Furthermore, functional impairment is required for diagnosis across disorders and the definition of functional impairment should not be greatly changed to accommodate certain disorders. In other words, if functional impairment consists of social-emotional impairment for LD diagnosis, it should consist of social-emotional impairment for attention deficit hyperactivity disorder (ADHD,) depression, anxiety, and other DSM disorders. This conception of functional impairment is unacceptable, though, since social-emotional difficulties are explicit symptom requirements for depression and other disorders, preventing functional impairment so defined from being measured independently of symptomatology (Brueggemann et al. 2008).

Fletcher et al. (2007) acknowledged that in order for a learning difficulty to be considered disabling, the disorder must be present based on criteria and must interfere with adaptive function. They posited that lack of response to instruction should be considered evidence of functional impairment. The most recent diagnostic criteria presented in DSM-5 (APA 2013) also indicate that the learning difficulties must significantly interfere with academic achievement, occupational performance, or activities of daily living that require the impaired academic skills.

In an attempt to determine what is meant by DSM-IV's impairment requirement, Lewandowski et al. (2006) referenced various instruments used to measure impairment. The review of seven measures suggested that functional impairment is actually roughly equivalent to adaptive functioning, including areas such as academic and social functioning. Fabiano et al. (2006) conducted several studies using the Impairment Rating Scale (IRS), which was determined to be reliable, correlate with other measures, and identify impairment beyond ADHD symptoms. The IRS includes the following six to seven domains depending upon the rater: relationships with peers, relationships with teachers/parents, relationships with siblings, academic progress, self-esteem, influence on classroom/family functioning, and overall impairment. Based on the accepted definition of functional impairment as adaptive functioning in the field of ADHD where most impairment research has been conducted, it follows that impairment for other disorders, including LD, can reasonably be considered synonymous with adaptive skills. A study determined that students with LD on average had lower adaptive behavior scores than average children but higher scores than children with mental retardation (Leigh 1987), which supports the notion that typical definitions of impairment can be applied to individuals with LD. Additional research is necessary to more precisely define functional impairment for LD to ensure that it does not restrict the diagnosis to children with comorbid conditions (Doll and Horn 2008).

A functional impairment approach to classification of children with LD will prevent the LD category from becoming a meaningless repository for all struggling students. To do so, it must effectively eliminate the continuance of placement decisions and only identify those students who are truly struggling in an academic subject, which raises issues concerning students who previously would have been considered in need of services. The two most contentious groups to no longer be considered learning disabled are likely to be “slow learners” and “gifted” students.

Differentiation of LD from “Slow Learner”

In order to avoid confounding the LD construct, students who are “slow learners” must not be identified as having an LD. Kaznowski (2004) defined slow learners as students with intelligence quotients (IQs) ranging from 70 to 85 and achievement scores in the same range, which thus does not represent a severe discrepancy between predicted and actual achievement. The National Association of School Psychologists (Carroll 1998) describes slow learners as “students with below-average cognitive abilities who are not disabled, but who struggle to cope with the traditional academic demands of the regular classroom” (p. 205) and estimates that they comprise at least 15 % of school populations.

According to Forness (1985), slow learners are stuck in a special education “no man’s land” (p. 39) due to a lack of consistent terminology, competing definitions, and differing prevalence rates. In one study conducted to determine the effectiveness of special education services for slow learners by comparing achievement of those receiving services as learning disabled and those who were not, it was discovered that few differences existed between the groups (Kaznowski 2004). In fact, the group of slow learners receiving special education were actually passing their academic classes and failing standardized achievement tests. The group not receiving services performed better on the Iowa Test of Basic Skills (ITBS) suggesting that the slow learners labeled learning disabled were receiving a watered-down curriculum and lower expectations (Kaznowski 2004). These findings may indicate that neither special education nor regular education is adequately meeting the needs of slow learners and special education may actually be detrimental for these students’ achievement. This is consistent with Kavale’s (2005) position that the concept of LD should not be threatened by the designation of slow learners as learning disabled despite the desire to see all students succeed academically.

While it is important that schools meet the needs of slow learners, as mentioned above, serving such students through classification as having an LD threatens the construct of LD and likely would not meet their needs (Kaznowski 2004). It is the authors' opinion that schools should develop programs independent of LD services to provide assistance for these slow learners. The discussion of such programs, however, is beyond the scope of this book.

Differentiation of LD from Learning Differences

Lewis Terman (1931), often considered the father of gifted education and research, stated that "superiority of one kind does not *necessarily* imply superiority in everything" (p. 568). Yet, it is not uncommon for gifted students who achieve only in the average range in one academic area to be identified as learning disabled. Reluctance to part with the notion of gifted LD stems in part from the idea of an "unexpected" academic failure, yet research has shown that in reading an idea of some type of unexplained reading failure being different from reading failure with an explanation is simply "folk psychology" (Stanovich 1999). As Stanovich (1999) pointed out, reading difficulties in a gifted individual would be expected if the person has deficits in phonological awareness.

The conceptualization of gifted LD is also based on the idea that measures of cognitive functioning actually tell us how much potential an individual possesses, which is also a holdout from the aptitude-achievement discrepancy model. If we have conceded that the discrepancy model is not a valid indicator of LD for average and below-average achievers, then we must also surrender the rationale of discrepancy as applied to gifted children. Even if one accepts the discrepancy model, Kavale (2005) points out that discrepancy indicates the *possibility* of a disability, but only significantly below-average achievement should be considered an LD.

Instead of referring to gifted students who do not perform as well as expected but have average or above-average achievement in one or more academic areas as having an LD, this author proposes that they be considered to have a "learning difference." This new terminology acknowledges that a gifted student displays a difference between achievement in various areas but does not imply that they suffer from an actual disability, thus reserving LD for students who display significantly below-average achievement despite average or better intelligence test scores.

The Research Study: An Impairment Model

Taylor et al. (2008) set out to identify the level of low achievement most associated with functional impairment using the person-oriented method of latent class analysis in a similar manner to that used by Hudziak et al. (1999) to demonstrate the continuous nature of ADHD represented by several classes of severity. The goal of latent class analysis is to classify cases into groups where members within a group are similar to each other and different from members of other groups (Vermunt and

Magidson 2002). Latent class methods identify cases using a model-based method, meaning an underlying statistical model is assumed to underlie the population. This model is used to identify groups of individuals similar with respect to a categorical latent variable (Muthén and Muthén 2000, 2004). The objective is to identify classes that differ with respect to their mean values for selected variables.

The profiles created based on academic achievement and behavioral adjustment can then be used as a categorical classification tool to identify individuals with LD. More specifically, for the group with the most functional impairment associated with low achievement, their pattern of low achievement and impairment would be hypothesized to have been caused by their membership in the LD group. In other words, LD is the latent variable causing their pattern of impairment and achievement. Thus, the cut score used in a low achievement model of LD diagnosis would be based on the mean score of this group. In order to accurately represent the members of the possible LD class, however, it will be necessary to select an achievement score range that will not exclude the half of the class members who have scores above the average.

Data for the study were collected as part of the federally funded Project A.C.T. Early.[1] The participating school district was composed of a large population of "at-risk" students. The sample included 523 kindergarten through fifth-grade children from three schools participating in the Project A.C.T. Early study during the 1999–2000 school year. In order to approximate adherence to the definition of LD, students who would be ruled out based on the exclusionary clause were omitted from the analyses. According to this clause, LD may not be primarily due to visual, hearing, or motor disabilities, mental retardation, emotional disturbance, or environmental, cultural, or economic disadvantage (Individuals with Disabilities Education Act Amendments of 1997, Sect. 602(26), p. 13). Thus, students classified as having an intellectual disability, emotional–behavioral disorder, traumatic brain injury, autism, other health impairment, or a native language other than English were removed from the sample. The sex distribution of the remaining sample was approximately half male ($N=228$) and half female ($N=260$). The resulting ethnic makeup was 57 % African American, 35 % Caucasian, 4 % Hispanic, 2 % Asian American, and 3 % multiracial.

In the study, both academic indicators and adaptive functioning indicators were used as variables in the latent class model to determine the low achievement score associated with significant levels of functional impairment. Academic indicators used included ITBS reading and mathematics scores. Functional impairment indicators included the Behavior Assessment System for Children Teacher Report Scale (BASC-TRS; Reynolds and Kamphaus 1992) Adaptive Skills composite scales, i.e., Adaptability, Leadership, Social Skills, Study Skills. Once the classes were obtained and the class representing students with possible LD was identified, other variables such as gender, special education placement, and pre-referral intervention history were used to determine if the class is accurately identified.

---

[1] Author note: Data collection was funded by Field-Initiated Studies grants (R306F60158, R305T990330) from the Institute for At-Risk Children of the Office of Educational Research and Improvement, US Department of Education awarded to R. W. Kamphaus, J. A. Baker, and A. M. Horne.

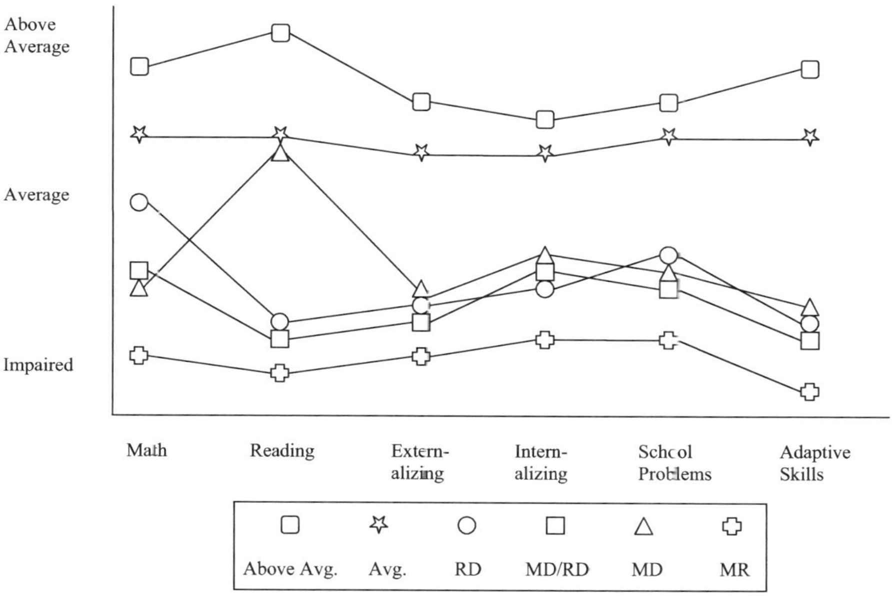

Fig. 6.1 Profile of hypothesized latent classes. *RD* Reading Disorder; *MD* Mathematics Disorder; *MR* Mental Retardation

Based on findings that students with achievement scores below about the 15th percentile do not respond to intervention (Vellutino et al. 2000, 2006; Berninger et al. 2002), it was expected that these LD groups would have scores below this percentile rank. Therefore, based on the prior review of the literature, it was hypothesized that at least six latent classes would be present. These classes, as shown in Fig. 6.1, were expected to include two representing normal and optimal academic development, another representing significantly poor academic development with percentile rank scores at or near the mental retardation range, one cluster with below-average reading, one cluster with below-average mathematics scores at or below the 15th percentile, and at least one cluster with achievement test scores at about the 15th percentile rank in reading and mathematics based on the findings of Vellutino and others (Speece and Cooper 1990; Rourke 1989; Barberesi et al. 2005). The latter three groups would be indicators of the presence of an LD consistent with the low achievement model.

MPlus Version 3.0 (Muthén and Muthén 2004) was used to perform the latent class analysis. Only continuous latent class indicators were used in the analyses. Automatic starting values were determined using maximum likelihood optimization. Prior to completing the Latent Class Analysis, the ITBS mathematics and reading scaled scores were converted to standardized *z* scores so that the achievement scores would be on a common metric across grades. This was necessary due to the ITBS's use of scaled scores, which are developmental norms that allow students' growth to be tracked within a given subtest or composite score as they progress through grades (Kamphaus 2001). Thus, scores cannot be compared between students in different grades, as age would be expected to be associated with score levels, with older students having higher scores.

Once the scaled scores had been transformed, the researchers fitted three-, four-, five-, six-, and seven-class models. Multiple fit indices were used to assess the models as well as comparing each of the models to the hypotheses to ensure correspondence with theory. Hence, because the goal of the study was to identify a group representing students with LD, the most parsimonious solution that contained the classes hypothesized based upon prior research and theory was chosen as the "best" solution. In addition, descriptive data including gender, race, age, special education status, and gifted program participation were considered for each class to provide more information about the class makeup. Finally, based on mean values for the six latent indicators (BASC scales: adaptability, leadership, social skills, study skills; ITBS composites: reading, mathematics) with reference to descriptive data, the class most likely to represent students who possibly have LD was identified.

In order to determine the cut score range that should be used to inform future research, the mean ITBS reading composite scores and the mean ITBS mathematics composite scores were identified. Scatterplots of scores for cases within the possible class indicating the presence of an LD were examined for a visual indication of scatter among scores to guide the determination of the best method to obtain the cut score. The options for obtaining such a score included simply using the mean, adding one standard deviation to the mean, adding two standard deviations to the mean, or using the maximum score in the class. All of these options involve possible drawbacks. For instance, the use of the mean would exclude half of the class from which it was obtained; adding one standard deviation may still exclude some class members; and, adding two standard deviations or using the maximum score would likely lead to overlap with other classes. Taking all of these considerations into account, adding one standard deviation to the mean was deemed to be the most appropriate option and resulted in the exclusion of 16% of students in the suspected LD class on average. After adding a standard deviation to the mean, the obtained scaled score was converted to a percentile rank to allow for meaningful comparison to other norm-referenced instruments.

Results

Each class solution was assessed for interpretability and fit with theory as recommended by Muthén (2003, 2004). In determining which solution was most interpretable, the goal of the study was considered to be of utmost importance. In order to comply with the exclusionary criteria in the LD definition, students who had been classified as having mental retardation were not included in the analyses. Thus, we would no longer expect to identify a group of well-below-average students, suggesting a five-class solution.

The three-class solution provided three nearly evenly distributed classes representing below-average, average, and above-average achievement with similar levels of associated adaptive skills and was rejected due to its oversimplification of students. Adding an additional class resulted in classes with below-average, slightly below-average, slightly above-average, and above-average achievement scores also with similarly increasing adaptive indicators, resulting in the rejection of the four-class

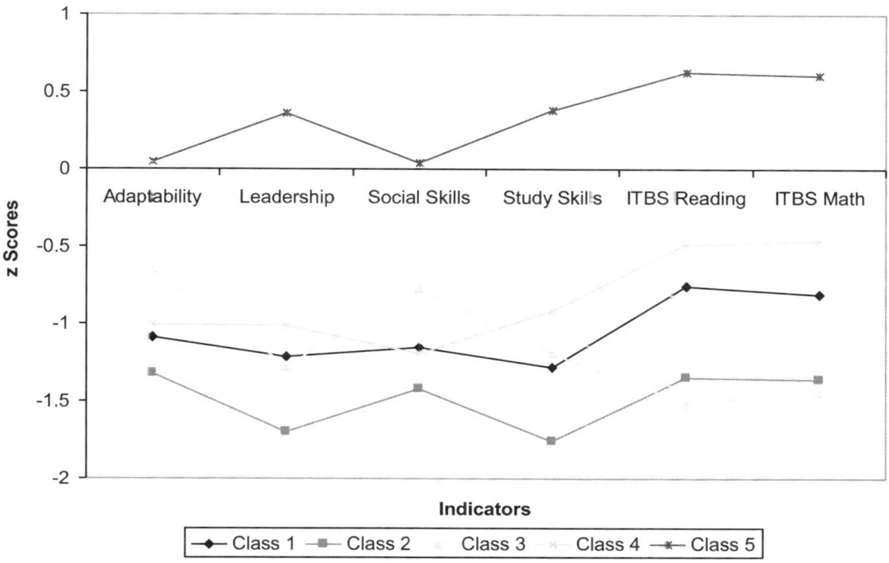

Fig. 6.2 Obtained latent class probabilities/means. *ITBS* Iowa Tests of Basic Skills

solution as well. The five-class solution resulted in a group with well-below-average achievement and adaptive scores, a somewhat impaired group, a class with average achievement and slightly above-average adaptive skills, a group with slightly above-average achievement and adaptive indicators, and a group with well-above-average scores. The six- and seven-class solutions provided similar low achieving groups but also included additional variations of groups with above-average achievement scores.

The six- and seven-class solutions were rejected because they did not provide additional information regarding a unique group of students that demonstrates a pattern of academic and functional performance that would be considered a marker of possible LD. Thus, the five-class solution was chosen as the best fit to data and theory across the five grades examined. Class sensitivity for the five-class solution, which is the average class membership probability after classification of all cases, was high (0.860–0.934), indicating that students were well classified.

The class-specific probabilities, which in the case of latent profile analysis are means obtained for the variables of interest, are illustrated in Fig. 6.2. Ninety-five (19%) cases were assigned to class 1, 148 (30%) to class 2, 85 (17%) to class 3, 62 (13%) to class 4, and 98 (20%) to class 5. Class 1 evidenced the lowest scores across the adaptive scales as well as the lowest reading and mathematics scores as can be seen in Table 6.1. This class was composed primarily of males and 38% of class members had been recommended for pre-referral intervention. Students in class 2 were below the mean but within one standard deviation for both impairment and academic indicators and contained nearly equal number of males (46%) and females (54%). Class 3 students demonstrated above-average adaptive skills and average achievement. Children in class 4 had nearly average adaptive skills and above-average achievement with 24% of group

Table 6.1 Latent class indicator means for model solution chosen as best fit

	Class 1	Class 2	Class 3	Class 4	Class 5
Adaptability	36.50	45.64	55.93	45.46	60.43
Leadership	35.93	44.48	55.13	52.85	66.04
Social skills	38.57	48.04	58.60	46.37	64.35
Study skills	35.71	44.25	55.27	52.22	63.11
Reading	−0.758	−0.589	−0.144	0.993	1.127
Mathematics	−0.805	−0.549	−0.068	0.969	1.066

members participating in the gifted program. Forty-nine percent of class 5 members were placed in the gifted program. This class had above-average adaptive and academic indicators. Table 6.2 provides information regarding gender, race, and age and Table 6.3 provides information regarding special education and gifted program status.

Careful review of the results described above led the researchers to conclude that class 2 was most likely to represent students with possible LD. The class 2 within class standard deviation (0.5313) was therefore added to the reading composite mean z score of −0.5887 to arrive at a reading cut score of −0.0570. In a similar manner, a mathematics cut score of 0.0762 (mean=−0.5486, standard deviation=0 .6248) was calculated. Single-sided cut scores were obtained in order to exclude as few cases as possible. These scores did result in the exclusion of 20 cases for the reading cut point and 25 cases for the mathematics cut point, which excluded the class members who had high achievement scores that would be considered outliers. Conversion to percentile ranks resulted in cut scores at the 48th percentile rank for reading and the 53rd percentile rank for mathematics performance. This study represents an incremental improvement toward Stanovich's (2005) goal of making LD a defensible category of disability. The derived cut scores, though, are far from Stanovich's recommendation of using the 10th–15th percentile rank and closer to Siegel's (1999) suggested cut score at the 25th percentile. The current study indicates that within an academic impairment framework, educators should focus their attention on children with academic achievement scores somewhere below the 25th–50th percentile rank as being at risk of having LD.

The results of the study imply that the use of subtyping and profiling with psychological and educational tests will not easily simplify the diagnostic approaches for identifying those with LD. It highlights the fact that diagnosis of LD and other disabilities is not a statistically simple procedure. Additionally, this study focuses on one approach to developing LD diagnostic criteria. It does, however, narrow down the group of students who should be considered at risk of having an LD by providing a broad cut score for use in an academic impairment model of identification. It is also likely that more gifted students may be diagnosed as having an LD than previously expected, since their achievement scores may fall closer to this upper limit. Thus, the academic impairment model of identification does not completely exclude gifted children from the LD category as some critics have suggested low achievement models would do.

In fact, one student who had been classified as gifted was included in the class representing the presence of a possible LD. This student was rated as demonstrating

Table 6.2 Gender, race, grade, and age statistics by mean/frequency and percentage

		Class 1		Class 2		Class 3		Class 4		Class 5	
		Mean/ FrEq.	%	Mean/ FrEq.	%	Mean/ FrEq.	%	Mean/ FrEq.	%	Mean/ FrEq.	%
Gender	Male	59	62	68	46	33	39	38	61	33	34
	Female	36	38	80	54	52	61	24	39	65	66
Race	White	12	13	26	18	25	29	41	66	65	66
	African American	79	83	103	70	52	61	18	29	24	25
	Hispanic	0	0	11	7	6	7	2	3	1	1
	Asian	0	0	4	3	1	1	0	0	5	5
	Multiracial	4	4	4	3	1	1	1	2	3	3
Grade	1	12	13	30	20	24	28	9	15	23	24
	2	20	21	32	22	18	21	15	24	24	25
	3	22	23	30	20	21	25	9	15	17	17
	4	15	16	24	16	8	9	11	18	16	16
	5	26	27	32	22	14	17	18	29	18	18
Age		9.57	–	9.1	–	8.85	–	9.37	–	8.92	–

FrEq frequency

Table 6.3 Special education and gifted program status

		Class 1		Class 2		Class 3		Class 4		Class 5	
		Mean/ FrEq.	%	Mean/ FrEq.	%	Mean/ FrEq.	%	Mean/ FrEq.	%	Mean/ FrEq.	%
Special education status	Pre-referral	36	38	21	14	6	7	6	10	2	2
	SPED placement	10	11	9	6	2	2	0	0	0	0
	SPED refer	10	11	7	5	1	1	2	3	1	1
	Eligibility	2	2	7	5	1	1	2	3	0	0
	LD	2	2	7	5	0	0	2	3	0	0
	SI	1	1	4	3	1	1	0	0	1	1
Gifted status	Placement	2	2	1	1	6	7	15	24	48	49
	Referral	3	3	0	0	1	1	5	8	5	5
	Eligibility	3	3	0	0	1	1	4	7	6	6

Cells refer to, in order, recommendation to pre-referral intervention, currently placed in special education, referred to special education, found eligible for special education, classified as having LD, classified as having speech impairment, placed in gifted program, referred to gifted program, and found eligible for gifted program, respectively
SPED special education, *SI* speech impairment, *FrEq* frequency

slightly above-average adaptability, average leadership, and slightly below-average social and study skills. Her reading and mathematics scores, however, were actually somewhat above average. Thus, this student demonstrated expected deficits in some areas of adaptive functioning, yet performed quite well on the school-wide standardized achievement test. It is not known whether she received accommodations during testing, capitalized on her ability to make the best of situations, or was served for an LD in an area other than reading or mathematics. Regardless of this child's particular pattern of achievement, this case and the relatively generous cut point suggested by this study indicate that gifted students will not be automatically excluded

Table 6.4 BASC (Behavior Assessment System for Children) data

	Behavior disorder (child)		Learning disability (child)		Mild mental retardation (child)		Autism (combined)		Current study (BASC)	
	BASC	BASC2	BASC	BASC2	BASC	BASC2	BASC	BASC2	Class 1	Class 2
Scale										
Atypicality	58.6	63.6	52.9	56.4	60.4	70.0	69.8	70.9	56.3	48.7
Withdrawal	60.4	61.9	55.6	55.3	61.7	62.8	74.9	71.4	58.7	49.0
Adaptability	38.4	37.9	44.1	44.9	40.7	39.5	43.7	35.9	36.2	45.9
Social skills	44.6	41.7	48.5	44.4	43.0	39.3	36.9	37.9	38.2	48.1
Leadership	42.1	41.8	46.6	42.5	38.7	37.5	35.1	39.3	35.6	44.5
Study skills	40.7	39.6	43.9	40.5	36.9	35.3	42.2	42.2	35.6	44.2
Composite										
Externalizing	66.9	64.4	54.9	54.2	52.8	60.7	52.8	57.9	62.4	53.1
Internalizing	61.1	62.3	53.9	53.8	56.7	58.3	50.7	59.9	55.1	51.0

from the LD diagnosis, but that the overidentification of gifted individuals with relative rather than absolute academic difficulties may be remedied.

The relatively high cut score for the class hypothesized to be organized around the latent construct of LD may indicate the need to consider the smaller and lower achieving class 1 as possibly being the most likely representative of an LD class. Upon further analysis, this does not seem to be the case. This option was explored by comparing the adaptive score patterns to those of the LD clinical sample in the BASC (Reynolds and Kamphaus 1992) and BASC-2 (Reynolds and Kamphaus 2004) manuals. This investigation revealed that class 1's adaptive functioning was most similar to the mild mental retardation (MMR) and autism clinical groups in the BASC studies, while class 2's adaptive functioning was similar to that of the LD group (see Table 6.4). The BASC studies also revealed that the distinguishing factors between the LD and MMR group appeared to be scores on the Atypicality and Withdrawal scales. One-way analyses of variance (ANOVAs) were performed and confirmed that class 1 was rated as displaying significantly more atypical ($F(4, 483)=48.809$, $p\leq 0.01$) and withdrawal ($F(4, 483)=38.644$, $p<0.01$) behaviors than class 2, indicating that class 1 is more likely composed of individuals with intellectual and adaptive functioning near the MMR range.

The lower adaptive functioning and higher rates of SST referral in class 1 also suggest that some members of the class may demonstrate a below-average pattern of performance across indicators due to an emotional or behavioral disorder. In order to test this possibility, one-way ANOVAs were conducted and confirmed that class 1 does in fact display more internalizing ($F(4, 483)=20.213$, $p<0.01$) and externalizing ($F(4, 483)=64.821$, $p<0.01$) behaviors in the school setting than class 2 members.

Overall, results of BASC studies and analyses utilizing BASC scales and composites indicate that class 1 is most likely composed of students with intellectual disabilities and emotional or behavioral disturbances that cause the pattern of high functional impairment and low academic achievement. This information also lends support to the credibility of class 2 as representing a group of students with possible LD. Additional support is provided by the assignment of 64 % of the students in the sample with LD to class 2, which is more than in any other class. While this difference is not statistically significant ($F(4, 483) = 2.169$, $p > 0.05$), the lack of significance is likely due to only 11 students in the sample being identified as having an LD.

Examination of the proportion of males versus females in class 2 is another method of ensuring the defensibility of labeling this class as representing potential LD. Several researchers have assumed that boys are about twice as likely to be identified as having a mathematics or reading LD than are girls (American Psychiatric Association 2004; Wagner et al. 2002). Epidemiological and neurological studies, however, have found that the incidence of LD in the population does not differ according to the sex of the child (Shaywitz et al. 1990; Alexander et al. 1993). Shaywitz et al. (1990) discovered that schools identified boys as having LD four times more often than girls, but when the school's role was deleted from the identification equation boys and girls were identified at equivalent rates. This epidemiological sex proportion is similar to that of our possibly LD class.

The high proportion of students identified as having a possible LD in the current study may also be a result of the type of test used. Specifically, the ITBS, which was the only achievement measure available in the existing database used for this study, does not measure discrete skills so those skills most associated with the presence of an LD are not the only constructs being measured. For instance, the reading composite includes the vocabulary and comprehension subtests and the mathematics composite includes the concepts, problems and data interpretation, and computation subtests for students in grades 2–5. Most research concerning the best measures for identifying reading and mathematics disabilities have employed tests that measure discrete skills, such as single word decoding or mathematics calculation. A test that measures multiple skills is more likely to identify students who may be struggling academically for a number of reasons.

Additionally, this study was conducted using an "at-risk" sample. For instance, in the school district attended by the children in this study, 70 % of students received a free or reduced lunch rate and a large percentage lived in public housing (Baker et al. 2006). The sample used was mainly composed of minority students and 4 % of the sample used in the data analysis was served by special education after eliminating students served in all but the LD and speech impairment categories. There was also a high rate of children served through pre-referral intervention. Given the sample demographics, the high rate of LD eligibility identified in this study is not unexpected. It is also likely that some children who are included in the possible LD class demonstrate concomitant functional impairment and low achievement due to other factors such as unidentified social–emotional disorders, ADHD, etc.

Review of Vellutino et al. (1996, 2000, 2006) work with at-risk readers reveals another possibility: The percentile ranks identified in the current study may identify students with LD as well as students who are at risk of developing a reading disability. Vellutino et al. (1996) found that the largest percentage of poor readers in their intervention program scored in the average or above-average range after being provided with remediation. In other words, these students appeared to have reading disabilities, but after intervention were able to read as well as average.

The scores for different skill level groups of readers from another intervention study (Vellutino et al. 2006) are actually quite similar to those found in the current study. From first through third grade, students labeled as difficult to remediate scored between the 8th and 38th percentile ranks on word identification, nonword decoding, and reading comprehension tests. Students considered less difficult to remediate received scores in the 40th–65th percentile rank range. Those students who responded to intervention and were labeled as no longer being at risk of reading difficulties scored in the 52nd–73rd percentile rank range. Thus, it would appear that the ITBS percentile ranks arrived at through latent class analysis may be identifying some students whose academic ability would improve with intensive intervention.

Yet another likely possibility is that the students in the sample would have benefited from intensive interventions, not simply because they had received inadequate instruction but because they are an at-risk population. This possibility was examined by converting the mean *z* score for the LD class to scaled scores for each grade and comparing the obtained scores to the normative sample for the ITBS to determine the associated percentile rank. As expected, adding one standard deviation to the scaled score means resulted in achievement percentile ranks similar to those found for students who persistently failed to respond to intervention in previous studies (Case et al. 2003; Vellutino et al. 2006). Based on these scores, it appears that Stanovich's (1999) suggested cut score at the 15th percentile may be appropriate for grades 1–3. The obtained scores also suggest that a more lenient cut score, such as the 25th percentile recommended by Siegel (1999), may be more appropriate for students in fourth through fifth grade since these students are beginning to use other strategies to compensate for their weaknesses (see Table 6.5).

It is important to note that the current study possessed several limitations. As mentioned previously, this sample consisted of an at-risk population and a less-than-ideal test was used as the measure of academic achievement. In addition to consisting of composites and subtests that assess multiple skills, the ITBS also only reports results as raw scores, scaled scores, and percentile ranks. Raw scores are meaningless and cannot be compared to other scores so scaled scores had to be used for the analyses. Scaled scores, though, are developmental scores that cannot be compared across grades. Due to this limitation, the achievement scores had to be converted to *z* scores and subsequently transformed to percentile ranks to make the results applicable to other achievement measures. Additionally, the interpretation of latent class analysis results relies heavily on individual judgment; thus, other researchers using different theories and hypotheses may have reached differing conclusions.

The study was also unable to identify all of the hypothesized classes of learning and adjustment. Specifically, we did not find three different types of LD as expected and instead only identified one class of students in each grade that was characterized by below-average achievement in reading and mathematics. One possible reason for

Table 6.5 Scaled score conversions by grade with associated ITBS (Iowa Test of Basic Skills) percentile rank

		Z score conversions for class 2		Corresponding ITBS percentile ranks	
		Scaled score mean	Mean plus 1 standard deviation	Scaled score mean	Mean plus 1 standard deviation
Grade 1	Reading	135.99	142.68	1	13
	Mathematics	137.00	144.35	2	16
Grade 2	Reading	144.15	155.72	1	10
	Mathematics	152.50	164.29	4	30
Grade 3	Reading	158.13	172.47	1	15
	Mathematics	168.67	180.10	7	29
Grade 4	Reading	178.52	191.54	6	26
	Mathematics	188.77	198.32	18	40
Grade 5	Reading	186.39	199.97	2	17
	Mathematics	190.95	210.80	4	39

the absence of a class of students with below-average achievement in solely mathematics or solely reading may be due to the demands of the ITBS. If the mathematics subtests require reading skill, then students with reading disabilities would perform poorly in the mathematics and reading tests. Similarly, studies have suggested that students' mathematics disabilities are often the result of difficulty with phonological representation, so these students would have low mathematics and reading achievement scores as well (Robinson et al. 2002). Since mathematics and reading disabilities influence other academic domains in addition to being comorbid, the majority of students with LD would likely manifest low achievement in more than just one academic subject. Those students who may have one type of LD that does not affect performance in other domains would represent a very small proportion of students with LD. This small proportion would likely not be sufficient for forming an independent class using latent class analysis with a small-to-moderate sample size and would have been assigned to a larger class with a similar pattern of probabilities.

Future research should employ a large community-sample-based dataset with multiple measures of functional impairment in different settings and individually administered, nationally normed measures of academic achievement across time. The academic tests should include at least two nationally normed tests of phonological processing, such as single word recognition and nonword decoding, to identify the core symptom of reading disability (Siegel 1999). In addition, because research has not yet yielded ideal measures for identifying mathematics disabilities, several types of arithmetic measures such as computation, fact retrieval, concepts and applications, and story problems tests should be included (Fuchs et al. 2005). Furthermore, in order to rule out competing explanations for low achievement, the sample should have research-based academic interventions like those found in RTI programs. Latent class analysis and similar statistical methodology could then be applied to better define cut points associated with the presence of an LD.

Best Practice: An Integrated Model of LD Identification

The use of a low achievement test score based on functional impairment for the diagnosis of LD does not preclude the use of RTI. While RTI does not provide a reliable means of diagnosis, it seems optimal to use some form of RTI as a means of guaranteeing quality pre-referral intervention. It would provide help for students without requiring the LD label, resulting in reduced need for educators to rely on a placement diagnosis rather than a construct diagnosis so students can receive services. In this situation, only those students who fail to respond to intervention would require evaluation for special education programs. This is in line with research showing that the use of pre-referral intervention services results in fewer children being tested for placement, and of the children who are tested using the pre-referral model, more are actually in need of services (Gutkin et al. 1988).

In addition to providing an efficient means of pre-referral intervention, RTI would also allow educators and clinicians to rule out ineffective instruction or lack of opportunity to learn as explanations for low achievement when performance of a group of students is in question. After a student is identified as having an LD, the curriculum-based measurement component of RTI may be used for teachers and special educators to monitor treatment progress (Dombrowski et al. 2004). Hence, while RTI is not useful as a defining feature of LD because it lacks norm-referenced scores that allow for professional communication, it is ideal for pre-referral intervention, hypothesis testing, and treatment monitoring.

Despite the advantages provided within an RTI framework, it is not appropriate as the sole means of diagnosis. Unresolved issues in RTI implementation include whether to use general education intervention (e.g., Fuchs et al. 2002) or intensive individual interventions (e.g., Vellutino et al. 1996) and how to define and measure responsiveness. The use of different interventions, definitions, and measures can lead to different prevalence rates and different children being identified (Fuchs et al. 2004). Further, it has been suggested that gains may not be maintained upon return to the regular classroom (Vaughn et al. 2003). In addition, RTI is unreliable across locations because it often relies on the collection of local norms and comparisons to those norms. Thus, once students have been identified as failing to respond to intervention, additional assessment, namely of academic achievement, should be conducted to verify that the child does in fact have an LD.

The proportion of the students in the study described previously with below-average achievement indicative of an LD combined with results of intervention research speaks to the need for implementation of response to intervention (RTI), as well as application of other exclusionary factors, to rule out other causes of learning difficulties, particularly ineffective instruction or lack of opportunity to learn. The use of RTI as a prevention strategy would eliminate the need for children to be labeled as having an LD to receive remediation. Those students who do not respond to intervention could receive an evaluation for special education so that more intensive remediation and accommodations could be made available. Despite the emphasis on RTI, special education regulations do not require RTI as *the* identification process, and actually require an evaluation to include many types and sources of information (Willis and Dumont 2006) so this type of approach is practical and allowable.

The use of low achievement scores will preclude comparison of children to local norm groups and to their own performance in other domains in addition to preventing students who do not have significantly below-average achievement from being mislabeled as having an LD. This method will also provide a reliable identification procedure that is uniform across locations and serves the purposes of classification. Instead of a simple cut point, a confidence band around the selected score would help to increase this utility.

The cut point would also not be based on some arbitrary number or only consider one indicator. The inclusion of functional impairment in the diagnostic procedure would identify students for whom actual distress is associated with their LD and consider more than just their achievement level, making it a more meaningful criterion. Using latent class analyses, Brueggemann and Kamphaus (2008) found that an academic achievement cutoff near the 15th percentile for both reading and mathematics achievement test scores was associated with below-average adaptive functioning in the first through third grades, but that higher cut scores at about the 25th percentile may be more appropriate for the fourth and fifth grades. While prior research findings similarly suggest that a normalized standard score of about 85 might be promising, others have argued that including too many individuals within the diagnostic category indicates normative functioning (e.g., Doll and Horn 2008). The important issue is to determine a cut score that would represent both poor academic achievement and problems functioning in the school environment. This will help to guarantee that special services are available to those students who are most in need.

As mentioned previously, while the LD diagnostic criteria would benefit from the suggested revision, it is still necessary to retain the exclusionary clause (i.e., a student's disability may not be the result of visual, hearing, or motor disabilities, of mental retardation, of emotional disturbance, or of environmental, cultural, or economic disadvantage). Without these exclusions, students whose academic difficulties are the result of other causes may receive the LD label inappropriately, thus reducing available resources for those who truly suffer from the disorder and further stalling scientific progress. It would be appropriate for many of these exclusions to be addressed during the pre-referral intervention or RTI phase.

Similar approaches using an academic impairment definition of LD that retains the exclusion of learning difficulties due to lack of educational opportunity or another disability have been advocated by Dombrowski et al. (2004), Siegel (1999), and Stanovich (1999). Each of these authors has suggested different arbitrary cut points, which is typically the main argument against this type of approach. Integrating impairment information would address this issue. It should be noted that impairment information is recommended for identifying a meaningful cut point within a low achievement approach to identification. It is not suggested that an impairment measure be used as an additional instrument when conducting evaluations for diagnosis. As noted by Doll and Horn (2008), there is no agreed-upon gold standard for assessing functional impairment.

Other researchers have generated alternative approaches that are similar in respect to utilizing RTI as a means of ruling out inadequate instruction and providing early remediation prior to comprehensive evaluations (e.g., Feifer 2008; Fletcher et al. 2007; Kavale et al. 2008), as well as pointing out the need to consider impairment. Similar to the practice proposed in this chapter, Fletcher (2005) concluded a review of LD identification practices by indicating that a hybrid model using RTI along with a low achievement model may be most useful. Similarly, as noted by Fletcher (2005) as well, a national research summit resulted in consensus statements from the participants indicating that current research suggests that multiple methods are best used in LD identification and should include RTI, evidence of academic deficit, and exclusionary rule-outs (Bradley et al. 2002). Flanagan et al. (2006) expanded upon and modified prior researchers' (Kavale and Forness 2002) efforts at an operational definition of LD by including impairment criteria, in addition to other changes.

The early framework for operationalizing LD conceptualized by Kavale and Forness (2000) consisted of five levels of assessment. First, an ability–achievement discrepancy is documented and, second, academic achievement is assessed to identify deficits in basic skill areas. At the third level, how the individual learns is explored in depth, followed by identification of processing deficits at the fourth level. The final level consists of addressing the exclusionary clause. Flanagan et al. (2002, 2006) proposed a modified version of this model with a greater focus on intelligence theory, removal of the ability–achievement discrepancy component, and integration of RTI as shown in Fig. 6.3.

Flanagan et al.'s (2006) model begins by assessing achievement in a normative manner, with deficits being considered to exist below the 16th percentile rank. The second phase of the first level consists of addressing exclusionary factors, which may be accomplished through RTI to some extent. Level II of Flanagan et al. (2006) involves a norm-referenced assessment of cognitive processing to identify deficits in broad Cattell–Horn–Carroll abilities that are linked to low achievement. Deficits in cognitive processes are considered to be represented by standard scores below 85. The second phase of this level involves ruling out exclusionary factors based upon results of cognitive testing. The third level analyzes the processing and achievement profile for consistency between cognitive and academic deficits as well as the presence of average or better functioning in some processes. Finally, observable impairments in academic performance or other areas of functioning that require academic skills must be determined to be present.

Hale et al. (2006) recommended a conceptually similar model with greater emphasis on RTI. Within their three-tier model, classroom-wide standardized benchmarking is conducted through curriculum-based measurement (CBM) to ensure children have been provided with quality instruction and evaluate progress in comparison to norms. If a student does not make progress at tier 1, they move to tier 2 and an individualized problem-solving RTI approach is implemented. If a child continues not to respond to interventions, a comprehensive evaluation is conducted. Hale et al. (2006) specified that cognitive processes are to be assessed at this stage with cognitive processing deficits that are related to academic underachievement meeting criteria for a specific LD and allowing them access to more intensive interventions and progress monitoring.

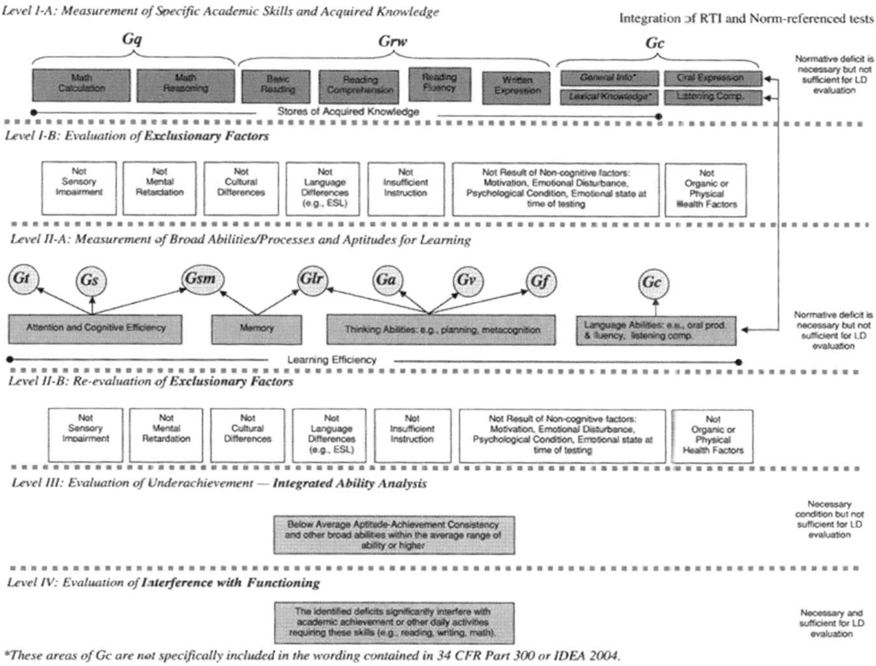

Fig. 6.3 Levels of Flanagan et al.'s operational definition of learning disabilities. *LD learning disability, RTI response to intervention.* (Source: Flanagan et al. 2006. Copyright 2006 by John Wiley & Sons, Inc. Reprinted with permission)

The work of Fletcher et al. (2007) moves closer still to a low achievement model; however, they do not recommend the use of a cut point or other score criteria. They recommend that children are first identified as at risk and provided with intervention and progress monitoring in the area of weakness. If the child fails to respond adequately to the instruction, norm-referenced assessment in the achievement area of concern is conducted along with additional comprehensive evaluation methods to address suspected comorbid conditions or conditions that could be causing poor achievement. Finally, exclusionary factors should be addressed.

It is worth reiterating that some experts have recommended discontinuing the use of cognitive tests for LD diagnoses. The primary complaint is the lack of aptitude × treatment interaction (e.g., Fletcher et al. 2007; Gresham et al. 2008). The consensus statement from the LD summit mentioned previously also noted that outside of the phonological processing and reading, evidence does not support measuring cognitive processes nor linking them to interventions (Bradley et al. 2002). While this author agrees that there is not enough research to link all cognitive processes and areas of academic achievement, there may be cases in which assessment of cognitive processing may be useful in developing useful accommodations for very difficult to remediate students. It is important to emphasize, however, that assessment of cognitive processes is supplemental within this framework and not necessary for the identification of an LD until that time when research proves a causal link between specific cognitive processes and LD.

In sum, it is suggested that a promising practice given the current available research evidence is to utilize a multistep approach to LD diagnosis. As proposed by Fletcher et al. (2012), academic achievement in the six areas of word reading/recognition, reading comprehension, reading fluency, mathematics computation, mathematics problem solving, and written expression should be considered when determining if a child has an LD. First, RTI methods should be implemented to ensure that adequate instruction has been provided and determine if students are performing at expected levels in comparison to peers and making progress. If a student is not achieving or progressing with intervention, then an evaluation of academic achievement, consisting of at least two measures for reliability, should be conducted. Throughout this process, necessary steps should be taken to determine that exclusionary factors do not account for the student's academic underachievement. Within this process, an individual is considered to have an LD if exclusionary factors are ruled out and the academic deficit is below the range of scores determined to be associated with functional impairment. Further research is necessary to identify the most appropriate range of scores to be used. Additionally, assessment of cognitive processing may be undertaken to assist in establishing useful accommodations for students if deemed necessary, and in the case of phonological processing, to select research-based interventions; however, cognitive processing should not be considered in the identification process. This approach is consistent with the DSM-5's criteria for specific learning disorder.

Below are two example reports using the proposed model. The first report presents an evaluation conducted in a private clinic setting. The reader should note that the clinician was in contact with the school to gain information regarding educational interventions that had been provided. The second report presents an evaluation for special education services conducted in a school. This report includes RTI data. Both evaluations address exclusionary factors without always doing so explicitly.

Case Examples

Student Name: Chelsea Adcock Date of Evaluation: 10/28/2009
Birthdate: 12/21/2000 **Grade**: 2
Age: 8 years, 10 months **Parent:** Erin Deal
Evaluation Procedures:
Parent interview
Teacher interview (by telephone)
Child interview
Kaufman Test of Educational Achievement, Second Edition (KTEA-II)
Wechsler Individual Achievement Test-Second Edition (WIAT-II)

Comprehensive Test of Phonological Processing (CTOPP)
Piers–Harris Children's Self-Concept Scale, Second Edition (Piers–Harris 2)

Referral Question and Background

Referral Question

Chelsea was referred to the University Psychology Clinic by her pediatrician due to her mother's concerns regarding persistent difficulties with reading assignments at school. Her mother was also interested in obtaining recommendations for helping Chelsea study at home and manage any anxiety or self-esteem issues that may arise from her learning problems.

Family History

Chelsea is an 8-year, 10-month-old female who resides with her mother, Erin Deal, and her 2-year-old sister, Stacie. Ms. Deal reported that the family's regular schedule involves Chelsea riding home from school with their neighbor who teaches in her school district, followed by playtime, dinner, homework, and bedtime. Ms. Deal reported that she and her husband divorced about a year ago and his job as a pharmacist results in long hours during some days of the week so Chelsea sees him sporadically. She noted that she and Chelsea's father both make efforts to engage in activities with the children such as having a movie night and playing in the park. According to Ms. Deal, Chelsea has a good relationship with all family members especially when she is in control and getting her way.

The family health history is significant for recurrent major depressive episodes for the maternal grandmother and great grandmother. Ms. Deal reported having a younger brother who had some difficulty with reading, but was unaware of any diagnosed LD on either side of the family.

Developmental History

Ms. Deal reported a difficult pregnancy with Chelsea due to placental abruption at 15 weeks, but the pregnancy was otherwise unremarkable. Chelsea was delivered at 42 weeks in meconium-stained amniotic fluid weighing 7 pounds, 9 ounces. Despite the placental abruption and meconium stain, the only sign of distress displayed by Chelsea at birth was a cone-shaped head. Her Apgar scores were within normal limits. Chelsea reached all developmental milestones within normal limits. She said her first word at 6 months, walked at 10 months, spoke in sentences at 18 months, and completed toilet training at 3 years of age.

Educational History

Chelsea's mother stated that prekindergarten got off to a good start but became more difficult as more "academic-like" tasks were required. Ms. Deal was concerned that Chelsea was slow to learn her letters in preschool and kindergarten, but felt she would catch up to the other children. She noted that more recently she was noticing frustration when Chelsea completed homework assignments as well as lower report card grades. Chelsea also acknowledged difficulty with reading tasks even though she felt she was trying her hardest. Ms. Deal reported that Chelsea's kindergarten teacher had considered recommending her to the school's pre-referral intervention program due to her appearing so bright but having difficulty with pre-reading skills. Chelsea's current teacher, Ms. Manheim, reported that she mainly earns As in her classes with the exception of slightly lower marks in reading. She reported that Chelsea had been receiving extra assistance in reading through the school's learning and behavior support team. Ms. Manheim noted that Chelsea had been participating in Peer-Assisted Learning Strategies (PALS) and receiving small-group Lindamood Bell reading instruction in addition to her daily classroom reading period. She reported that Chelsea had made some progress; however, it was not considered adequate growth in comparison to other second graders at the school. Additionally, she noted that Chelsea had not met her winter benchmark goal on recent curriculum-based testing.

Affect and Social Characteristics

Ms. Deal described Chelsea as a basically happy child who sometimes seems unhappy because she likes to do things well and is easily discouraged academically. Chelsea also endorsed being happy, except when she cannot do something that she needs to do. She noted that she is happiest when she makes other people happy too. According to Chelsea and her mother, she has many friends and easily adapts to new social situations. Ms. Deal stated that Chelsea's greatest strengths are her outgoing and affectionate nature as well as her great creativity that she demonstrates by art activities and song lyrics she develops as she sings.

General Behavioral Observations Chelsea was evaluated on October 28, 2009, at the University Psychology Clinic. She appeared to be happy, well kempt, and in good health. Chelsea readily accompanied the evaluators. She engaged in frequent spontaneous conversation, evidencing well-developed language skills. During the assessment, Chelsea was motivated and only took breaks when encouraged. When Chelsea found a task interesting or felt particularly successful, she became much more animated and tended to say, "Yes!" under her breath. The following evaluation appears to be a valid assessment of Chelsea's current level of functioning based on descriptions of her daily performance.

Academic Achievement Chelsea was administered the KTEA-II to determine current levels of academic achievement. These tests are individually administered, norm-referenced tests that assess performance in the essential academic areas of reading, mathematics, and written language. Standard scores are based upon a mean of 100 and a standard deviation of 15. Scores that fall between 85 and 115 are considered to be within the average range.

Subtest/composite	Standard score	Percentile
Letter and Word Recognition	84	14
Reading Comprehension	86	18
Reading Composite	*83*	*13*
Mathematics Concepts and Applications	102	55
Mathematics Computation	99	47
Mathematics Composite	*99*	*47*
Written Expression	95	37
Spelling	92	30
Written Language Composite	*92*	*30*

In the area of reading skills, Chelsea obtained a Reading Composite score of 83 (13th percentile), which is in the average range of functioning. This composite included two subtests. On the Letter and Word Recognition subtest, Chelsea obtained a standard score of 84, which is in the below-average range. She tended to guess at words based on their structure rather than sounding them out on this task. On the Reading Comprehension subtest, she obtained a standard score of 86, which is also in the below-average range. She appeared to reread passages in an attempt to understand their meaning, but when unable to sound out key words guessed at the correct answer.

In the area of mathematics skills, Chelsea obtained a Mathematics Composite score of 99 (47th percentile), which is in the average range of functioning. Her ability to complete mathematics calculation and use those skills to solve applied problems was within the average range.

In the area of written language, Chelsea obtained a Written Language Composite score of 92 (30th percentile), which is in the average range of functioning. Chelsea's written language and spelling scores were within the average range. She commented that she has worked "extra hard" to learn spelling words.

Chelsea was also administered the reading subtests of the WIAT-II to provide a second measure of her reading ability. As with the KTEA-II, standard scores are based upon a mean of 100 and a standard deviation of 15.

Subtest/composite	Standard score	Percentile
Word Reading	82	12
Reading Comprehension	84	14
Pseudoword Decoding	85	16
Reading Composite	*81*	*10*

The CTOPP was also completed given Chelsea's weakness in reading. The CTOPP is an instrument that is designed to measure the ability to use phonological information, especially the sound structure of one's oral language, in processing written language. A deficit in some aspect of phonological processing ability has been linked to the presence of reading disability. Standard scores obtained on the CTOPP composites are based upon a mean of 100 and a standard deviation of 15. Standard scores obtained on the subtests of the CTOPP are based upon a mean of 10 and a standard deviation of 3. The following scores were obtained on the CTOPP:

Subtests/areas	Standard score	Percentile
Elision	8	25
Blending Words	8	25
Phonological Awareness	*88*	*21*
Memory for Digits	5	5
Rapid Digit Naming	9	37
Phonological Memory	*82*	*12*
Nonword Repetition	8	25
Rapid Letter Naming	9	37
Rapid Naming	*103*	*58*

Chelsea's Phonological Awareness Composite Score (PACS) was within the below-average range, which indicates that she may have difficulty identifying and separating discrete sound "chunks" as well as synthesizing or blending sounds together to form words. She performed similarly on the two Phonological Awareness subtests, one of which measures the ability to remove phonological segments from spoken words to form other words and the other that measures the ability to synthesize and form words.

Chelsea's Phonological Memory Composite Score (PMCS) was also within the below-average range. She primarily demonstrated difficulty on the Memory for Digits subtest, which measures the ability to store and recall a series of numbers. She performed better on the Nonword Repetition subtest, which measures the ability to accurately repeat nonsense words.

Chelsea's Rapid Naming Composite Score (RNCS) was within the average range, indicating expected levels of efficiency of retrieval of phonological information from long-term memory and the ability to execute a series of operations quickly and repeatedly.

The Piers-Harris 2 was also administered due to parent concerns regarding self-esteem. The Piers-Harris 2 is a self-report questionnaire designed to assess how children and adolescents feel about themselves. The Piers-Harris 2 measures an individual child's self-evaluative attitudes and behaviors which have a bearing on self-concept. The Piers-Harris 2 yields six "cluster scales" and an overall assessment of self-concept. The cluster scales include: Behavioral Adjustment, Intellectual and School Status, Physical Appearance and Attributes, Freedom from Anxiety, Popularity, and Happiness and Satisfaction. Raw scores on the Piers-Harris 2 are converted to T—scores with a mean of 50 and a standard deviation of 10. A T—score between 35 and 39* is considered to be below average, while a T—score below 35** is considered significantly low. High scores indicate favorable self-concept, whereas lower scores are associated with lower self-concept.

Scale	T-scores	Percentile
Behavioral adjustment	48	43
Intellectual and school status	37*	12
Physical appearance and attributes	52	57
Freedom from anxiety	65	93
Popularity	50	50
Happiness and satisfaction	51	52
Total score	48	40

Chelsea reported an overall positive self-concept, including the areas of behavior, physical appearance, and social acceptance. She did, however, report a below-average perception of her intellectual and school status. She indicated that she does not feel she is as smart as her peers and has more difficulty learning. Despite these negative perceptions, Chelsea still described herself as being a good person who has many strengths.

Summary and Conclusions Chelsea is an 8-year-old second grade student who was referred for evaluation due to difficulties with reading. Background information indicated that Chelsea has received adequate education as well as intensive remediation for reading without notable improvement. While Chelsea's mother expressed some concern with anxiety and self-concept, Chelsea does not appear to exhibit emotional difficulties at this time. The home environment seems to provide sufficient enrichment. Evaluation results revealed that Chelsea's mathematics and writing ability is within the average range, while she displays a consistent weakness in reading with scores a standard deviation below the population mean. Given this information, a diagnosis of Reading Disability appears to be warranted. Chelsea's mother and teacher are encouraged to carefully review and implement the attached recommendations.

Student Name: Tristan James Parent(s): Lisa and Cullen James
Date of Birth: March 3, 1994 Date of Evaluation: February 17, 2008
Age: 13 years, 11 months
Grade: 7
Evaluation Methods
Record review
Progress monitoring
Woodcock-Johnson III Tests of Achievement (WJ-III ACH)
Kaufman Test of Educational Achievement, Second Edition (KTEA-II)
Behavior Assessment System for Children, Second Edition (BASC-2)
Parent Rating Scale (BASC-2-PRS)
Teacher Rating Scale (BASC-2-TRS)
Student Observation System (BASC-2-SOS)

Interview

Referral and Background Information

Tristan was referred for a psychological evaluation by the RTI team due to poor and inconsistent academic performance in mathematics.

Tristan is a 13-year-old seventh-grade student at Brighton Middle School. He lives at home with his mother, father, 17-year-old brother, 9-year-old sister, 8-year-old sister, 4-year-old brother, and two 4-year-old sisters. Tristan was born at term despite brief toxemia shortly before his birth following an uncomplicated pregnancy. Medical history is unremarkable and developmental milestones were met within normal limits.

According to Tristan's mother, he had academic difficulties since beginning school in kindergarten. Tristan was retained in second grade at his previous school in Maryland. Tristan began receiving RTI services at the end of August after beginning seventh grade at Brighton Middle School. Interventions resulting from RTI team services included mathematics remediation through the mathematics connections class and daily computerized mathematics instruction in the classroom in addition to his classroom mathematics instruction. These strategies continue to be used currently with no improvement in his grades. Tristan's grades for the second quarter of his seventh grade year were as follows: 87 in science, 89 in social studies, 68 in mathematics, 72 in mathematics remediation, and 90 in language arts.

The results of hearing and vision screening indicated the following:

Hearing	11/17/2008	Result	Passed
Vision	11/17/2008	Result	Passed

Response to Intervention Progress Monitoring Data As can be seen from the data below, Tristan did not achieve his target rate and/or intervention outcome:

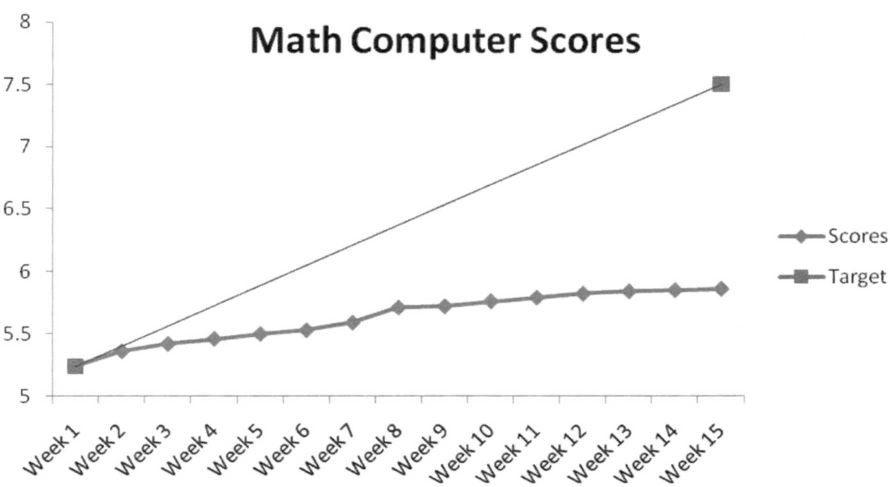

Test Behavior and Observations Prior to the evaluation, Tristan was observed in his mathematics classroom for one session of approximately 50 min using the *BASC, Second Edition Student Observation System (BASC-2-SOS)* and informal observation methods. During this time, students silently worked problems and then reviewed together as a class. Tristan appeared to work on the assignment, despite looking around the room on two occasions as if he did not know what to do. Tristan seemed to follow along during the review and almost constantly wrote notes on his own paper. He raised his hand once to volunteer an answer and was called on by the teacher twice. The first time the teacher had to assist Tristan in working the problem to arrive at the correct answer and the second time he immediately supplied the correct answer. After the assignments had been reviewed, the students paired off for partner work. The teacher stopped at Tristan's desk several times to ask him questions about his assignment and to encourage him to continue. He and his partner worked separately and then came together occasionally to discuss their answers. Tristan frequently looked at his partner's paper to determine how to complete problems. After completing the assignment, Tristan quietly waited to go to lunch. The BASC-2-SOS 15-minute observation did not reveal problem behaviors, although there were three instances at the beginning of the partner assignment when he was engaged in individual seatwork, rather than choosing and working with another student.

At the time of the evaluation, Tristan appeared appropriately dressed and seemed to be in good health. He wore glasses throughout the evaluation. Rapport during testing was easily established and effectively maintained. Tristan was cooperative, motivated, and pleasant, needing little encouragement to provide his best effort. Overall test results are considered to be an accurate estimate of Tristan's current functioning.

Standardized Academic Achievement The *Woodcock Johnson III Tests of Achievement (WJ-III ACH)* was administered to determine Tristan's current level of academic ability. The WJ-III ACH is an individually administered achievement test containing various subtests that are combined to provide composite scores. The WJ-III ACH yields standard scores with a mean of 100 and a standard deviation of 15. Standard scores between 85 and 115, which include 68 % of the general population, are considered to be within the average range.

Subtest/cluster	Standard scores	Percentile rank
Letter–Word Identification	96	39
Reading Fluency	103	57
Passage Comprehension	90	25
Broad Reading	*94*	*35*
Calculation	92	30
Mathematics Fluency	87	20
Applied Problems	80	9
Broad Mathematics	*82*	*12*
Spelling	97	42
Writing Fluency	101	52

Subtest/cluster	Standard scores	Percentile rank
Writing Samples	97	41
Broad Written Language	*97*	*42*
Academic Skills	*95*	*37*
Academic Fluency	*98*	*46*
Academic Applications	*84*	*14*

In the area of Broad Reading ability, Tristan earned a standard score of 94 (35th percentile), which is within the average range. His ability to read words in isolation (Letter–Word Identification), quickly read and understand what he has read (Reading Fluency), and comprehend text without time constraints (Passage Comprehension) was within the average range.

Tristan earned a standard score of 82 (12th percentile) on the Broad Mathematics Cluster, which is within the low average range of performance. His mathematics calculation skills were within the average range, while his ability to quickly complete arithmetic problems and apply his mathematical knowledge (Applied Problems) was within the low average range.

On the Broad Written Language Cluster, Tristan earned a score of 97 (42nd percentile), which is within the average range. His abilities to spell words, quickly produce short sentences in response to prompts, and write complete thoughtful responses were within the average range.

Overall, Tristan's academic achievement was within the average range when compared to other students his age. His academic skills and fluency with academic tasks were both within the average range, while his ability to apply academic skills was within the low average range.

Tristan was administered the KTEA-II to provide additional mathematics achievement data. The KTEA-II is an individually administered, norm-referenced test that yields standard scores with a mean of 100 and a standard deviation of 15. Scores that fall between 85 and 115 are considered to be within the average range.

	Standard score	Percentile
Mathematics Concepts and Applications	76	5
Mathematics Computation	88	21
Mathematics Composite	*80*	*9*

Tristan's performance on the KTEA-II was consistent with results of the WJ-III presented above. His ability to solve mathematics problems was within the below-average range while his ability to solve applied mathematics problems requiring mathematical reasoning was less well developed and within the low range.

Behavioral Rating Scales: Tristan's father and mother, Mr. and Mrs. James, and mathematics teacher, Ms. Jackson, completed the *BASC-2*, a measure that evaluates levels of behavioral, emotional, and social competencies relative to other children. On the Clinical scales and Composite scores of the BASC-2, T-scores of 70 and above** are considered clinically significant, scores between 60 and 69* are in the at-risk range, and scores of 41–59 are in the average range. Adaptive scale scores of

30 or less** are considered clinically significant, scores of 31 through 40* are at risk, and scores between 41 and 59 are average.

Skill area	T-score (parents)	T-score (teacher)
	61*	52
Aggression	57	63*
Conduct Problems	67*	54
Externalizing Problems	*63**	*57*
Anxiety	47	42
Depression	49	53
Somatization	61*	43
Internalizing Problems	*53*	*45*
Attention Problems	–	55
Learning Problems	–	64*
School Problems	–	*60**
Atypicality	52	56
Withdrawal	56	52
Attention Problems	51	–
Behavioral Symptoms Index	*55*	*56*
Adaptability	41	48
Social Skills	44	40
Leadership	46	49
Activities of Daily Living	44	–
Study Skills	–	34*
Functional Communication	42	31*
Adaptive Skills	*42*	*39**

*At risk

** Clinically significant/high level of maladjustment

Mr. and Mrs. James's F, Response Pattern and Consistency indexes were within the acceptable range. The Externalizing Problems Composite was within the at-risk range due to some hyperactivity and rule breaking. Additionally, Tristan's parents endorsed that he is usually fearful of becoming sick, resulting in an at-risk Somatization scale.

Ms. Jackson's ratings also yielded acceptable F, Response Pattern, and Consistency indexes. Similar to Tristan's parents, she did not identify any composites as being within the significant range. The Aggression scale was within the at-risk range, primarily due to endorsing that Tristan occasionally teases peers. The Learning Problems scale was within the at-risk range due to Tristan's difficulties with academic performance and contributed to the School Problems composite being within the at-risk range. Ms. Jackson rated Tristan's adaptive skills as being within the at-risk range due to the Study Skills and Functional Communication scales. The Study Skills scale reflected Tristan's difficulty completing assignments while the Functional Communication scale reflected Tristan's difficulty finding needed information.

Overall, behavioral ratings indicate that Tristan displays some minor difficulties. At school, he primarily exhibits slightly impaired functioning related to his difficulty with mathematics.

Conclusions Tristan is a 13-year-old seventh grade student who was referred for an evaluation for special education services due to poor mathematics performance. After intensive intervention, Tristan did not meet his goal for improvement. His academic performance in reading and writing was within the average range and suggested he is capable of completing grade-level academic tasks. His mathematics calculation skills were within the low average to average range, and his mathematics reasoning ability was within the low to low average range, which his considered significantly low in comparison to same-age peers. Parent and teacher behavioral ratings indicated only minor difficulties, with the most prominent including some impairment in adaptive skills at school. Taken together, this information indicates that Tristan would be most appropriately served through the specific LD program due to mathematics disorder.

Summary of Key Points

- The research model presented proposes the incorporation of a low achievement model with functional impairment.
- Functional impairment is a standard requirement for diagnosis of disabilities and is a broader concept than severity.
- Use of functional impairment is likely to decrease the identification of relative poor achievers and conserve resources for absolute poor achievers. Individuals considered to be gifted with average or above achievement scores and those considered to be slow learners with low achievement scores across academic subjects would not be identified as having an LD within such a model.
- Functional impairment may be considered equivalent to adaptive functioning.
- The current study use latent class analysis to identify a group with low achievement with associated functional impairment to determine a meaningful cut score range for use within a low achievement model of LD identification.
- Results of the study indicated use of cut scores closer to the 25th percentile as recommended by Siegel (1999). This higher than expected cut score range is also likely identifying at-risk students.
- Different cut scores may be required for accurate identification at different grade levels.
- Future research should include a large sample with multiple measure of functional impairment, at least two individually administered nationally normed achievement tests, and the use of RTI to rule out alternative explanations for learning problems.
- Best practice should include RTI to rule out competing explanations and provide remediation, a low achievement approach with at least two tests of academic achievement, consideration of functional impairment, and, if necessary for accommodation decisions, use of *research-supported* cognitive assessment.

Questions and Answers with the Expert: Kenneth Kavale

Meet the expert: Dr. Kenneth Kavale most recently served as a distinguished professor at Regent University and had previously been a faculty member at the University of Iowa, University of Georigia, University of Colorado, and University of California at Riverside. Dr. Kavale has been known for his exemplary contributions in meta-analysis research within the education field and learning disabilities (LD) research and practice. He was the founding editor of *Learning Disabilities* Research (now *Learning Disabilities: Research & Practice*). He has authored numerous books, research articles, and scholarly reviews. Dr. Kavale passed away on December 13, 2008. For more information go to http://www.regent.edu/acad/schedu/faculty_staff/kavale.cfm.

Question 1: What do you see as response to intervention (RTI)'s main role in learning disability (LD) diagnosis?

Answer 1: I believe that the main role of RTI in LD diagnosis is to serve as a pre-referral activity. It is not itself a diagnostic process. The advantage of RTI is the rigor it brings to the pre-referral process. Until RTI was introduced, pre-referral was often a rather unsystematic activity which often failed to achieve the goal of limiting unnecessary referrals. With RTI, it will now be possible to identify students whose academic struggles may be potentially related to LD. The emphasis here is on "potentially LD" because RTI alone provides little insight into the possibility of LD. When a student fails to respond, the presence of significant low achievement is affirmed, but no other critical markers of LD have been identified. To provide information that might confirm an LD diagnosis, a comprehensive psychometric evaluation is required. Thus, RTI serves as a rigorous and systematic instructional activity that provides a means to determine the potential of LD status.

Question 2: What is the most important area, or areas, of assessment in the accurate identification of LD?

Answer 2: Specific LD is a complex phenomenon that is not easily identified by any single variable. Most of the past difficulties in identifying LD originated when the notion of "severe discrepancy" became the sole diagnostic marker. Discrepancy is a necessary but not sufficient criterion for LD determination. Although discrepancy documents the presence of "unexpected" learning failure, more evaluation information is necessary before there can be confidence in an LD diagnostic. The primary LD marker requiring documentation is the presence of process deficits which indicate the student's difficulty in efficient information processing. When a student is identified as an underachiever (not simply low achiever) and possesses deficits in cognitive processing, more confidence about LD status is achieved. The findings from a comprehensive evaluation can also be used to assess the "exclusion" criterion which should assure a reliable LD diagnosis.

Question 3: What do you consider best practice for LD identification?

Answer 3: For LD identification, best practice seems predicated on a comprehensive psychometric evaluation. Although clinical judgment is important, "hard" data is necessary to document the primary markers of LD. The LD construct is complex and not easily identified by any single variable. A comprehensive psychometric evaluation provides the most efficient means to obtain the data for confident decision-making about LD status. With a full evaluation, all facets of the LD construct are assessed and greater confidence in LD diagnoses is achieved. Without a full evaluation, reliance on single variables like discrepancy (underachievement) or RTI (nonresponsiveness) cannot capture the complexity of LD and LD diagnosis remains incomplete.

Question 4: What do you recommend for practitioners within schools whose practices may be restricted by limited resources and state laws?

Answer 4: A very difficult problem to resolve. With a continuing problem of overidentification, efforts should be directed at enhancing the diagnostic process instead of limiting the ability to achieve a confident diagnosis. When limited, however, practitioners need to collect as much information (both formal and informal) as possible. Additionally, observation of the student in different settings is critical. Under such circumstances, the student in question becomes a case study and clinical judgment becomes an essential feature of the diagnostic process. Although not as efficient as comprehensive psychometric evaluation (which also includes informal and observational information), the outcome can still be a confident LD diagnosis.

Chapter 7
Comorbidity and Differential Diagnosis

A comorbid disorder is one that coexists with and yet is unrelated to another disorder. The topic of comorbidity raises the question of whether diagnostic criteria are flawed, with comorbid disorders actually representing symptoms of one disorder. Angold et al. (1999) posit that this is due to the status of psychological and psychiatric conditions being less well established than physical disease categories. For a more in-depth discussion of such issues related to comorbidity in children and adolescents, readers are referred to the above-referenced researchers' work.

There is evidence that learning disabilities (LD) occur concomitantly with other disorders, but little research specifically addresses comorbidity and differential diagnosis with LD (Rosenberg 1997). Instead, the focus is typically on exclusionary factors, which increases the risk of not identifying students who may actually have a LD along with a co-occurring disorder. One possible reason that LD and comorbidity are not frequently addressed may be that it is considered a mild disorder that is more difficult to distinguish than more severe forms of disability. While mild disorders, such as mild mental retardation and emotional/behavioral disorders, are marked by less severe impairments, individuals with mild disorders are distinguishable from typically developing individuals (Shepard 1977). In general, the more extreme the symptoms the more valid is the identification.

This chapter discusses several conditions that may co-occur with or present similar symptoms to those of an LD. The main issue is determining whether the LD is secondary to, or the result of, another disorder or if the LD is primary and co-occurring with or contributing to the symptoms of the other disorder. Based upon the symptom presentation, the clinician must determine if multiple disabilities or only one should be diagnosed. This decision may, in part, take into consideration the treatment options for one or both conditions. For example, will treating one issue result in improvement in the other or are they completely unrelated requiring separate interventions?

A. E. B. Taylor, *Diagnostic Assessment of Learning Disabilities in Childhood*, Contemporary Issues in Psychological Assessment, DOI 10.1007/978-1-4939-0335-1_7,
© Springer Science+Business Media New York 2014

Disorders and Conditions To Be Considered

Exclusionary factors The logical starting point in the differential diagnosis of LD is the exclusionary factors in the federal definition:

> Such term does not include a learning problem that is primarily the result of visual, hearing, or motor disabilities, of mental retardation, of emotional disturbance, or of environmental, cultural, or economic disadvantage. (IDEA, S.1248, 2003, sect. 602(29)) mainly use RTI for latter three—provide experiences that would have been lacking and monitor progress.

Several of these disabilities are discussed in more detail in the following sections. For the remaining disadvantage categories, the response to intervention (RTI) process will be critical in determining if a student's academic performance improves after being provided learning opportunities that were previously lacking. Additionally, the response to intervention and evaluation process should include a thorough review of records to determine if environmental, cultural, or economic disadvantages are viable possible explanations for a child's low achievement.

Mental retardation/Intellectual Disability As noted earlier, there is frequent confounding between high-incidence mild disabilities, with the primary confounding occurring between LD and mild intellectual disability (ID). This is particularly true when cut scores are used in determining if an individual meets criteria for the disorders (Kavale 2002). Some states identify more students as having LD and fewer with ID, while others identify more students as having ID and fewer with LD. It has been determined that the correlation between the percentage of children classified with mild ID is inversely related to the percentage of students classified with specific LD (Gresham 1996). This basically means that a child identified as having an LD in one state may be identified as having mild ID in another state.

Studies have shown that children with LD and those with mild ID may demonstrate similar behavioral characteristics, including adaptive functioning (Gresham 1996; Polloway et al. 1997). Gresham (1996) conducted a study comparing students identified as being low achieving, having an LD, and having mild mental retardation. He determined that there were few differences between the groups in terms of teacher behavioral ratings and school history; however, they did differ according to cognitive ability and achievement. Students with mental retardation performed more poorly across all academic areas as compared to the low-achieving students and students with LD. The researcher concluded that there are more similarities than differences between mild disability groups and suggested that mild mental retardation would be better termed "generalized learning disability." In other words, an LD is underachievement in one or a few specific academic areas, while mental retardation is underachievement across all academic areas.

While ID would typically rule out the possibility of an LD, some argue that LD may co-occur with mild ID, although LD would always be considered secondary to ID (Polloway et al. 1997). For example, an individual may have significantly impaired functioning in one academic area as compared to academic functioning in another area. In this case, it may be useful to apply RTI strategies as would be done with any individual to determine the appropriateness and utility of the additional label of LD.

As indicated above, differential diagnosis of LD and mild ID requires assessing achievement, intelligence, and adaptive functioning. When a child or adolescent displays a significant deficit in one (or several limited) academic area(s), it may be determined that the individual has a *specific* LD. On the other hand, when an individual displays deficits across all or most academic areas, intelligence and adaptive functioning should be assessed to determine if the individual has mild ID.

Slow learner Similar to the situation in which a clinician must determine if an individual has an LD or mild ID, one may also be faced with discriminating between a slow learner and a student with an LD. Kaznowski (2004) defined slow learners as students with IQs ranging from 70 to 85 and achievement scores in the same range, which thus does not represent a severe discrepancy between predicted and actual achievement. With the decreasing emphasis on intelligence testing in LD assessment, the pattern of academic performance may be considered more pertinent. As described above, these students likely display generalized academic deficiencies while specific LD is one or more academic deficiency but not all (Kavale 2002). Again, achievement testing, and intelligence testing if indicated, will be critical in accurate differential diagnosis.

ADHD Attention-deficit/hyperactivity disorder (ADHD) is a clinical disorder that is diagnosed based upon the *Diagnostic and Statistical Manual for Mental Disorders, 5th Edition* (DSM-5; APA 2013). ADHD is divided into three subtypes: ADHD, predominantly hyperactive/impulsive presentation; ADHD, predominantly inattentive presentation; and ADHD, combined presentation. Most frequently, the latter two subtypes are most likely to require differential diagnosis from LD. The current criteria for ADHD are presented in Fig. 7.1.

Approximately 82.2 % of children with LD in one study had ADHD, while 69.8 % of students with ADHD had LD (Mayes et al. 2000). In this study, children with ADHD performed more poorly on achievement than expected given intelligence compared to children without ADHD. As might be expected, students with comorbid LD and ADHD performed most poorly on achievement tasks, followed by children with LD only, then ADHD only. On attention tasks, children with comorbid LD and ADHD performed most poorly, followed by ADHD only, then LD only. The researchers demonstrated that both disability groups have attention problems distinguished by severity level, and ADHD populations have more learning problems than typically developing individuals.

Stanford and Hynd (1994) compared children with ADHD inattentive type (ADHD-I), ADHD hyperactive-impulsive type (ADHD-H), and LD. The researchers' hypothesis that behavioral profiles for ADHD-I and LD would be similar was supported to some extent, but there were symptoms specific to each ADHD group that were not displayed similarly in the LD group. Their study suggested different causes for learning difficulties across groups with ADHD-I related to inattention

A. A persistent pattern of inattention and/or hyperactivity-impulsivity that interferes with functioning or development, as characterized by (1) and/or (2) (Note: Symptoms are not solely a manifestation of oppositional behavior, defiance, hostility, or failure to understand tasks or instructions. For older adolescents and adults (age 17 and older), at least five symptoms are required):

(1) Inattention: Six (or more) of the following symptoms have persisted for at least 6 months to a degree that is inconsistent with developmental level and that negatively impacts directly on social and academic/occupational activities:

(a) Often fails to give close attention to details or makes careless mistakes in school work, work, or other activities.

(b) Often has difficulty sustaining attention in tasks or play activities.

(c) Often does not seem to listen when spoken to directly.

(d) Often does not follow through on instructions and fails to finish school work, chores, or duties in the workplace.

(e) Often has difficulty organizing tasks and activities.

(f) Often avoids, dislikes, or is reluctant to engage in tasks that require sustained mental effort (such as schoolwork or homework).

(g) Often loses things necessary for task or activities.

(h) Is often easily distracted by extraneous stimuli.

(i) Is often forgetful in daily activities.

(2) Hyperactivity and impulsivity: Six (or more) of the following symptoms have persisted for at least 6 months to a degree that is inconsistent with developmental level and that negatively impacts directly on social and academic/occupational activities:

Fig. 7.1 *Diagnostic and Statistical Manual for Mental Disorders, 5th Edition* (DSM-5; APA 2013) diagnostic criteria for attention-deficit/hyperactivity disorder (ADHD)

(a) Often fidgets with or taps hands or feet or squirms in seat.

(b) Often leaves seat in situations when remaining seated is expected.

(c) Often runs about or climbs excessively in situations where it is inappropriate (in adolescents or adults, may be limited to feeling restless).

(d) Often unable to play or engage in leisure activities quietly.

(e) Is often "on the go," acting as if "driven by a motor".

(f) Often talks excessively.

(g) Often blurts out an answer before a question has been completed.

(h) Often has difficulty waiting his or her turn.

(i) Often interrupts or intrudes on others.

B. Several inattentive or hyperactive-impulsive symptoms were present prior to age 12 years.

C. Several inattentive or hyperactive-impulsive symptoms are present in two or more settings.

D. There is clear evidence that the symptoms interfere with, or reduce the quality of, social, academic, or occupational functioning.

E. The symptoms do not occur exclusively during the course of schizophrenia or another psychotic disorder and are not better accounted for by another mental disorder (e.g., mood disorder, anxiety disorder, dissociative disorder, or a personality disorder).

Fig. 7.1 (continued)

and internalizing behaviors, ADHD-H related to impulsive and externalizing behaviors, and LD related to processing deficits, although the LD group also displayed some withdrawal and social isolation characteristics similar to the ADHD-I group.

The studies described above indicate that children with LD and children with ADHD may demonstrate similar types of underachievement; however, there may be distinguishable characteristics. If it is determined that ADHD-related behaviors are present, it is necessary to consider the severity of the attention and/or hyperactivity symptoms as well as the academic deficit. Very severe difficulties may be indicative of a comorbid disorder, while more mild learning difficulties may suggest only one disorder. One way to determine the appropriate diagnosis is to provide accommodations for the attention difficulties, such as small group and limited distractions, and determine if academic performance improves. Regardless of whether the diagnosis of LD is made, the individual is likely to need academic remediation.

Emotional Emotional disorders are typically distinguished from LD in terms of severity. If a behavior is extreme and pervasive, then learning problems are considered secondary (Shepard 1977). Research, however, has shown that some types of social-emotional and behavior difficulties are more frequently found in students with LD than average children (Rourke and Fuerst 1991). It has been estimated that 24–52 % of children with LD have social, emotional, and behavioral problems, while 38–75 % of children with serious emotional disturbance have LD or serious learning problems (Rock et al. 1997). As in the case of other so-called mild disabilities, it is important to look at the pattern of academic performance. In many cases, a child whose academic performance is depressed by an emotional disturbance will display deficits across academic areas, thus not meeting criteria for a specific LD. Frequently, emotional and behavioral difficulties, particularly those of an internalizing nature are overlooked, so a broad assessment measure should be administered to screen for difficulties if there is any suspicion of emotional and behavioral problems.

Language Differences Across disability categories, culturally and linguistically diverse groups may be over- or under-identified due to language differences. This is another area where RTI is important in using less formal measures within the classroom to determine whether a student is displaying actual learning differences or is having difficulty learning or communicating knowledge due to English being a second language. Additionally, the use of local norms may allow the comparison of the individual's performance to a similar reference group in order to rule out cultural diversity as an explanation for the academic difficulties (Ortiz 1997). The typical best practice in formal evaluation when working with an individual whose first language is not English is to assess proficiency in both the native language and English to determine the child's dominant language (Ortiz 1997; Rhodes et al. 2005). The Woodcock-Munoz Language Survey-Revised (Woodcock et al. 2005) is one example of an instrument that may be used. If a student is not proficient in English, the first hypothesis should be that language is the difficulty. In addition to determining language dominance, a clinician should also compare performance across languages. If a child or adolescent demonstrates academic deficits in the dominant language as well as English, it is likely the student truly has an LD. For a more in-depth discussion of assessing diverse populations, the reader is referred to Rhodes, Ochoa, and Ortiz (2005).

In addition to the difficulty of identifying culturally diverse students as having an LD, the conceptual and practical overlap of LD with communication disorders further complicates matters. The Individuals with Disabilities Education Act (IDEA) definition of LD explicitly states that LD is related to psychological processes involved in understanding written or spoken language as well as including oral language and listening comprehension as areas of specific LD. The American Speech-

Oral and Written Language Scales[1]	Test of Auditory Processing Skills-Third Edition[2]
Peabody Picture Vocabulary Test, Fourth Edition[3]	Expressive Vocabulary Test, Second Edition[4]
Clinical Evaluation of Language Fundamentals-4 Screening Test[5]	Woodcock-Johnson III Tests of Achievement[6]

Fig. 7.2 Possible language screening instruments

Language-Hearing Association (1993) provides the following definition of a language disorder:

> A language disorder is impaired comprehension and/or use of spoken, written and/or other symbol systems. The disorder may involve (1) the form of language (phonology, morphology, syntax), (2) the content of language (semantics), and/or (3) the function of language in communication (pragmatics) in any combination.

- Form of Language
  - Phonology is the sound system of a language and the rules that govern the sound combinations.
  - Morphology is the system that governs the structure of words and the construction of word forms.
  - Syntax is the system governing the order and combination of words to form sentences, and the relationships among the elements within a sentence.
- Content of Language
  - Semantics is the system that governs the meanings of words and sentences.
- Function of Language
  - Pragmatics is the system that combines the above language components in functional and socially appropriate communication.

It is not uncommon for children to be identified as having a communication disorder at younger ages and as having an LD when older (Schoenbrodt et al. 1997). Similar to the discrepancy method that has been used for identifying LD, discrepancy scores are frequently used to assess for language disabilities. Schoenbrodt, Kumin, and Sloan (1997) have suggested that the following areas should be assessed to determine whether a language-based LD is more accurately classified as an LD or a communication disorder: intelligence, problem solving, attention, concentration, memory, receptive and expressive vocabulary, listening comprehension, auditory processing, and academic ability. Within a school setting, the school psychologist

[1] Carrow Woolfolk (1995)

[2] Martin & Brownell (2003)

[3] Dunn & Dunn (2007)

[4] Willliams (2007)

[5] Semel, Wiig, & Secord (2004)

[6] Woodcock, McGrew, & Mather (2001)

may complete screening measures such as those shown in Fig. 7.2 and/or refer the student for evaluation by a speech-language pathologist.

Visual Impairment According to Erin and Koenig (1997), 14–65% of students with visual disabilities also have LD. They reported that visual problems are often identified earlier with any learning problems being attributed to the visual deficits, possibly because visual disability is more easily understood and it may be easier for parents to accept a physiologically based disorder rather than a learning problem that is associated with cognitive abilities. Historically, the use of discrepancy formulas has made the identification of LD in individuals with visual impairments difficult because intelligence cannot be accurately assessed with traditional means. The use of RTI methods, however, allows for visual accommodations and academic remediation to be put in place without labeling the student as having an LD. If the learning problems continue, it would be necessary to use appropriate formal achievement measures to determine if the student displays a significant learning problem beyond that caused by visual challenges. One would be most confident in identifying an LD in an area unrelated to vision, for example, if a student has difficulties with phonological processing when reading and pronouncing works read in Braille despite being able to identify the letters, it would be reasonable to determine that the child has a reading disability (Erin and Koenig 1997).

Case Examples

Below are two sample reports that required the clinician to differentiate between an LD and another disorder. In the first case, the child had previously diagnosed emotional disabilities with the evaluation indicating the likelihood of a coexisting LD. The second case presents an initial evaluation with the presence of significant ADHD symptoms that were determined to be the primary reason for learning problems.

NAME: Andrew Richards **PARENT/GUARDIAN: Tamara Richards**

BIRTH DATE: 01/03/1996 **REFERRED BY: IEP Team**

AGE: 12 years, 2 months **SCHOOL: Barnard Middle**

SEX: Male **GRADE: 6**

DATES EVALUATED: 03/28/2008, 03/31/2008

VISION & HEARING PASSED: 03/25/2008

Assessment Tools:

Review of records
Wechsler Individual Achievement Test, Second Edition (WIAT-II)
Wide Range Achievement Test-4 (WRAT-4)
The Behavior Assessment System for Children, Second Edition (BASC-2)

Parent Rating Scales (PRS)
Teacher Rating Scales (TRS)
Adolescent Psychopathology Scale (APS)
Clinical interview

Referral Reason Andrew was referred for a comprehensive psychoeducational reevaluation in order to evaluate academic progress, to determine instructional needs, and to determine possible eligibility for future special education services. He has been served through the Emotional and Behavioral Disorder program. Additional evaluation of academic functioning was requested due to concerns with his reading and writing performance.

Background Information According to an eligibility report dated March 24, 2003, Andrew was initially referred to special education by his parents based upon a private psychological assessment conducted by Angela Dixon, Ph.D., a clinical psychologist. Dr. Dixon's report from November 3, 2002, noted that Andrew was referred for evaluation due to attention difficulties and low frustration tolerance. According to Dr. Dixon, prior to the evaluation, Andrew saw Mr. David Joyce on four occasions for counseling due to symptoms of obsessive-compulsive disorder (OCD) and Attention-deficit/hyperactivity disorder (ADHD) and was then referred to Dr. Timothy Jackson, a psychiatrist, who prescribed Luvox for the OCD symptoms. Dr. Dixon reported that Andrew continued to fidget, have nervous habits, engage in repetitive untying of his boots, and be strongly opinionated at the time of his evaluation. He also reported that Andrew struggled in school and tended to become self-deprecatory when frustrated by academic tasks. Dr. Dixon administered the Wechsler Intelligence Scale for Children, Second Edition (WISC-III), and Andrew earned a Verbal Comprehension score of 108, Perceptual Organization score of 97, Freedom from Distractibility score of 90, Processing Speed score of 88, and Full Scale IQ score of 101. On the Bender Visual-Motor Gestalt Test, Andrew completed nine drawings in 6 minutes and 35 s with nine errors, yielding a perceptual age score of 6 years, 0 months, which Dr. Dixon concluded represented a spatial weakness. Andrew also completed the Wechsler Individual Achievement Test (WIAT) and earned the following standard scores: Basic Reading 84, Mathematics Reasoning 94, Spelling 82, Reading Comprehension 78, Numerical Operations 90, Listening Comprehension 108, and Oral Expression 109. Dr. Dixon reported that the parent Achenbach Child Behavior Checklist indicated significant anxious/depressed behaviors and attention problems and the Teacher Report Form indicated significant inattention and thought problems and some withdrawn behaviors. Other teacher rating scales reported by Dr. Dixon, including the ADHD Rating Scale and School Situations Questionnaire, also indicated difficulties with impulsivity and overactivity. Andrew was administered the Connors' Continuous Performance Test by Dr. Dixon and results were considered indicative of inattentiveness and impulsive responding, as well as possible visual-perceptual difficulties. Dr. Dixon concluded that Andrew exhibited a profile for OCD, a learning problem, and ADHD. Based on the results of Dr. Dixon's report and observations that Andrew exhibited perfectionistic tendencies, nervous behaviors, psychosomatic illnesses, inattention, and self-abuse at school that all seemed to impact his learning, particularly in reading, the eligibility committee concluded that Andrew met the criteria for an emotional and behavioral disorder.

School records indicated that Andrew spent 5 days in the Appalachian Hospital in Fall 2006 due to increased anxiety, self-injurious behavior, and suicidal ideation. While hospitalized, he was reportedly diagnosed with major depression and ADHD. His medications at the time were noted to consist of Zoloft, Focalin, Wellbutrin, and Trileptal. Andrew was also reported to have attended weekly counseling sessions with his previous school counselor.

During the current school year, Andrew has been participating in intensive interventions for reading and writing. These have included daily Wilson reading lessons with the school reading specialist, an additional 60 min daily of writing instruction, and tutoring at a private clinic after school. Andrew's teacher reported that his reading skills have only minimally improved as a result of the extra instruction. They also indicated that the lack of improvement had led to increases in Andrew's negative statements about his intelligence.

Parent Interview Andrew's mother, Ms. Tamara Richards, completed an interview on April 24, 2008. Ms. Richards noted that Andrew lives at home with her, his father, Mr. William Richards, and his 10-year-old brother. She reported that Andrew was the product of an uncomplicated pregnancy and delivery and was born weighing 7 pounds, 12 ounces. He reached developmental milestones within normal limits, walking at 11 months, speaking at 12 months, achieving toilet training at 24 months, and dressing himself at 36 months. Andrew's early childcare included a babysitter for 1 year, preschool from ages 3 through 5 years, and additional care from his mother, grandparents, and aunt. No serious childhood illnesses or injuries were reported. In terms of Andrew's current health, Ms. Richards endorsed that he is healthy, overweight, and has some vision problems. She noted that his current medications include Lamictal (200 mg) and Klonopin (0.5 mg). She also noted that in the past, Andrew has taken many different medications for ADHD, depression, anxiety, and bipolar disorder.

Ms. Richards endorsed that reading and writing are the most difficult subjects for Andrew and that it is very hard for him to study at home. She specified reading and writing as also being her greatest concerns for Andrew at school. Ms. Richards endorsed that Andrew is overly anxious to please, loud, easily frustrated, shy/withdrawn, and trustworthy. She also noted that he has few close friends, has difficulty adjusting to change, and acts younger than other children his age. Ms. Richards endorsed that Andrew gets along well with his friends and family members. She reported that he enjoys golf and that she most enjoys Andrew's sense of humor. She disclosed that being hospitalized was a significant event in Andrew's life that may have a lasting effect on him. She reported his eating habits as her greatest concern for him at home.

Testing Observations Andrew is a 12-year-old sixth grader who is noted to be of somewhat above average height and weight for his chronological age. He was tested at Barnard Middle School over three sessions. Andrew entered the testing situation willingly and rapport was easily established and maintained, although he stated that he is nervous around unfamiliar people. His affect was appropriate to the testing situation and his mood was pleasant and cooperative. He attempted all tasks and put forth adequate effort despite frustration with reading tasks. Andrew stated that he enjoyed completing rating scales and other question-and-answer tasks about himself, but that he did not like to read and that it made him feel dumb and unable to continue other types of tasks. While Andrew enjoyed completing rating scales, it should be noted that he was very concerned with his performance and appeared to be careful to respond in socially desirable ways. During the second testing session, academic testing was initiated and after having difficulty on a reading task, Andrew pushed the materials away, was visibly upset, and stated that he could not go on. On several occasions, he called himself "stupid" and "retarded." After being allowed a calming period, Andrew agreed to continue with tasks other than reading. He agreed to complete reading tasks at the end of the testing session so it would not affect his performance on other activities. At the end of the session, he completed the reading tasks despite his frustration, although it should be noted that the reading comprehension subtest was discontinued to prevent further undue distress. Andrew was alert and appeared oriented throughout the evaluative sessions. He was allowed to get up and move about the room or take breaks between tasks if he felt the need to move around. He approached tasks in an organized and logical manner. His eye contact was appropriate and no disturbances in his thought processes were observed. Overall test results appear to be a valid estimate of Andrew's current level of functioning.

Test Results and Interpretation *Academic Achievement*

Andrew was administered selected subtests of the *Wechsler Individual Achievement Test, Second Edition (WIAT-II)* to determine current levels of academic achievement. These tests are individually administered, norm-referenced tests that assess performance in the essential academic areas of reading and mathematics. Standard scores are based upon a mean of 100 and a standard deviation of 15. Scores that fall between 85 and 115 are considered to be within the average range.

Subtest/composite	Standard score	Percentile
Word reading	45	<1
Reading comprehension	–	–
Pseudoword decoding	63	1
Reading composite	–	–
Numerical operations	90	25
Math reasoning	85	16
Mathematics composite	*86*	*18*
Spelling	54	<1
Written expression	55	<1
Written language composite	*45*	*<1*
Listening comprehension	112	79
Oral expression	87	19
Oral language composite	*98*	*45*

A Reading Composite score was not calculated due to the discontinuation of the Reading Comprehension subtest. On the Word Reading subtest, Andrew obtained a standard score of 45, which is in the extremely low range. On the Reading Comprehension subtest, Andrew picked out words he could recognize and then guessed at the answer to questions related to the passage. Attempting to decode the passages and guess the answers quickly became very distressing and the test was discontinued. On the Pseudoword Decoding subtest, Andrew obtained a standard score of 63, which is in the extremely low range. On both subtests, Andrew tended to insert extra phonemes into words he was decoding and/or substituted a similar word for the target word.

In the area of mathematics skills, Andrew obtained a Math Composite score of 86 (18th percentile), which is in the below average range of functioning. This composite included two subtests—Numerical Operations and Math Reasoning. On the Numerical Operations subtest, Andrew obtained a standard score of 90, which is in the average range. On the Math Reasoning subtest, Andrew obtained a standard score of 85, which is in the below average range. Andrew was able to complete mathematics problems within a paper and pencil format, but struggled with a variety of problems presented in pictorial and word problem formats.

Within the area of written language, Andrew earned a Written Language Composite score of 45 (<1st percentile), which is in the extremely low range. The Written Language Composite included the Spelling and Written Expression subtests. Andrew obtained a standard score of 54 on the Spelling subtest, which is in the extremely low range. He correctly spelled most three- and four-letter words, but provided incorrect, although phonetically accurate, representations of other words. On the Written Expression subtest, Andrew earned a score of 55, which is in the extremely low range. Andrew's poor score is primarily due to his frustration level and resulting inability to complete the essay portion of the subtest, instead writing only "no opinion."

Andrew obtained an Oral Language Composite score of 98 (45th percentile), which is within the average range. The Oral Language Composite included the Listening Comprehension and Oral Expression subtests. On the Listening Comprehension subtest, Andrew earned a score of 112, which is in the above average range. He obtained a score of 87 on the Oral Expression subtest, which is within the below average range. Andrew was able to name many objects and actions rapidly, but did not include many details when telling stories or giving directions.

Andrew was also administered the *Wide Range Achievement Test, Fourth Edition (WRAT-IV),* which measures academic functioning, rendering a Math Computation score and Word Reading and Sentence Comprehension scores that are combined to provide a Reading Composite score.

Subtest/composite	Standard score	Percentile
Word reading	63	1
Sentence comprehension	66	1
Reading composite	*63*	*61*
Math computation	104	1

Andrew's reading scores on the WRAT-IV were within the extremely low range, which is commensurate with results of the WIAT-II. He continued to add extra letter sounds, transpose sounds, and substitute visually similar words when reading. Taking his reading and spelling results from both instruments into consideration, it seems that Andrew struggles to decode words and as a result has difficulty gaining meaning from text. Andrew's mathematics score on the WRAT-IV was somewhat higher than his scores on the WIAT-II. It should be noted that the mathematics portion of the WRAT-IV was administered at a separate time from other achievement tests. It is possible that Andrew's overall performance on the WIAT-II was impaired by his frustration and emotional upset regarding reading tasks.

Due to concerns with Andrew's written expression skills, he was also administered the *Oral and Written Language Scales (OWLS), Written Expression Scale.* Andrew earned a written expression standard score of 68 (2nd percentile), which is within the below average range and consistent with his performance on the WIAT-II. Item and task analyses indicated that Andrew demonstrated weaknesses in capitalization, punctuation, and spelling and failed to use complex sentences and details to make his writing more descriptive and meaningful.

Social/Emotional/Behavioral Rating Scales Andrew's mother, Ms. Linda Richards, and his teacher, Ms. Libby Shook, completed the *Behavior Assessment System for Children, Second Edition (BASC-2),* a measure that evaluates levels of behavioral, emotional, and social competencies relative to other children their age and gender. On the Clinical scales and Composite scores of the BASC-2, T-scores of 70 and above** are considered clinically significant, scores between 60 and 69* are in the at-risk range, and scores of 41–59 are in the average range. Adaptive scale scores of 30 or less** are considered clinically significant, scores between 31 and 40* are at risk, and scores between 41 and 59 are average.

Skill area	T-score (mother)	T-score (father)	T-score (teacher)
Hyperactivity	80**	70**	85**
Aggression	53	61	81**
Conduct problems	40	51	61*
Externalizing problems	*59*	*62*	*78***
Anxiety	66*	74**	94**
Depression	65*	80**	103**
Somatization	47	60	80**
Internalizing problems	*61**	*76***	*99***
Attention problems	–	–	72**
Learning problems	–	–	79**
School problems	–	–	*78***
Atypicality	56	63	78**
Withdrawal	77**	75**	78**
Attention problems	64*	61*	–
Behavioral symptoms index	*71***	*74***	*92***
Adaptability	26**	33*	31*
Social skills	29**	39*	45
Leadership	32*	35*	44
Activities of daily living	48	48	–
Study skills	–	–	38*
Functional communication	43	34*	38*
Adaptive skills	*33**	*36**	*38**

*At risk

** Clinically significant/high level of maladjustment

Mr. and Ms. Richards's F, Response Pattern, and Consistency indexes were within the acceptable range. Ms. Shook's Response Pattern and Consistency indexes were within the acceptable range, while her F index, which is a measure of negative responding, was within the caution range. This was due to endorsing that Andrew almost always worries and is nervous. Given Andrew's preoccupation with his academic performance, it seems that Ms. Shook's responses were not extreme and results should be considered valid.

On the clinical scales, Ms. Shook indicated that Andrew demonstrates more types of and more severe difficulties with internalizing and externalizing symptoms at school than were reported by Mr. and Ms. Richards at home. All raters agreed that Andrew demonstrates significant Hyperactivity across settings, particularly interrupting other individuals. At school, Ms. Shook also endorsed a short temper and arguing (Aggression), as well as some rule breaking (Conduct Problems). In terms of Internalizing Problems, Ms. Shook identified significant difficulties, including worrying and nervousness (Anxiety), negativity and loneliness (Depression), and several occasional health complaints (Somatization). Ms. Richards also indicated observing significant depression and anxiety symptoms. With the exception of somatization, Ms. Richards endorsed observing similar issues at home but not as often. The Behavioral Symptoms Index, which is a global indicator of behavioral issues, was significant according to all raters' results. This composite reflects several internalizing and externalizing behaviors, as well as Atypicality, Withdrawal, and Attention Problems. Mr. Richards, Ms. Richards, and Ms. Shook identified significant Withdrawal tendencies. Ms. Shook also indicated significant Atypicality, which is likely related to Andrew's OCD behaviors, and Attention Problems, which are associated with his diagnosis of ADHD.

Ms. Shook and Mr. and Ms. Richards agreed that Andrew's overall Adaptive Skills were within the at-risk range. At home, this appears to mainly be due to mild to significant difficulties with adapting to changes (Adaptability) and engaging in common courtesies (Social Skills). At school, Ms. Shook endorsed that Andrew has some difficulties adapting to situations (Adaptability), efficiently engaging in academic tasks (Study Skills), and expressing himself clearly and finding information (Functional Communication). Mr. Richards also indicated that Andrew tends to have difficulty locating information at home.

Andrew completed the *Behavior Assessment System for Children, Second Edition – Self-Report of Personality (BASC-2-SRP)* in order to provide his perception of his behavioral, emotional, and social relative to other children his age. Andrew's F, Response Pattern, Consistency, V, and L indexes were within the acceptable range. It should be noted that, as with all social-emotional measures administered, the evaluator read the items to Andrew and he appeared very careful to reply in a socially desirable manner. Thus, it is possible that results do not provide an accurate portrait of Andrew's actual social-emotional experience. As with the parent and teacher forms, the Clinical scales and Composite T-scores of 70 and above** are considered clinically significant, scores between 60 and 69* are in the at-risk range, and scores of 41–59 are in the average range. Adaptive scale scores of 30 or less** are considered clinically significant, scores of 31–40* are at-risk, and scores between 41 and 59 are average. Specific T-scores obtained on the BASC are listed below:

Skill area	T-score
Attitude to school	40
Attitude to teachers	34
Sensation seeking	30
School problems	*30*
Atypicality	45
Locus of control	41
Social stress	47
Anxiety	48
Depression	41
Sense of inadequacy	47
Somatization	40
Internalizing problems	*42*
Attention problems	41
Hyperactivity	48
Inattention/hyperactivity	*44*
Emotional symptoms index	*50*
Relations with parents	55
Interpersonal relations	36*
Self-esteem	47
Self-reliance	38*
Personal adjustment	*42*

*At risk
** Clinically significant/high level of maladjustment

On this self-report, Andrew did not endorse any significant or at-risk difficulties on the clinical scales. On the Personal Adjustment scale, Andrew indicated at-risk Interpersonal Relations and Self-Reliance. The Interpersonal Relations scale represents Andrew's perception that it is somewhat difficult for him to make friends. The Self-Reliance scale reflects Andrew's belief that he cannot always solve problems by himself and that friends do not come to him for help.

The *Adolescent Psychopathology Scale (APS)* was also completed by Andrew as a means of assessing psychopathology and psychosocial problems as compared to males his same age. The summary is based on the adolescent's responses to the 346-item APS. T-scores between 65 and 69* represent a mild clinical symptom range, while T-scores from 70 to 79** represent a moderate clinical symptom range and T-scores above 80*** indicate the severe clinical symptom range.

Clinical disorder scales	T-score
Attention-deficit/hyperactivity disorder (ADH)	41
Conduct disorder (CND)	40
Oppositional defiant disorder (ODD)	35
Adjustment disorder (AJD)	44
Substance abuse disorder (SUB)	45

Clinical disorder scales	T-score
Anorexia nervosa (ANV)	52
Bulimia nervosa (BNV)	46
Sleep disorder (SLP)	53
Somatization disorder (SOM)	42
Panic disorder (PAN)	53
Obsessive-compulsive disorder (OCD)	49
Generalized anxiety disorder (GAD)	52
Social phobia (SPB)	49
Separation anxiety disorder (SEP)	46
Posttraumatic stress disorder (PTS)	45
Major depression (DEP)	41
Dysthymic disorder (DYS)	52
Mania (MAN)	45
Depersonalization disorder (DPR)	48
Schizophrenia (SCZ)	45
Personality disorder scales	*T-Score*
Avoidant personality disorder (AV)	48
Obsessive-compulsive personality disorder (OC)	66*
Borderline personality disorder (BD)	41
Schizotypal personality disorder (SZ)	44
Paranoid personality disorder (PD)	49
Psychosocial problem content scales	*T-Score*
Self-concept (SC)	54
Psychosocial substance use difficulties (PS)	–
Introversion (IN)	70**
Alienation-boredom (AL)	53
Anger (AN)	36
Aggression (AG)	39
Interpersonal problems (IP)	47
Emotional lability (EL)	37
Disorientation (DO)	44
Suicide (SU)	45
Social adaptation (SA)	65*
Response style indicator scales	*T-score*
Lie response (Si)	65*
Consistency response (Cn)	51
Infrequency response (If)	46
Critical item endorsement (Cr)	41
Factor scales	*T-Score*
Internalizing disorder factor (Int FS)	47
Externalizing disorder factor (Ext FS)	39
Personality disorder factor (Per FS)	50

It should be noted that items represent symptoms of diagnoses and are not diagnostic in themselves. Results should be used in conjunction with other assessment information in forming diagnostic impressions and treatment planning. Andrew's responses indicated some moderate and mild clinical symptoms. On the Psychosocial Problem Content scales, Andrew endorsed moderate symptoms of Introversion and mild symptoms of Social Adaptation. High scores on the Introversion scale may indicate concern about lack of friends, extreme shyness, active avoidance of evaluative situations, intense feelings of loneliness, perceived rejection by others, and significant depressive symptoms. Adolescents with high scores on the Social Adaptation scale are generally distrustful, socially isolated, unresponsive, and anhedonic. On the Clinical Disorder scales, Andrew indicated mild symptoms of obsessive-compulsive personality disorder. Adolescents with scores in this range tend to have a perfectionistic attitude, a need for orderliness, a strong need for structure, and an overdependence on rules and schedules. Some of these individuals may have difficulty turning in assignments on time due to perfectionism and may find it difficult to throw away old, worn, or used items. It should also be noted that Andrew's responses resulted in a mildly elevated Lie Response scale. The Lie Response scale serves to identify endorsement of highly unlikely behavior and/or an overly positive image. As noted with other self-report instruments, Andrew seemed quite concerned with providing desirable responses.

Clinical Interview In a separate interview, Andrew was oriented to person, time, and place. His thoughts appeared logical and organized. He was somewhat guarded in responding, but was more open than in his responses to the rating scales reported earlier. Andrew endorsed being satisfied with his decisions at times, but sometimes regretted making mistakes if he is doing something in front of a group. When asked to provide three words that best describe him, Andrew replied that he is dependable at times, obsessive, and likes to feel like he is in control. He reported that he feels his greatest strength is his memory.

Andrew disclosed that he lives at home with his mother, father, and 10-year-old brother and that they all get along well. He reported that he has lived in the area his entire life and is close to his family, particularly his parents from whom he has no secrets. He went on to state that he has to get along with his brother because they do not have any neighbors, so he serves as a companion. He did not feel that his parents are overly strict and reported that they usually punish him by "grounding."

Andrew described his current mood as nervous and his usual mood as upbeat, although he worries about a lot of stuff and cannot control it. When asked what he worries about, Andrew replied that he worries about politics and "stuff other people my age don't usually worry about." He reported that he was happiest when he went to his grandmother's. Andrew stated that he does not think the future will be "doom and gloom," but that he just worries. He said that he obsesses about things and then forgets about them in a few minutes. Andrew reported that he becomes upset due to things people say and do, particularly when he sees others being picked on. He stated that this makes him feel "really depressed" but he bounces back in about an hour.

Andrew reported that he takes medication for bipolar disorder and stress and that the combination has been working. He disclosed that the medication helps to regulate his moods and also helps with his "ADD." He endorsed being healthy with the exception of some sinus problems. He also reported that he had recently lost 10 pounds after joining the Weight Watchers program. He stated that he has not received sexual education, but believes in abstinence so is not concerned about such issues. Andrew described himself as needing everything to be in its place in his room and could not verbalize what he would do if he were unable to put things where they belong. He stated that he is a "little OCD."

Andrew disclosed that he does not do things outside of school. He reported that he does not have friends because he does not believe in "true friends," which he described as individuals who are loyal and trustworthy. Andrew stated that he does have "acquaintances" with whom he talks and socializes. He endorsed enjoying "tinkering," which he described as making stuff with various materials. He then described how he made a tree stand even though he does not hunt, because an acquaintance had made one and he wanted to make a better one. He also reported enjoying watching TV, particularly music channels, and playing video games on the Xbox 360. Andrew described school as being "fine" and said that he makes "really good grades." He reported history as his favorite subject because he already knows half of the material in the first chapters. He reported his least favorite school activity as anything involving computers because he has never really used them before. This led him to disclose that he worries about the possibility of an EMP and the effect on America's ability to function. When asked what he would like to do after high school, Andrew stated that he was not sure. He stated that he may want to study culinary arts to become a chef because he has never messed up when cooking.

Summary Andrew is a 12-year-old, sixth grade student who was referred for a comprehensive reevaluation to assist in determining continuing eligibility for special education services. Previous test results suggested that Andrew's intellectual functioning is in the average range. Academically, Andrew's performance in reading and written expression were in the extremely low range, while his oral language and mathematical skills were in the below average to average range.

Andrew's parents and teacher completed behavioral rating scales. In terms of externalizing behaviors, parent and teacher ratings identified significant concerns with hyperactivity, with the teacher report also indicating some verbal aggression issues at school. Internalizing difficulties were endorsed across raters, with depression and anxiety being most prominent. Andrew was also noted to withdraw from social interaction at home and school.

Andrew also completed ratings scales and an interview. His self-ratings primarily reflected his effort to respond in socially acceptable ways. He did, however, indicate some introversion, social isolation, and perfectionistic tendencies that may at times be obsessive. In an interview, he endorsed worrying to the point of obsession about various issues, having difficulty sitting still, and not trusting other people, particularly his peers. Throughout the testing session, Andrew exhibited perfectionistic attitudes and a desire to please others.

Determination of Andrew's eligibility for placement in a special education program must be made by the eligibility team and must be based upon eligibility criteria. Andrew is demonstrating a significant number of behaviors/emotions consistent with the criteria for an emotional and behavioral disorder. More specifically, Andrew is unable to form meaningful and lasting relationships with others, and he displays a pervasive negative mood and heightened levels of anxiety under normal circumstances. Based on the current evaluation, Andrew's academic performance in reading and writing is significantly below the normative group mean. The severity of his impaired reading and writing skills and ability to perform within the average range other academic tasks indicates that his learning difficulties are not simply a result of his emotional difficulties. His academic abilities also do not appear to have improved in response to intensive and individualized instruction. These results suggest that Andrew has a specific learning disability in the areas of reading and writing. Determination of eligibility, however, should not be made exclusively or principally upon the results of the present psychological evaluation. The eligibility team must consider all pertinent data.

NAME: Aaron Rawlings PARENT: Rita Criss

BIRTH DATE: 12/27/1998 GRADE: 4

AGE: 10 years, 1 month DATES EVALUATED: 04/01, 04/03/2009

SEX: Male

EVALUATION INSTRUMENTS:

Parent and teacher interviews

Reynolds Intellectual Assessment Scales (RIAS)

Woodcock-Johnson III Tests of Achievement (WJ III ACH)

Delis-Kaplan Executive Function System (D-KEFS)

Behavior Rating Inventory of Executive Function (BRIEF)

Clinical Assessment of Attention Deficit-Child (Cat-C)

Integrated Visual and Auditory Continuous Performance Test (IVA+)

The Behavior Assessment System for Children, Second Edition (BASC-2)

Clinical Interview

Referral and Background Information Aaron was referred by his mother, Ms. Rita Criss, due to school difficulties. She reported that Aaron had a very hard time completing academic tasks, received poor grades, and was frequently "written up" at school. She was interested in determining if a learning disability (LD) explained his school problems.

Ms. Criss reported that Aaron lives at home with her, his stepfather, and his 18-year-old brother. She reported that she and Aaron's biological father divorced when Aaron was 5 years old and that Aaron has seen his father once or twice a year because they live in different states. Ms. Criss endorsed receiving regular prenatal care during her pregnancy and delivered Aaron prematurely through cesarean section at a weight of 4 pounds, 15 ounces. She disclosed that Aaron was born with hyaline membrane disorder, or immature lungs, and suffered frequent respiratory infections and allergies as a toddler. Aaron was reported to have met all developmental milestones within normal limits, walking at 18 months, saying his first words between 18 and 24 months, speaking clearly at 36 months, achieving daytime toilet training at 4 years, and achieving nighttime toilet training and dressing himself at 6 years.

Ms. Criss described Aaron's general health as being good. She endorsed that he is often irritable or grouchy, has good coordination, is a picky eater, and has a normal energy level although at times he is overly active and always on the move. She described him as not falling asleep quickly, wanting to stay up late, and being difficult to awaken. His time of going to sleep was 9–10 p.m. and his time of awakening was 5 AM. Ms. Criss noted that Aaron frequently experiences headaches and stomachaches. She also indicated that Aaron fractured his collarbone in a bicycle accident when he was 8 years old. She noted that the family health history is significant for depressive episodes in herself and Aaron's maternal aunts as well as attention problem in the father's family.

According to Ms. Criss, Aaron was not eager and excited to start school and had difficulties separating. She reported that he was cared for by his mother, father, and grandfather from birth until age 5 and attended a preschool when he was 4 years old. She noted that he has repeated kindergarten and ninth grade. She noted that writing and mathematics are the most difficult academic subjects for Aaron and that she has difficulty getting him to study at home. Ms. Criss reported that Aaron currently goes home with his family after school and is expected to complete his homework as soon as he arrives.

Ms. Criss endorsed that Aaron often requires discipline for not completing tasks. Ms. Criss described Aaron as interacting with his family and being appropriate at times and argumentative at other times. She described him as getting along well with his classmates most of the time, but becoming irritable, defensive, and argumentative sometimes. His relationships with friends were described as being good and cooperative.

Ms. Criss endorsed that Aaron may have been affected by his parents' divorce and that she is most concerned about his ability to care for himself independently, do his work and graduate from school, get along with his family, and become more responsible. Ms. Criss indicated that Aaron may need extra assistance staying on task and not worrying about others' behaviors. She reported that Aaron's interests include guitars and cars. Some of her descriptions of Aaron included seeming happy with himself, being talented, being motivated, and being trustworthy, caring, and compassionate. Ms. Criss endorsed most enjoying how loving, smart, and funny Aaron can be.

A phone interview was conducted with Aaron's teacher, Mr. Writ, who reported that Aaron was frequently off-task, fidgety, and disruptive in class. He indicated that Aaron would express good intentions but frequently did not complete his work, forgot to turn in work he completed, or lost his work. He noted that Aaron attended remediation classes during connections classes, such as art and music, but the teacher in that class had reported similar difficulties getting Aaron to pay attention and do his work. Aaron's grades were reported as follows: reading 60, mathematics 60, science 82, social studies 75, language arts 70, and life skills 90.

Testing Observations

Aaron is a 10-year-old male who is noted to be of average height and weight for his chronological age. He was tested at the clinic over two sessions. He entered the testing situation willingly and rapport was easily established and maintained. Aaron displayed a full range of affect appropriate to the testing situation and his mood was pleasant and cooperative. He attempted all tasks and put forth adequate effort. He stated several times that he was tired and was very distractible, which he apologized for more than once. The quality of Aaron's expressive language was considered to be within the average range. He often spontaneously initiated conversation with the examiner. Aaron was alert and appeared oriented throughout the evaluative sessions, with the exception of looking around the room when distracted. He approached tasks in an organized and logical manner. His eye contact was appropriate and no disturbances in his thought processes were observed. Overall test results appear to be a valid estimate of Aaron's current level of functioning.

Test Results and Interpretation

Intelligence Aaron was administered the Reynolds Intellectual Assessment Scales (RIAS) in order to provide an estimate of his cognitive ability. The RIAS is an individually administered test designed to provide subtest and composite scores that represent intellectual functioning in specific cognitive domains.

The following scores reflect Aaron's performance on individual subtests. Each subtest score is scaled to a mean of 50 and a standard deviation of 10. Subtest scores that fall between 45 and 54 are considered average. The various indexes are scaled to a mean of 100 and a standard deviation of 15. Composite scores that fall between 90 and 109 are considered average.

Index score	Standard score	Percentile
Verbal intelligence index (VIX)	102	55
Nonverbal intelligence index (NIX)	103	58
Composite intelligence index (CIX)	102	55
Composite memory index (CMX)	72	3
Verbal subtest	*T-Score*	
Guess what (GWH)	52	
Verbal reasoning (VRZ)	50	
Nonverbal subtest	*T-Score*	
Odd-item out (OIO)	45	
What's missing (WHM)	57	
Memory subtest	*T-Score*	
Verbal memory (VRM)	47	
Nonverbal memory (NVM)	17	

In the area of verbal skills, Aaron obtained a Verbal Intelligence Index (VIX) composite score of 102 (55th percentile), which is in the average range of functioning. He performed similarly across the subtests.

In the area of nonverbal skills, Aaron obtained a Nonverbal Intelligence Index (NIX) composite score of 103 (58th percentile), which is in the average range of functioning. He performed somewhat better on the Odd-Item Out subtest than the What's Missing subtest, but the resulting composite score is considered valid.

Aaron's overall performance was within the average range of intellectual functioning. His Composite Intelligence Index (CIX) score was a standard score of 102, which corresponds to the 55th percentile, which means that Aaron is functioning equal to or better than 55 % of children his same age. The chance that the range of scores from 96 to 108 includes Aaron's true IQ is 95 out of 100.

In the area of memory, Aaron obtained a Composite Memory Index (CMX) composite score of 72 (3rd percentile), which is in the moderately below average range. Within the subtests making up the CMX, Aaron's performance in the verbal memory domain significantly exceeded his level of performance within the nonverbal memory domain. This difference is reliable and indicates that Aaron functions at a significantly higher level when asked to recall or engage in working memory tasks that are easily adapted to verbal linguistic strategies, as opposed to tasks relying upon visual-spatial cues and other nonverbal memory features. This discrepancy between verbal and nonverbal memory was of a relatively infrequent magnitude, occurring in 7.8 % of the population at Aaron's age.

When compared to his general level of intelligence as measured by his CIX, Aaron's CMX falls significantly below his CIX. This result indicates that Aaron's level of working memory skill is not as well developed as his general intelligence. The magnitude of this difference is relatively infrequent in the general population, occurring in only 4.9 % of the population.

Academic Achievement The Woodcock-Johnson III Tests of Achievement (WJ III ACH) was administered to determine Aaron's current level of academic ability. The WJ III ACH is an individually administered achievement test containing various subtests. The subtest scores are combined into a number of composite scores. The composites calculated and presented here depend on the subtests given. The WJ III ACH yields standard scores with a mean of 100 and a standard deviation of 15. Standard scores between 85 and 115, which include 68 % of the general population, are considered to be within the average range.

Subtest/cluster	Standard scores	Percentile rank
Letter-word identification	86	18
Reading fluency	56	<1
Passage comprehension	90	25
Broad reading	*76*	*5*
Calculation	62	1
Mathematics fluency	36	<1
Applied problems	85	16
Broad math	*61*	*<1*
Spelling	80	9
Writing fluency	42	<1
Writing samples	76	5
Broad written language	*59*	*<1*
Academic skills	*76*	*6*
Academic fluency	*36*	*<1*
Academic applications	*86*	*17*

In the area of Broad Reading ability, Aaron earned a standard score of 76 (5th percentile), which is within the low range. His ability to read words in isolation (Letter-Word Identification) was within the low average range, while his ability to comprehend text without time constraints (Passage Comprehension) was within the average range. His ability to quickly read and understand what he has read (Reading Fluency) was within the very low range.

Aaron earned a standard score of 61 (< 1st percentile) on the Broad Math cluster, which is within the very low range of performance. His ability to apply his mathematical knowledge (Applied Problems) was within the low average range, while his mathematics calculation skills (Calculation) and ability to quickly complete arithmetic problems (Math Fluency) was within the very low range. When completing the latter two tasks, Aaron stated that mathematics is his least favorite subject and he was very distractible and only attempted tasks that required little effort and/or sustained mental processing. Based upon his attempt at these tasks and his performance on the applied mathematics tasks, it is likely that these scores are an underestimation of his actual mathematical ability.

On the Broad Written Language cluster, Aaron earned a score of 59 (< 1st percentile), which is within the very low range. His ability to spell words (Spelling) was within the low average range, while his ability to quickly produce short sentences in response to prompts (Writing Fluency) and write complete thoughtful responses (Writing Samples) was within the very low range. Aaron again seemed very distractible and unable to apply sustained mental effort completing these tasks.

Overall, Aaron's academic achievement was within the very low range when compared to other students his age. His fluency with academic tasks was within the extremely low range. His academic skills were within the low range, while his ability to apply academic skills was within the low average range.

Executive Functioning/Attention Based upon teacher reports of attention difficulties and observations of distractibility during testing, Aaron was also administered several tasks from the Delis-Kaplan Executive Function System (D-KEFS). The first test Aaron completed was the D-KEFS Trail Making Test, which consists of a visual cancellation task and a series of connect-the-circle tasks. There are five tasks including visual scanning, number sequencing, letter sequencing, letter-number sequencing, and motor speed. Aaron's completion time scores across conditions were below to well below the expected level. The contrast scores suggest that Aaron's cognitive flexibility is within the expected range given his sequencing ability and motor speed. His overall performance suggests that slow processing speed interferes with his functioning across tasks.

The D-KEFS Verbal Fluency Test consists of three conditions: Letter Fluency, Category Fluency, and Category Switching. All conditions require generating words meeting a certain criteria within 60 s. Letter Fluency requires words that begin with a particular letter, Category Fluency requires words from a designated semantic category, and Category Switching requires words from alternating semantic categories. Aaron's category fluency score was well below expected levels, his letter fluency score was below expected levels, and his category switching scores were borderline. His contrast score indicated a somewhat better performance on the more cognitively demanding switching task than the fluency task, suggesting more difficulty with verbal skills and rapid retrieval of lexical items than cognitive flexibility. The pattern of his responses over time indicated difficulty initiating responses with increased but still lower than expected responding over time. He maintained the instructional set throughout the tasks.

Aaron also completed the D-KEFS Design Fluency Test, which consists of three conditions requiring the examinee to draw different designs in each box in rows of boxes using four lines to connect dots located in the boxes. In condition 1, Filled Dots, only filled dots are presented and the examinee draws designs to connect those dots providing a measure of basic design fluency. In condition 2, Empty Dots Only, the boxes contain filled and unfilled dots and the examinee is required to connect only the unfilled dots, measuring design fluency and response inhibition. Condition 3, Switching, presents boxes with filled and unfilled dots and the examinee is asked to draw designs by alternating between filled and empty dots, which measure design fluency and cognitive flexibility. Aaron's performance was below expectations across tasks and again was more suggestive of initiation and fluency deficits more than cognitive flexibility and higher order skills.

The D-KEFS Color-Word Interference Test is a variant of the Stroop procedure and measures the examinee's ability to inhibit an overlearned verbal response (i.e., reading the printed words) in order to generate a conflicting response of naming the dissonant ink colors in which the words are printed. The conditions 1 and 2 are baseline measures of basic naming of color patches and basic color-words printed in black ink, respectively. The third condition, Inhibition, is the traditional Stroop task in which the examinee inhibits reading words in order to name the dissonant ink color. Condition 4, Inhibition/Switching, requires the examinee to switch back and forth between naming the dissonant ink colors and reading the words. Aaron performed well below expectations across task demands, suggesting that he does not have impairments in verbal inhibition and cognitive flexibility over and above his deficiency in naming and reading speed. Aaron's rate of corrected errors and lack of uncorrected errors indicated the cognitive capacity to monitor and modify his behavior in order to produce a correct response.

Aaron's parent and teacher also completed the Behavior Rating Inventory of Executive Function (BRIEF), a questionnaire designed to provide a better understanding of a child's self-control and problem-solving skills by measuring eight aspects of executive functioning. The executive functions are mental processes that direct a child's thought, action, and emotion, particularly during problem solving. Raw scores obtained on the BRIEF are converted to T-scores, which have a mean of 50 and a standard deviation of 10. T-scores between 60 and 64* are considered mildly elevated and T-scores at or above 65** indicate clinically significant difficulties.

Index/scale	Parent T-scores	Teacher T-scores
Inhibit	81**	75**
Shift	65**	79**
Emotional control	72**	62*
Behavioral regulation index (BRI)	*77***	*74***

Index/scale	Parent T-scores	Teacher T-scores
Initiate	73**	76**
Working memory	82**	84**
Plan/organize	75**	84**
Organization of materials	72**	110**
Monitor	62*	76**
Metacognition index (MI)	*76***	*88***
Global executive composite (GEC)	*79***	*87***

Ms. Criss' and Mr. Writ's ratings were reasonably consistent and were not overly negative indicating that they are valid. Both parent and teacher ratings resulted in an elevated composite index, the Global Executive Composite (*GEC*). Both the Behavioral Regulation Index (*BRI*) and the Metacognition Index (*MI*) were also elevated (*BRI*).

Both raters noted concerns with Aaron's ability to inhibit impulsive responses (Inhibit), adjust to changes in routine or task demands (Shift), initiate problem solving or activity (Initiate), sustain working memory (Working Memory), plan and organize problem-solving approaches (Plan/Organize), and organize his environment and materials (Organization of Materials). Parent and teacher ratings differed in terms of severity of Emotional Control and Monitoring deficits, with Ms. Criss reporting significant difficulties modulating emotions (Emotional Control) and Ms. Murphy reporting difficulties monitoring his own behavior (Monitor).

Current models of self-regulation suggest that behavioral regulation, particularly inhibitory control, underlies most other areas of executive function. Essentially, one needs to be appropriately inhibited, flexible, and under emotional control for efficient, systematic, and organized problem solving to take place. Aaron's elevated scores on the Inhibit scale, and the BRI and MI, suggest that Aaron has poor inhibitory control and/or suggest that more global behavioral dysregulation is having a negative effect on active metacognitive problem solving. The elevated BRI score, however, does not negate the meaningfulness of the elevated MI score. Instead, one must consider the influence of the underlying behavioral regulation issues while simultaneously considering the unique problems with the metacognitive problem-solving skills.

Aaron was administered, by computer, the Integrated Visual and Auditory Continuous Performance Test (IVA+) as a measure of his visual and auditory attention. The test presents 500 intermixed visual and auditory signals 1.5 s apart. Aaron was asked to click the mouse when he saw or heard the number 1 presented. The IVA+ gives a sustained auditory quotient and a sustained visual attention quotient as indicators of his performance. Quotient scores are based upon a mean of 100 and a standard deviation of 15. Quotient scores between 0 and 59 reflect extreme weaknesses. Aaron's performance is presented in the following table:

IVA+plus sustained attention scales	Quotient
Sustained auditory attention quotient	4
Sustained visual attention quotient	0
Combined sustained attention	*12*

Aaron's performance on this measure demonstrated sufficient understanding of the task for the test results to be considered valid in both the auditory and visual modalities. The Combined Sustained Attention score provides a global measure of a student's ability to accurately and quickly respond in a reliable manner to stimuli under low demand conditions. In addition, it includes the ability to sustain attention and be flexible when things change under high-demand conditions. Aaron's Combined Sustained Attention, Sustained Auditory Attention, and Sustained Visual Attention were within the extremely impaired range. Based on Aaron's performance on this test, he demonstrated responding characteristic of individuals with attention-deficit/hyperactivity disorder (ADHD). He displayed relative weaknesses in consistency, vigilance, and focus. He displayed a relative strength in stamina, indicating good attentional endurance.

Behavioral Rating Scales Aaron's mother and teacher also completed the Clinical Assessment of Attention Deficit-Child (Cat-C) as a measure of his attention. The Cat-C uses T-scores to measure attention in three clusters: clinical, context, and locus. A clinical index is also provided as an indicator of clinical significance. T-scores below 59 are considered to be normal or within the average range scores. Scores ranging from 60 to 69* are considered as indicators of mild clinical risk, whereas scores ranging from 70 to 79** are indicative of significant clinical risk and scores above 80*** are very significant clinical risk.

Scale/cluster	T-score (parents)	T-score (teacher)
Clinical scale		
Inattention	74**	69*
Impulsivity	69*	64*
Hyperactivity	70**	71**
Cat-C clinical index	*73***	*69**
Context cluster		
Personal	70**	67*
Academic/occupational	72**	74**
Social	70**	62*
Locus cluster		
Internal	75**	68*
External	69*	70**

*At risk
** Clinically significant
*** Very significant

Overall, the Cat-C Clinical Index was in the at-risk to clinically significant range as indicated by Aaron's mother and teacher. Further examination of the subscales suggested that Aaron's parents and teachers similarly viewed him as having slightly higher levels of inattention and hyperactivity as compared to impulsivity. The Context subtests revealed that Aaron's ADHD-related behaviors primarily impact his academic performance at school, while these behaviors are equally impairing across daily task performance, academic/work, and interpersonal domains. In terms of Locus, Aaron was indicated to have approximately equal amounts of covert and overt ADHD-related behaviors and symptoms, although slightly more in internalizing attention at home versus externalizing attention at school.

Aaron completed the Behavior Assessment System for Children, Second Edition – Self-Report of Personality (BASC-2-SRP) to provide his perception of his social and emotional functioning. As with the parent and teacher forms, the Clinical scales and Composite T-scores of 70 and above** are considered clinically significant, scores between 60 and 69* are in the at-risk range, and scores of 41 through 59 are in the average range. Personal Adjustment scale scores of 30 or less** are considered clinically significant, scores of 31 through 40* are at risk, and scores between 41 and 59 are average. Specific T-scores obtained on the BASC-2-SRP are listed below:

Skill area	T-score
Attitude to school	45
Attitude to teachers	46
Sensation seeking	33
School problems	*39*
Atypicality	42
Locus of control	46
Social stress	40
Anxiety	38
Depression	40
Sense of inadequacy	40
Somatization	40
Internalizing problems	*38*
Attention problems	59
Hyperactivity	54
Inattention/hyperactivity	*57*
Emotional symptoms index	*41*
Relations with parents	51
Interpersonal relations	52
Self-esteem	57
Self-reliance	41
Personal adjustment	*50*

*At risk
**Clinically significant/high level of maladjustment

Aaron's F, Response Pattern, V, L, and Consistency indexes were within the acceptable range. On this self-report, Aaron did not report any significant or at-risk areas of social, emotional, or behavioral functioning. He indicated that he is satisfied with his relationships, has a positive self-concept, and is generally well adjusted.

Clinical Interview In a separate interview, Aaron reported that he is 10 years old and in the fourth grade. He was oriented to person, place, time, and situation. Aaron shared that he was born in Kansas City and lived there until his parents divorced when he was 5 years old and he moved with his mother. Aaron reported that his family moved out of the state because his stepfather, whom his mother has been married to for 3 or 4 years, lived there. He endorsed being "cool" with the move because it made his mother happy and he likes his stepfather. Aaron went on to report that he gets along well with his stepfather because he is supportive, has things in common with him, and does nice things for him. Aaron disclosed that he stays in touch with his biological father by telephone and visits him in Kansas for 1–2 weeks in the summer.

Aaron reported currently living with his mom, his stepfather, and his 18-year-old brother. He endorsed having a good relationship with all of his family members, with his mother being the person he goes to when "something is going on" and his brother being there to talk to and help him with computer problems. Aaron described his parents as being structured rather than strict and noted that they take things away, such as phone and guitar privileges, when he is in trouble. Aaron shared that his family was planning to sell their house next year during better economic times and then move back to Kansas. He stated that he was not upset about the move and actually wanted to go back, but has a lot of friends here.

Aaron described his current mood as good and on a scale of 1 to 10, where 1 is the worst and 10 is the happiest he has ever been, rated himself as a 10. He endorsed that his mood is usually a 10 and that life in general makes him happy. He reported rarely feeling very sad and that it only happens when there is an issue in his life. He stated that he has found ways to relieve stress and is more open to talking to others, so this is quite infrequent. Aaron denied experiencing compulsions, delusions, hallucinations, dissociation, obsessions, and paranoia. Aaron reported that his current health is good and endorsed trying to eat a balanced diet. He reported sleeping well and having no difficulties with falling asleep or awakening.

According to Aaron, he is unable to keep up in his classes. Aaron stated that his favorite subjects are science and reading. Mathematics is his least favorite subject because it is complicated, but he has to try. He stated that he would not change anything about his school or teachers because he likes everything just as it is.

Aaron described himself as being a social person and having many friends. He stated that most of his friends are his age or older. When asked which three words best describe him, Aaron stated that he is silly, happy, and energetic. He endorsed that his strengths as a person are being helpful to people and his knowledge of guitars. He reported that finding something he is good at, i.e., guitars, has been the most important thing to happen to him.

Summary Aaron is a 10-year-old, fourth grade student who was referred for evaluation due to school difficulties. Current test results suggest that Aaron is functioning intellectually in the average range. Academically, Aaron's performance in reading was in the average to below average range, with low average spelling ability and low writing performance. In mathematics, Aaron demonstrated extremely low calculation skills but his ability to apply his mathematical knowledge was within the low average range. Aaron's academic fluency was a significant deficit across subjects. Aaron's performance on mathematics and writing tasks is likely an underestimation of his actual ability due to difficulty focusing and maintaining attention, but is likely an accurate representation of his functioning in the classroom.

The results of the D-KEFS indicated deficits in verbal and motor fluency, task initiation, ability to remain attentive to task, and abstract categorical processing, while he seemed to have a slight verbal bias with expected levels of abstract thinking, deductive reasoning, and cognitive flexibility. Aaron's sustained verbal and auditory attention were significantly impaired.

Aaron's mother and his teacher completed behavioral rating scales and interviews. Both indicated significant difficulties with inattention and related executive functioning impairments, including behavioral regulation and metacognition deficits. Aaron's teacher also indicated that he has difficulty effectively completing academic tasks and classroom routines.

Aaron also completed a self-report measure and a clinical interview. He indicated that he is currently satisfied with his personal and affective functioning at this time. Despite his school difficulties, he endorsed being happy there.

Based upon parent and teacher reports, Aaron's test performance, and testing observations, Aaron meets DSM-IV criteria for attention-deficit/hyperactivity disorder, combined type (314.01). While Aaron also demonstrated significant academic impairments, his learning difficulties appear to be due to ADHD-related behaviors. Aaron's mother is encouraged to share this information with his school to assist in developing appropriate interventions and accommodations.

Summary of Key Points

- Comorbidity is the existence of two or more unrelated disorders within one individual.
- LD do exist with other disorders or characteristics of LD may result from another disorder or condition.
- Differential diagnosis is necessary to determine if a disorder is comorbid with an LD or if the disorder is causing symptoms of the LD.
- Exclusionary factors in the LD definition are the first factors that must be considered when assessing for an LD.
- Conditions to consider when making a differential diagnosis of LD include mental retardation, functioning within the slow learner range, ADHD, emotional disability, language differences, and visual impairment.

Questions and Answers with the Expert: Stefan C. Dombrowski

Meet the expert: Stefan C. Dombrowski, Ph.D., is a Full Professor and Director of Training in the School Psychology Program at Rider University in Lawrenceville, NJ. As a licensed psychologist and certified school psychologist, Dr. Dombrowski maintains an active psychological evaluation practice. Dr. Dombrowski completed his undergraduate studies at the College of William and Mary and his graduate work at the University of Georgia. He also completed a postdoctoral fellowship in clinical child psychology at the University of California, Davis Medical Center. Dr. Dombrowski has published three books and more than three dozen articles in the areas of learning disabilities (LD) assessment, child psychopathology, and prenatal exposures as they adversely impact children's psychological, behavioral, and educational functioning.

Question 1 What types of assessment do you recommend to differentiate LD from other disorders?

Answer 1 LD is one of the most ubiquitous disorders of childhood, yet its definition and diagnostic approach (e.g., IQ-Achievement Discrepancy) is predicated upon outdated science as well as a law (IDEIA 2004) and diagnostic code (*Diagnostic and Statistical Manual of Mental Disorders* (DSM)) that needs to revise how the construct of LD is defined and diagnosed. Certainly, the discrepancy approach, in whatever iteration, is inappropriate. I also think that the definition should stick to the three "Rs" of reading, writing, and arithmetic and divest itself from difficulties with speaking and listening. This would more fully align the Individuals with Disabilities Education Improvement Act (IDEIA) definition with that of the DSM.

I recommend a comprehensive assessment of cognitive, academic, behavioral, social, and emotional functioning. Why is a comprehensive assessment recommended as opposed to a targeted evaluation that focuses solely on academic domains? Because there are comorbid disorders and exclusionary conditions that contribute to learning difficulties but are sometimes mistaken for LD. Response to Intervention and Instruction (RTII) may also be useful in ruling out children's reading disabilities. The technology for differentiating an LD in mathematics and writing using RTII is not sufficiently advanced to be useful for this purpose, although the technology may be on the horizon.

Question 2 What advice would you give clinicians with limited resources and administrative support for making differential diagnosis?

Answer 2 I think that a comprehensive psychoeducational evaluation utilizing multiple methods and sources of data including standardized tests, rating forms, teacher interviews, parent interviews, child interviews, classroom observations, review of academic and medical records, curriculum-based measurement (CBM) probes (where available), and response to intervention (RTI) data (where available) is necessary. I do not think that neurological tests such as a magnetic resonance imaging (MRI) or computed tomography (CAT) scan are fruitful at this point for differentiating LD from non-LD. The relationship between particular brain areas and LD is far too equivocal to justify the cost. Neuropsychological research has uncovered what is called a neural signature for reading that may potentially differentiate good readers from poor readers. This line of investigation portends a possible scientific breakthrough, but may still be too expensive to be used as a common diagnostic procedure for reading disabilities.

Question 3 What disorders are most often mistaken for an LD, and vice versa?

Answer 3 Rat her than offering a simple list of narrow disorders such as attention-deficit/hyperactivity disorder (ADHD) or intellectual disability (formerly mental retardation (MR)), I would like to posit that there are a number of features and conditions that must be ruled out prior to offering a classification of LD. First, psychologists need to be sensitive to cultural nuance and cautious about offering a diagnosis when cultural factors may be involved. Second, psychologists must differentiate between an LD and an ESL condition. Third, intellectual disability (formerly MR) must be ruled out. Although many clinicians feel that they "can just tell" whether a child has an intellectual disability through solely clinical interaction and observation, this practice is inappropriate and possibly unethical. Therefore, I recommend the use of a rapidly administered IQ test to rule out MR. Fourth, children with behavioral and emotional issues sometimes present with learning difficulties but these difficulties may be better accounted for by the emotional or behavioral issue. This may be the case with a child with ADHD, a disorder of conduct, or a condition that warrants a classification of emotional disturbance. Fifth, there may be health, vision, or hearing issues that contribute to the learning difficulty and these must be considered. Finally, speech-language delays must be ruled out although they are highly correlated with reading and writing delays.

Question 4 What do you consider the best practice for LD identification?

Answer 4 With some modification, the dual-deficit model proposed by Dombrowski, Kamphaus, and Reynolds (2004) is sufficiently inclusive to meet the diagnostic needs of the clinical and school psychology community. This model requires two elements:

1. A deficit in standardized achievement in reading, writing, or mathematics of somewhere from 80 to 85 (some flexibility in the achievement cut score may be necessary to account for local differences)
2. A documentation of academic impairment in reading, writing, and mathematics based upon classroom grades; teacher reports (if in kindergarten where grades are not assigned); CBM probes (if their technical adequacy has been documented); or RTI results in reading (if determining a reading disability)

The typical exclusionary features would still apply (e.g., intellectual disability, lack of educational exposure, medical issues, cultural aspects, visual impairment). As noted above, I also recommend the use of an IQ test that can be rapidly administered. This test should not be used in the context of the discrepancy model, but should be used to rule out intellectual disability and to get a sense of a child's cognitive capacity. I know that some researchers and clinicians may favor eschewing the use of IQ testing in the context of LD diagnosis, but the construct of IQ is one of the most researched in the field of psychology and has been linked with not only academic outcomes but also vocational and other life outcomes. Certainly, probability would generally suggest that a child with an IQ of 78 has a poorer prognosis than a child with an IQ of 108.

The above dual-deficit academic impairment model of LD is parsimonious, objective, and may be adopted by both the educational and psychiatric/clinical communities and incorporated into their respective diagnostic nosology (e.g., *DSM* and IDEIA). This definition will also permit consistency of diagnosis, enhance communication, and may reduce much of the idiosyncratic approaches to diagnosis undertaken both across and within states and between educational and clinical settings. Importantly, it will capture those children who might otherwise fall through the cracks. Ideally, the evaluation for LD would follow a rigorous monitoring system such as RTI without which there may be an increase in false positive identifications. The assessment of cognitive processes (e.g., phonological awareness, attention, executive function, memory) may also play a role in understanding how and why a child might be struggling. Any diagnostic decision using this model should always be filtered through clinical judgment.

Appendix

Appendix A States' Previous Discrepancy Models and Current Identification Models

This table contains identification methods as described on each state's department of education website or through email/phone communication. Each state department of education was contacted to allow them to submit information. This list is not intended to provide exact identification criteria, but to provide a general idea.

State	Previous Discrepancy Approach	Current Approach
Alabama (Alabama Administrative Code, 2009)	1.5 standard deviation between intelligence and achievement; tables available for various IQ tests using regression formula	Must show underachievement (districts may use discrepancy of at least 1 standard deviation or 16 points), lack of progress in response to intervention, and a pattern of strengths and weaknesses
Alaska D. Enoch (personal communication, September 4, 2009) (State of Alaska, 2009)	Each school district allowed to use approved system—choose own definition of severe discrepancy	Response to scientific, research-based instruction or pattern of strengths and weaknesses in performance, achievement, or both; not required to use discrepancy and may use other alternative research-based procedures for identification
Arizona (Arizona Administrative Code, 2003) (Arizona Department of Education, n.d.)	Severe discrepancy (no further description provided)	Severe discrepancy or failure to respond to scientifically-based interventions with an identified pattern of strengths and weaknesses

A. E. B. Taylor, *Diagnostic Assessment of Learning Disabilities in Childhood*, Contemporary Issues in Psychological Assessment, DOI 10.1007/978-1-4939-0335-1,

© Springer Science+Business Media New York 2014

Arkansas (Arkansas Department of Education, n.d.) (Arkansas Department of Education, 2008)	1.75 or more standard deviations at the 50 % or above level of probability as determined by regression analysis	Failure to respond to intervention as well as pattern of strengths and weaknesses. Must use intelligence test, achievement test, adaptive measure, and language screener. May use discrepancy with regression formula
California (California Administrative Code, n.d.)	Difference between IQ and achievement is greater than 1.5 x the standard deviation of computed differences of students taking the tests (allowing adjustment of 1 SEM), or team may prove discrepancy through deficit in psychological process(es)	Not required to use discrepancy and may use response to intervention with reference to federal code
Colorado C. Myers (personal communication, July 17, 2009)	Previously "Perceptual/Communicative Disability"—significant discrepancy using regression tables between estimated intellectual potential and actual level of performance with cognitive and/or language processing difficulties and significantly impaired achievement in one of the seven areas	In a response to intervention model, shows an academic deficit and does not respond to intervention in 1 of 8 areas, or severe discrepancy with disorder in a psychological process and significantly impaired achievement allowed until 08/14/2009
Connecticut (Connecticut State Department of Education, 1999) P. Murdica (personal communication, July 31, 2009)	After tiers of intervention and monitoring designed by Planning and Placement Team, 1.6 standard deviation discrepancy between intelligence and achievement with use of regression tables	Under development as of 07/31/2008—expected to be completed early 2009
Delaware (Delaware Administrative Code, 2007)	Discrepancy using correlation between tests and regression—if lower than value in table, meets criteria	Eliminated use of discrepancy; child fails to respond to scientific, research-based instruction plus processing strengths and weaknesses
Florida (Florida Administrative Code, 2009)	Disorder in one or more of the basic psychological processes and significant discrepancy based upon standard deviation criteria varying according to age grouping	Failure to respond to appropriate instruction as evidenced by a performance discrepancy, rate of progress, or educational need as measured by RTI data

Georgia (Official Code of Georgia, 2007)	20 standard score point discrepancy between achievement and intelligence and pattern of processing strengths and weaknesses	Supplementary instruction and progress monitoring prior to referral show lack of progress in response to intervention, deficit in basic psychological process(es), and pattern of strengths and weaknesses related to area of underachievement
Hawaii (Hawaii Administrative Code, 2002)	Severe discrepancy of 1.5 standard deviations between achievement and intelligence or evidence of discrepancy in one or more basic psychological process	Severe discrepancy between actual achievement and intellectual ability by a difference of at least one and one-half standard deviations
Idaho (Idaho State Department of Education, 2007)	A pattern of strengths and weaknesses and an achievement standard score 15 points below a regressed full-scale intelligence score	Resistance to general education intervention and discrepancy from peers' performance, or standard discrepancy approach
Illinois (Illinois Administrative Code, n.d.) D. Camacho (personal communication, September 1, 2009)	Must comply with federal regulations	No later than the 2010–2011 school year, must use a process to determine if student responds to scientific research based intervention; may also use discrepancy
Indiana (Indiana Administrative Code, 2008) G. Cochran (personal communication, November 5, 2009)	Pattern of strengths or weaknesses in performance or achievement or both	Insufficient progress to meet age or grade standards when using response to intervention or pattern of strengths or weaknesses in performance or achievement or both (may not use severe discrepancy in making this determination)
Iowa E.Neessen (personal communication, July 9, 2009)	Never used – (general school-wide response to intervention) problem-solving method for struggling students in general education. If moved to an evaluation, use multiple sources, which may include cognitive and academic assessments, to determine if child meets criteria for special education in general	Categorical designation Specific Learning Disability allowed, but must include: scientific and/or alternative research-based intervention as part of RTI, discrepancy between performance and accepted standards of academic performance, lack of sufficient progress to age- or grade-level standards or pattern of strengths and weaknesses in performance and/or achievement, and observation. If this process not followed, may only qualify as Eligible Individual

Kansas E. D. Lincoln (personal communication, July 22, 2009)	Severe discrepancy between achievement and ability with LEA's able to choose from a variety of indicators such as difference of 25 standard points or 1.75 standard deviations below mean among others	Use of response to scientific research-based intervention or discrepancy/pattern of strengths and weaknesses
Kentucky (Kentucky Administrative Code, 2007)	Information not provided	Insufficient progress to meet age or grade standards when using response to intervention or pattern of strengths or weaknesses in performance or achievement or both; must have received instruction with progress monitoring data showing lack of progress
Louisiana N. Hicks (personal communication, November 5, 2009)	Severe discrepancy between achievement and ability evidenced by at least one standard deviation between strongest and weakest academic area as shown by a deficit of more than 1- 11/2 standard deviations below mean (depending on grade) and strength of no more than 1- 11/2 standard deviations below mean (depending on grade)	If inadequate response to intervention then standardized achievement test to determine if child meets criteria in definition with evidence of pattern of strengths and low achievement demonstrated by achievement more than 1- 11/2 standard deviations below mean (depending on grade) and strength of no more than 1- 11/2 standard deviations below mean (depending on grade)
Maine (Maine Administrative Code, 2009) (Maine Administrative Code, 1999)	Student does not achieve commensurate with age and ability level and a severe discrepancy of 1.5 SDs between intelligence and achievement	May not require discrepancy and may allow use of RTI—must score 1.5 SDs below mean for age in one area of psychological processing or 1 SD below in two or more areas and in grades 4–12 must obtain cognitive standard score no lower than 1.5 SDs below mean along with preferral interventions showing lack of progress or RTI
Maryland (Maryland Administrative Code, n.d.) (Maryland State Department of Education, 2001)	Severe discrepancy between achievement and intellectual ability (chart provides ranges of intellectual ability with corresponding expected achievement range and discrepant achievement range)	May use RTI; pattern of strengths and weaknesses in performance, achievement or both that is relevant to LD; or alternative research-based procedures

Massachusetts L. Tarmy (personal communication, July 15, 2009)	Discrepancy between intelligence and achievement with each district defining magnitude and measurement of discrepancy	Process based on the student's response to scientific, research-based intervention OR exhibits a pattern of strengths and weaknesses in performance, achievement or both based on a discrepancy between intelligence and achievement
Michigan (Michigan Department of Education, 2009) (Michigan Administrative Code, 2004)	Severe discrepancy between achievement and intellectual ability (magnitude not stated)	Proposed: Does not make sufficient progress when using a process based on response to scientific research-based instruction; or exhibits a pattern of strengths or weaknesses in performance, achievement, or both relevant to SLD
Minnesota (Minnesota Administrative Rules, 2008) V. Weinberg (personal communication, July 15, 2009)	Information processing deficit and discrepancy of at least 1.75 standard deviations between intellectual ability and achievement	Lack of adequate progress in response to meet age or grade state-approved standards in a process based on response to scientific, research-based intervention (SRBI) OR pattern of strengths and weaknesses in performance, achievement, or both as well as disorder in one or more of the basic psychological processes. Also either discrepancy of at least 1.75 standard deviations between general intellectual ability and achievement OR inadequate rate of progress in SRBI
Mississippi D. Munday (personal communication, July 10, 2009)	Does not achieve commensurate with age or ability level and has severe discrepancy between achievement and intellectual ability of at least one standard deviation. Additional guidance provided for decision-making if IQ does not appear to be valid and/or reliable	Preferral requirement of data-based progress documentation ensuring appropriate instruction. First, consider process using response to scientific, research-based intervention then may use alternative research-based procedures or severe discrepancy between intelligence and achievement, operationalized as a difference of 1.5 standard deviations. Also an observation
Missouri (Missouri Department of Education, 2008) (Missouri Department of Education, 2007)	Current and former discrepancy: severe discrepancy between intellectual ability and achievement of at least 1.5 standard deviations plus additional data from observation, interview, records, etc. Must have pattern of cognitive and achievement strengths and weaknesses	Response to scientific, research-based intervention process or pattern of strengths or weaknesses/discrepancy; districts may choose either or various combinations

Montana (Montana Administrative Rules, 2007)	50% or higher probability of a two standard deviation discrepancy between general cognitive ability and achievement when adjusting for regression to the mean	Insufficient response to scientific research-based intervention or severe discrepancy
Nebraska C. McClain (personal communication, August 4, 2009)	Discrepancy between IQ and achievement of at least 20 standard score points, and academic standard score used must be below 84	If child does not achieve adequately for age or grade then may continue to use previous severe discrepancy criteria until full RTI transition (by 8/2012 for reading in grades k-12) , response to intervention process, or other scientific research-based intervention
Nevada (Nevada Administrative Code, 2009)	Information not provided	Process based on response to scientific research-based instruction; pattern of strengths and weaknesses in performance and/or achievement; if pattern of strength or weakness then determine if discrepancy between achievement and intellectual ability through use of a "statistically valid formula, as prescribed by the Department, which takes into account the age and level of ability of the pupil, the correlation between tests of ability and achievement, and the reliability of each test used"
New Hampshire (New Hampshire Administrative Code-proposed, 2009)	Information not provided	LEA must choose from one or more of the following criteria: discrepancy between intellectual skills and achievement, process that determines if child responds to scientific research-based intervention, or other alternative research-based procedures. Also failure to achieve adequately based on age or state standards when using a process based on response to intervention OR a pattern of strengths and weaknesses in performance, achievement, or both that is indicative of a learning disability
New Jersey (New Jersey Administrative Code, n.d.)	Information not provided	A severe discrepancy between current achievement and intellectual ability or may use a response to scientifically based interventions methodology. If using discrepancy, the district must use a statistical formula and criteria to determine

New Mexico B. Tennyson (personal communication, October 5, 2009)	Exclusive use of severe discrepancy using 1.5 standard deviations between intelligence and achievement	Response to intervention with SLD criteria met when there is dual discrepancy, meaning performance below grade-level peers and learning rate below grade-level peers
New York (New York State Education Department, n.d.) (New York State Education Department, 2004)	Student who exhibits a discrepancy of 50 % or more between expected and actual achievement must be deemed to have a learning disability	Student does not achieve adequately for age or standards and either does not make progress or exhibits a pattern of strengths and weaknesses in performance, achievement, or both relative to age, standards, or intellectual development; after July 2012 may not use discrepancy to identify reading disability for grades K-4
North Carolina S. A. Abernethy (personal communication, July 10, 2009)	Simple discrepancy of 15 points between general intelligence and achievement	Continued difficulties after at least two interventions implemented in regular education, discrepancy of at least 15 standard score points between general intelligence and achievement and exhibits characteristics of LD consistent with definition
North Dakota (North Dakota Department of Public Instruction, 2007) B. K. Oas (personal communication, July 15, 2009)	Discrepancy approach left up to districts	Failure to achieve adequately based on age or state standards when using a process based on response to intervention OR a pattern of strengths and weaknesses in performance, achievement, or both that is indicative of a learning disability (i.e., discrepancy model). Intervention team process is started as soon as student demonstrates difficulty and further evaluation if at least 2 or 3 interventions do not result in progress. Also observation
Ohio B. Murphy (personal communication, July 17, 2009) (Ohio Administrative Code, 2009)	Severe discrepancy between achievement and ability and based on a specified formula (Subtract mean of intelligence score from obtained score and divide by standard deviation; repeat for achievement scores and then subtract number obtained from achievement from number obtained from intelligence. If equal to two or greater, than discrepancy.). Plus additional supporting data. No specific formula required after 2002	Must have referral process using scientific, research-based instruction with data showing discrepancy between expected and actual performance or lack of progress. With written approval a district may use any alternative research-based assessment procedure to determine if there is a pattern of strengths and weaknesses in performance, achievement, or both

Oklahoma (Oklahoma State Department of Education, 2007)	Information not provided	Does not achieve adequately for the child's age or to meet State approved grade-level standards and does not make sufficient progress to meet age or grade-level standards when using a process based on the child's response to scientific, research-based intervention or a severe discrepancy of 1.5 standard deviations between achievement and intellectual ability
Oregon (Oregon Administrative Rules, 2008)	Information not provided	Does not make sufficient progress to meet age or Oregon grade-level standards based on the student's response to scientific, research-based intervention OR exhibits a pattern of strengths and weaknesses in classroom performance, academic achievement, or both, relative to age, grade-level standards, or intellectual development
Pennsylvania (Pennsylvania Administrative Code, 2008)	Information not provided	Process based on the child's response to scientific, research-based intervention or process that examines whether a child exhibits a pattern of strengths and weaknesses, relative to intellectual ability as defined by a severe discrepancy between intellectual ability and achievement, or relative to age or grade
Rhode Island (Rhode Island Department of Education, 2008)	Information not provided	May use severe discrepancy (achievement gap and pattern of strengths and weaknesses) until August 31, 2010 for elementary and August 31, 2011 for middle and high schools and must use response to intervention process (achievement gap and educational process) by September 1, 2010 for elementary and September 1, 2011 for middle and high schools
South Carolina B. Davis (personal communication, August 26,2009) (South Carolina Administrative Code, 2004)	Significant discrepancy between achievement and ability with each LEA submitting its definition of severe discrepancy for approval	Child does not make sufficient progress when using a process based on response to scientific, research-based instruction or exhibits a pattern of strengths or weaknesses in performance, achievement, or both

South Dakota (South Dakota Administrative Rules, 2007)	Information not provided	Does not make sufficient progress to meet age or grade-level standards when using a process based on the child's response to scientific, research-based intervention; OR a pattern of strengths and weaknesses in performance, achievement, or both, relative to age, state-approved grade-level standards, or intellectual development as measured by a discrepancy of 1.5 standard deviations between achievement and ability considering regression (table provided)
Tennessee (Tennessee State Department of Education, 2008)	Information not provided	May use state-approved RTI approach (with comprehensive evaluation if other results are inconclusive) or IQ/achievement discrepancy method using 1.5 standard deviation difference using a regression table
Texas P. Carrasquillo (personal communication, September 24, 2009)	Severe discrepancy greater than one standard deviation between ability and achievement	Must determine appropriate instruction through repeated assessments, demonstrate student does not achieve adequately for age or grade-level standards, and does not make progress as indicated through a response-to-intervention process OR exhibits a pattern of strengths and weaknesses in cognitive functioning
Utah J. Gibbs (personal communication, August 26, 2009) (Utah State Office of Education, 2008) (Utah State Board of Education, 2007)	Discrepancy approach using complex formula to account for correlation between tests, regression, and test unreliability—use Estimator online to determine if severe discrepancy	Choose from response to scientific, research-based intervention, severe discrepancy between achievement and ability, or a combination of RTI and discrepancy as used previously
Vermont (Vermont Administrative Code, 2007)	Information not provided	Discrepancy model using 1.5 standard deviation discrepancy between ability and performance or subject to using procedures to correct for regression (iii), a problem solving, response to instruction model that determines if the student responds to scientific, research-based instruction as a part of the evaluation

Virginia (Virginia Administrative Code, 2009)	Information not provided	Does not achieve adequately for age or grade standards and does not make sufficient progress to meet age or grade standards when using a process based on response to intervention or exhibits a pattern of strengths or weaknesses in performance, achievement, or both relative to age, grade standards, or intellectual development; does not require use of severe discrepancy
Washington H. Unger (personal communication, December 9, 2009) (Washington Administrative Code, 2007)	Severe discrepancy between intellectual ability and achievement using discrepancy tables taking correlation and regression into account	Each school district shall develop procedures for the identification of students with specific learning disabilities which may include the use of: a severe discrepancy between intellectual ability and achievement (using discrepancy tables taking correlation and regression into account); a process based on the student's response to scientific, research-based intervention; or a combination of both within a school district, provided that the evaluation process used is the same for all students within the selected grades or buildings within the school district and is in accordance with district procedures
West Virginia L. Palenchar (personal communication, December 10, 2009) (West Virginia Department of Education, 2007)	Severe discrepancy of at least 1.75 standard deviations between ability and achievement using a regression formula, with general intellectual functioning at or above 1 standard deviation below the mean	Low academic performance compared to standard & progress monitoring data showing growth rate substantially below peers (RTI) or pattern of strengths and weaknesses in performance, achievement, or both relative to age, grade standards, or intellectual development (may use severe discrepancy model requiring intellectual functioning at or above 1 SD below mean with discrepancy defined as minimum of 1.75 standard deviations difference, taking regression and 1.0 standard error measurement into account—for elementary until June 30, 2009, middle June 30, 2010, high school June 30, 2011

Wisconsin V. A. Ashby (personal communication, September 2, 2009) (Wisconsin State Administrative Code, 2001)	Severely delayed achievement, significant discrepancy equal to or greater than 1.75 standard errors of the estimate below expected achievement, using a standard regression procedure that accounts for the correlation between ability and achievement measures and information processing deficit linked to academic delay	Proposed rule: does not achieve adequately based on insufficient progress in process based on scientific, research-based intervention, or pattern of strengths and weaknesses in performance, achievement or both, significant discrepancy between academic achievement and intellectual ability based on 1.75 standard errors of the estimate below expected achievement using regression procedure accounting for correlation between tests until July 30, 2012
Wyoming P. Brown-Clark (personal communication, August 25, 2009) (Wyoming Administrative Code, n.d.)	Does not achieve adequately for age or grade-level standards using Wyoming Severe Discrepancy Formula—difference greater than or equal to 1.5 standard deviations or 22 points between expected achievement level and actual achievement level) using a table to determine expected achievement level that accounts for correlation between achievement and intelligence measures as well as regression to the mean	Does not achieve adequately for age or grade-level standards using lack of sufficient progress when using a process based on response to scientific, research-based intervention or the Wyoming Severe Discrepancy Formula

Appendix B State Response to Intervention Models

This table contains overviews of states' response to intervention models as described on each state's department of education website or through email/phone communication. Each state department of education was contacted to allow them to submit information. This list is not intended to provide exhaustive RTI model information, but to provide a general idea.

State	Tier I	Tier II	Tier III	Other
Alabama (Alabama Department of Education, 2009)	Research-based core instruction (80 %)	Targeted interventions (15 %)	Intensive interventions (5 %)	
Alaska D. Enoch (personal communication, September 4, 2009) (Alaska Department of Education and Early Development, 2007)	Universal core curriculum (80 %)	Strategic targeted group/individual interventions (15 %)	Intensive individual interventions (5 %)	RTI guidance still in draft format
Arizona (Arizona Department of Education, 2009)	Universal education	Targeted interventions (20–30 %)	Intensive intervention (small percentage of Tier II students)	
Arkansas (Arkansas Department of Education, 2007)				Model consisting of 4 levels of evaluation for identifying dyslexia
California (California Department of Education, 2009)	Benchmark interventions (80–90 %)	Targeted group interventions	Intensive individual interventions (1–5 %)	Response to Instruction and Intervention (RTI2)
Colorado C. Myers (personal communication, July 17, 2009)	Universal core curriculum (80–90 %)	Targeted level for at-risk students with problem-solving team involvement (5–15 %)	Intensive level with one-on-one or small group instruction and possible diagnostic assessment (1–5 %)	

Connecticut (State Department of Connecticut, 2008)	Core curriculum (80 %)	Small group focused interventions for 8–20 weeks	Greater intensity and individualization for 8–20 weeks	Scientific Research-Based Intervention (SRBI)
Delaware (Delaware Department of Education, 2008)	All students receive core class instruction (80 %)	Group and individual interventions after insufficient progress in tier 1 (15 %)	Sustained intensive intervention and possible special education identification (5 %)	
Florida (Florida Department of Education, 2008)	Core curriculum and universal interventions (~80 %)	Strategic/targeted group interventions (~15 %)	Comprehensive and intensive interventions (~5 %)	
Georgia (Georgia Department of Education, 2008)	Standards-based classroom learning/ Universal intervention	Needs-based learning/ smaller groups	Student support team driven learning/ intensive intervention	Tier IV: Specially designed learning/Special education, alternative instruction, or targeted placement (Georgia Pyramid of Interventions)
Hawaii (Hawaii Department of Education, 2008)				General Comprehensive Student Support System (CSSS) with no specific reference to RTI
Idaho				
(Idaho State Department of Education, 2009)	Core curriculum (80 %)	Additional instruction (15 %)	Intensified instruction (5 %)	
Illinois (Illinois State Board of Education, 2008) D. Camacho (personal communication, September 1, 2009)				General guidance with districts developing their own plans
Indiana (Indiana Department of Education, 2009)	Core curriculum and instruction	Targeted supplemental supports	Intense individual support	

Iowa E.Neessen (personal communication, July 14, 2009)				Encourage response to intervention process in general education called Instructional Decision Making but not mandated. RTI only required as part of comprehensive evaluation
Kansas (Kansas State Department of Education, 2009)				Multi-Tier System of Supports (MTSS)—provide resources and guidance but schools choose exact model
Kentucky (Kentucky Department of Education, 2009)	Quality academic and behavior instruction in the classroom based on state curriculum framework: (80%)	Quality academic and behavior instruction in the classroom based on state curriculum framework in addition to core instruction (15%)	Individualized intensive academic or behavior interventions (5%)	Kentucky System of Interventions (KSI)
Louisiana N. Hicks (personal communication, November 5, 2009)				Each LEA must submit plan including high quality research based instruction in general education, universal screening, benchmarks/progress monitoring, multi-tiered interventions, and shared ownership of all students

Maine (Maine Parent Federation, Inc., 2009)	Qualified instruction for all students (80–90 %)	Additional interventions and supports for students who struggle to meet benchmarks (5–10 %)	More intense instructional support in areas of need for students who continue to struggle (1–5 %)	
Maryland (Maryland State Department of Education, 2008)	High quality research-based classroom instruction	Supplemental targeted interventions in small group or individual in addition to core instruction	Specifically-designed individualized interventions with more intense frequency and duration	
Massachusetts L. Tarmy (personal communication, July 15, 2009)	General education	Supplemental services	Intensive intervention	
Michigan (Michigan Department of Education, 2009)				Some guidance regarding determining significant deficits after instruction
Minnesota V. Weinberg (personal communication, July 15, 2009)				General guidance
Mississippi D. Munday (personal communication, July 10, 2009)	Quality instruction for all (100 %)	Focused supplemental instruction (15 %)	More intensive instruction specifically designed to meet individual needs (5 %)	
Missouri (Missouri Department of Education, 2008)				Broad view of RTI as general education process at beginning of determination or narrow view to only identify SLD at end of determination; general guidance provided

Montana (Montana Office of Public Instruction, 2009)	ALL: Core classroom instruction (80–90 %)	SOME: Strategic targeted instruction (5–10 %)	FEW: Intensive targeted intervention (1–8 %)	
Nebraska C. McClain (personal communication, August 4, 2009)				In early stages of development. Nebraska RTI Consortium providing training statewide
Nevada (Nevada Department of Education, 2007)				Schools allowed to use RTI for students not suspected of disability, but must provide intervention plan for parents
New Hampshire (New Hampshire Department of Education, 2009)				Provides guidance and sample frameworks
New Jersey				Information not provided. No website available
New Mexico B. Tennyson (personal communication, October 5, 2009)	High-quality, whole–group, research-based general instruction delivered by qualified personnel, combined with the general screening process. Intervention is a general education function to include all students	Scientific, research-based intervention. Targeted at small-group or individual instruction in deficit areas. Intervention still the function of general education teacher, but a Student Assistant Team (SAT) would assist as a resource and would also assist in gathering instructional strategies	Individualized supports and IEP process begins after multi-disciplinary evaluation. Instruction and intervention through special education and related services	

New York (Buffalo State University of New York, n.d.)	Core instruction or primary intervention intended for all students in general education classroom	Secondary intervention for 10–15% of students who are not making adequate progress with core instruction at Tier 1	Tertiary intervention intended for 1–5% of students who are not responding to instruction at Tiers 1 and 2	
North Carolina S. A. Abernethy (personal communication, July 10, 2009)	Implement scientific research-based intervention plus vision and hearing screening	Modify Tier 1 or new intervention	Modify Tier II or new intervention plus speech-language screening, developmental history form, and observation	Tier IV: Modify Tier III or refer for evaluation. Based on pyramid with 80% at core, 15% at strategic, and 5% at intensive
North Dakota (North Dakota Department of Public Instruction, 2007) B. K. Oas (personal communication, July 15, 2009)				Optional process. Districts choose decision points and criteria
Ohio B. Murphy (personal communication, July 17, 2009)				General guidance provided
Oklahoma (Oklahoma State Department of Education, 2007)	Intervention in/with general education classroom/resources; at least 4–6 weeks	Intervention in/with general education classroom/resources; at least 9–12 weeks	Likely special education resources; no more than 4 weeks	
Oregon (Oregon Department of Education, 2009)				Examples from participating school districts
Pennsylvania (Pennsylvania Department of Education, 2009)	Standards-aligned instruction for all students	Strategic interventions for some students	Intensive interventions for some students	Response to Intervention and Instruction (RtII) is part of Pennsylvania's Standards Aligned System (SAS)

Rhode Island (Rhode Island Department of Education, n.d.)				Model guidance for general intervention process; final guidelines not yet released for determining if SLD
South Carolina B. Davis (personal communication, August 26, 2009)				Currently developing implementation guidelines to help LEAs operationalize
South Dakota (South Dakota Department of Education, 2007)	Core curriculum with screening three times per year, additional instructional strategies (80–85 %)	Core curriculum with progress monitoring twice per month, strategic interventions (for 10–15 %)	Core or core replacement curriculum, intensive interventions (5 %)	Tier IIIB: Special Education
Tennessee (Tennessee State Department of Education, 2009)	Effective instruction in general education classroom for all students	Students scoring 10 % or below on universal screening receive small group instruction for at least 30 min per day	Students who have not made adequate progress in Tier 2 after 8 weeks receive 60 min of small group, intensive instruction for at least 6 weeks	Tier 4: Special education (Hardeman County) LEAs must submit application to state describing RTI approach This is an example from Hardeman County
Texas P. Carrasquillo (personal communication, September 24, 2009)				No specific model—may or may not be used. Refer to National Association of State Directors of Special Education IDEA partnership for guidance

Utah J. Gibbs (personal communication, August 26, 2009) (Utah State Office of Education, 2008)	Core classroom instruction for all	Supplemental targeted instruction for 10–15 % of students	Intense targeted intervention for most at-risk readers which is 3–5 % of students, smaller group, 60 min daily with specialist	
Vermont (Vermont Administrative Code, 2007)				School must submit specific plan to state department
Virginia (Virginia Department of Education, 2007)				Provide guidance with several pilot schools
Washington (Washington Administrative Code, 2007) (Washington Office of Superintendent of Public Instruction, 2006)				General guidance for implementation
West Virginia (West Virginia Department of Education, 2006)	Core classroom reading instruction (at least 80 %)	Specialized small group reading instruction 30 min daily (about 15 %)	Two 30 minute reading intervention sessions daily in group of less than 3 students (about 5 %)	Pilot process implemented in 2005–2006 with plan for phasing from elementary to middle and high over time
Wisconsin (Wisconsin Department of Education, 2009)				General guiding framework
Wyoming (Wyoming Department of Education, 2011)	Classroom or universal level (80–85 %)	Strategic or supplemental level	Intensive level	

Appendix C Links to Useful Websites

Links to RTI/CBM websites

http://www.interventioncentral.org/ Intervention Central
Provides interventions for a variety of academic areas as well as CBM materials
http://www.rtinetwork.org RTI Action Network
Information describing RTI and its implementation
http://www.jimwrightonline.com/php/rti/rti_wire.php RTI Wire
A collection of RTI resources available online
https://dibels.uoregon.edu/DIBELS
Links to RTI information as well as free sample progress monitoring materials

Links to Discrepancy websites:
http://estimator.srlonline.org/Utah Estimator
Information regarding the online discrepancy calculator, including sample reports.
http://state.rti4success.org National Center on Response to Intervention: RTI State Database
Information regarding information and regulations available for each state for RTI and current SLD identification

Best practices:
http://www.cldinternational.org Council for Learning Disabilities
Links and information regarding various aspects of learning disabilities.
http://www.cec.sped.org Council for Exceptional Children
A variety of general special education information, including learning disabilities resources.
http://www.nrcld.org National Research Center on Learning Disabilities
Extensive collection of research and other information about learning disabilities.
http://www.LDOnLine.org LD OnLine
A variety of information regarding learning disabilities.

Comorbidity:
http://www.asha.org American Speech-Language-Hearing Association
Variety of resources about communication and communication disorders.
http://www.aamr.org American Association on Intellectual and Developmental Disabilities
(previously American Association of Mental Retardation)
Information and resources about intellectual disability/mental retardation.
http://www.chadd.org Children and Adults with Attention Deficit Disorder
ADHD information and resources.
http://www.nichd.nih.gov/National Institute of Child Health and Human Development
Information and resources about multiple physical and mental disabilities affecting

children and adolescents.

http://www.navh.org National Association for Visually Handicapped

Information regarding eyes, vision, and medical conditions related to eyes and vision.

Low Achievement:

http://www.nifl.gov National Institute for Literacy

Information regarding reading research, including links to *Put Reading First*

http://www.ada.gov Office of the American's with Disabilities Act

Information about the American's with Disabilities Act.

Introduction:

http://www.idea.ed.gov Building the Legacy: IDEA 2004

Individuals with Disabilities Education Act information from the U.S. Department of Education

http://www.ldonline.org/about/partners/njcld National Joint Committee on Learning Disabilities

Information about and resources provided by the National Joint Committee on Learning Disabilities

http://www.psychiatry.org/practice/DSM American Psychiatric Association: Diagnostic and Statistical Manual

General information regarding the DSM and the DSM-IV TR.

http://www.dsm5.org American Psychiatric Association: DSM-5 Development.

Information about the development process and implementation of the DSM-5.

References

Aaron, P. G., Joshi, M. R., Gooden, R., & Bentum, K. E. (2008). Diagnosis and treatment of reading disabilities based on the component model of reading. *Journal of Learning Disabilities, 41*, 67–84.

Alabama Administrative Code Title 16, Chapter 39 § 290-8-9.3(10) (pp. 514–518) (2009). https://docs.alsde.edu/documents/65/-0%20AAC%20Chapter%20290%208%209%20(5-14-2009).pdf. Accessed 12 Dec 2009.

Alabama Department of Education. (2009). Response to instruction (RtI). https://docs.alsde.edu/documents/54/response_to_instruction_alabama%20core%20support%20for%20all%20students.pdf. Accessed 31 July 2012.

Alaska Department of Education and Early Development. (2007). Response to instruction part II: Linking the data to instruction. http://www.eed.state.ak.us/nclb/Response/Response%20to%20InstructionPart2.ppt. Accessed 4 Sept 2009.

Alaska Department of Education and Early Development. (2009). State of Alaska special education handbook. http://www.eed.state.ak.us/tls/sped/Handbook.html. Accessed 4 Sept 2009.

Alexander, D., Gray, D. B., & Lyon, G. R. (1993). Conclusions and future directions. In G. R. Lyon, D. B. Gray, & J. F. Kavanagh (Eds.), *Better understanding learning disabilities: New views from research and their implications for education and public policies* (pp. 343–350). Baltimore: Paul H. Brookes.

Al Otaiba, S., & Fuchs, D. (2002). Characteristics of children who are unresponsive to early literacy intervention. *Remedial and Special Education, 23*, 300–316.

American Association on Mental Retardation Ad Hoc Committee on Terminology and Classification. (2002). *Mental retardation: Definition, classification, and systems of supports* (10th ed.). Washington, D.C.: American Association on Mental Retardation.

American Psychiatric Association. (2013). *Diagnostic and statistical manual of mental disorders* (5th ed.). Washington, D.C.: American Psychiatric Association.

American Psychiatric Association (2012 May 1). DSM-5 development: Specific learning disabilities. http://www.dsm5.org/ProposedRevision/Pages/proposedrevision.aspx?rid=429. Accessed 12 Aug 2012.

American Psychiatric Association. (2000). *Diagnostic and statistical manual of mental disorders* (4th ed., text revision). Washington, D.C.: American Psychiatric Association.

American Speech-Language-Hearing Association. (1993). *Definitions of Communication Disorders and Variations* [Relevant Paper]. Available from http://www.asha.org/policy.

Angold, A., Costello, E. J., & Erkanli, A. (1999). Comorbidity. *Journal of Child Psychology and Psychiatry, 40*, 57–87.

Arizona Administrative Code Title 7, Chapter 2 §R7–2-401E6d (p. 20). (2003). http://www.ade.state.az.us/ess/resources/lawsRegs/7-02.pdf. Accessed 13 Dec 2009.

Arizona Department of Education. (2009 Nov 20). *Arizona RTI: Academic and behavioral system of support*. http://www.azed.gov/azrti/. Accessed 13 Dec 2009.

A. E. B. Taylor, *Diagnostic Assessment of Learning Disabilities in Childhood*, Contemporary Issues in Psychological Assessment, DOI 10.1007/978-1-4939-0335-1,

© Springer Science+Business Media New York 2014

Arizona Department of Education. (n.d.). *Evaluation and eligibility policy and procedures checklist*. http://www.ade.state.az.us/Guidelines/Federal/EX-08. Accessed 13 Dec 2009.

Arkansas Department of Education. (2007). *Resource guide for specific learning disabilities (SLD)/ dyslexia*. http://arksped.k12.ar.us/documents/stateprogramdevelopment/DyslexiaGuideApril30.pdf. Accessed 13 Dec 2009.

Arkansas Department of Education. (2008). *Specific learning disability* http://arksped.k12.ar.us/rules_regs_08/3.%20SPED%20ELIGIBILITY%20CRITERIA%20AND%20PROGRAM%20GUIDELINES%20FOR%20CHILDREN/PART%20I%20ELIGIBILITY%20CRITERIA%20AGES%205-21/I.%20SPECIFIC%20LEARNING%20DISABILITY.pdf. Accessed 13 Dec 2009.

Arkansas Department of Education. (n.d.). *SLD eligibility: Method for determining discrepancy analysis*. http://arksped.k12.ar.us/documents/policy/rulesandregulations/D1.pdf. Accessed 13 Dec 2009.

Baker, J.A., Kamphaus, R.W., Horne, A.M., & Winsor, A.P. (2006). Evidence for population-based perspectives on children's behavioral adjustment and needs for service delivery in schools. *School Psychology Review*, *35*, 31–46.

Bateman, B. D. (1965). An educational view of a diagnostic approach to learning disabilities. In J. Hellmuth (Ed.), *Learning disorders* (Vol. 1, pp. 219–239). Seattle: Special Child Publications.

Bird, H. R. (1999). The assessment of functional impairment. In D. Shafer, et al., C. Lucas (Eds.), *Diagnostic assessment of child and adolescent psychopathology* (pp. 209–229). New York: Guilford.

Berninger, V. W., Abbott, R. D., Vermeulen, K., Ogier, S., Brooksher, R., Zook, D., & Lemos, Z. (2002). Comparison of faster and slower responders to early intervention in reading: Differentiating features of their language profiles. *Learning Disability Quarterly*, *25*, 59–76.

Blashfield, R. K. (1998). Diagnostic models and systems. In A. S. Bellack, M. Hersen, & C. R. Reynolds (Eds)., *Comprehensive clinical psychology: (Vol. 4) Assessment* (pp. 57–80). New York: Elsevier Science.

Boden, C. & Kirby, J. R. (1995). Successive processing, phonological coding and the remediation of reading. *Journal of Cognitive Education*, *4*, 19–31.

Bracken, B. A., & McCallum, R. S. (1998). *Universal Nonverbal Intelligence Test*. Itasca: Riverside.

Bradley, R., Danielson, R. L., & Hallahan, D. P. (2002). *Identification of learning disabilities: Research to practice*. Mahwah: Erlbaum.

Brody, L. E., & Mills, C. J. (1997). Gifted children with learning disabilities: A review of the issues. *Journal of Learning Disabilities*, *30*, 282–296.

Brueggemann, A. E., Kamphaus, R. W., & Dombrowski, S.C. (2008). An impairment model of learning disability. *Professional Psychology: Research and Practice*, *39*, 424–430.

Buffalo State University of New York. (n.d.). *New York state response to intervention technical assistance center*. http://www.nysrti.org/Accessed 13 Dec 2009.

Burns, M. K., & Senesac, B. V. (2005). Comparison of dual discrepancy criteria to assess response to intervention. *Journal of School Psychology*, *43*, 393–406.

California Administrative Code Title I, Part 30 § 56337 (n.d.) http://www3.scoe.net/speced/laws_search/searchDetailsLaws.cfm?id=256&keywords=learning%20dis. Accessed 13 Dec 2009.

California Department of Education. (2009). Determining specific learning disability eligibility using response to instruction and intervention (RTI^2). http://www.cde.ca.gov/sp/sr/documents/sldeligibilityrti2.doc. Accessed 13 Dec 2009.

Carlson, J., & Das, J. P. (1997). A process approach to remediating word decoding deficiencies in Chapter 1 children. *Learning Disabilities Quarterly*, 20, 93–102.

Carroll, S. (1998). Slow learners in the regular classroom: A handout for teachers. In A. S. Canter & S. A. Carroll (Eds.), *Helping children at home and school: Handouts from your school psychologist* (pp. 205–206). Bethesda: The National Association of School Psychologists.

Carrow Woolfolk, E. (1995). *Oral and written language scales: Listening comprehension and oral expression*. Circle Pines: American Guidance Service, Inc.

Carrow Woolfolk, E. (1996). *Oral and written language scales: Written expression*. Circle Pines: American Guidance Service, Inc.

Case, L. P., Speece, D. L., & Molloy, D. E. (2003). The validity of a response-to-instruction paradigm to identify reading disabilities: A longitudinal analysis of individual differences and contextual factors. *School Psychology Review, 32*, 557–582.

Ceci, S. J. (2000). So near and yet so far: Lingering questions about the use of measures of general intelligence for college admission and employment screening. *Psychology, Public Policy, and Law, 6*, 233–252.

Connecticut State Department of Education. (1999) *Draft guidelines for identifying children with learning disabilities*. http://www.sde.ct.gov/sde/lib/sde/PDF/DEPS/Special/LDGuide_1999.pdf. Accessed 13 Dec 2009.

Connecticut State Department of Education. (2008). *Using scientific research-based interventions: Improving education for all students: Connecticut's framework for RTI*. http://www.sde.ct.gov/sde/lib/sde/pdf/Pressroom/RTI_Executive_Summary.pdf. Accessed 13 Dec 2009.

Conners, C. K., & MHS staff. (2000). Conners' Continuous Performance Test II. North Tonawanda: Multi-Health Systems, Inc.

Connolly, A. J. (2007). *Keymath-3 Diagnostic Assessment*. Minneapolis: Pearson.

Cronbach, L. J. (1975). Beyond the two disciplines of scientific psychology. *American Psychologist, 30*, 116–127.

Dana, J., & Dawes, R. (2007). Comment on Fiorello et al. "Interpreting intelligence test results for children with disabilities: Is global intelligence relevant?" *Applied Neuropsychology, 14*, 21–25.

Das, J. P. (2002). A better look at intelligence. *Current Directions in Psychology, 11*, 28–32.

Das, J. P., Kirby, J. R., & Jarman, R. (1979). *Simultaneous and successive cognitive processes*. New York: Allyn & Bacon.

Das, J. P., Mishra, R. K., & Pool, J. E. (1995). An experiment on cognitive remediation or word-reading difficulty. *Journal of Learning Disabilities, 28*, 66–79.

Das, J. P., Parrila, R. K., & Papadopoulos, T. C. (2000). Cognitive education and reading disability. In A. Kozulin & Y. Rand (Eds.), *Experience of mediated learning* (pp. 276–291). Amsterdam: Pergamon.

Dean, V. J., & Burns, M. K. (2002). Inclusion of intrinsic processing difficulties in LD diagnostic models: A critical review. *Learning Disability Quarterly, 25*, 170–176.

Dehn, M. J. (2006). *Essentials of processing assessment*. Hoboken: Wiley.

Delaware Administrative Code Title 14 § 925.6.1 & § 925.9.0 (2007). http://regulations.delaware.gov/AdminCode/title14/900/925.shtml#TopOfPage. Accessed 13 Dec 2009.

Delaware Department of Education. (2008). *Delaware response to intervention*. http://www.doe.k12.de.us/infosuites/staff/profdev/rti_files/corrected%20rti%20desk%20ref.pdf. Accessed 13 Dec 2009.

Delis, D. C., Kaplan, E., & Kramer, J. H. (2001). *Delis-Kaplan Executive Function System*. San Antonio: The Psychological Corporation.

Delis, D. C., Kramer, J. H., Kaplan, E., Ober, B. A., & Fridlund, A. J. (1994). *California Verbal Learning Test, Children's Version*. San Antonio: The Psychological Corporation.

Deno, S. L., Fuchs, L. S., Marston, D., & Shin, J. (2001). Using curriculum-based measurement to establish growth standards for students with learning disabilities. *School Psychology Review, 30*, 507–524.

Dombrowski, S.C., Kamphaus, R. W., & Reynolds, C. R. (2004). After the demise of the discrepancy: Proposed learning disability diagnostic criteria. *Professional Psychology: Research and Practice, 35*, 364–372.

Dunn, L. M., & Dunn, D. M. (2007). *Peabody Picture Vocabulary Test* (4th ed.). Bloomington: Pearson.

Elliott, C. D. (2007). *Differential ability scales* (2nd ed.). San Antonio: PsychCorp.

Erin, J. N., & Koenig, A. J. (1997). The student with a visual disability and a learning disability. *Journal of Learning Disabilities, 30*, 309–320.

Fabiano, G. A., Pelham, W. E., Waschbusch, D. A., Gnagy, E. M., Lahey, B. B., Chronis, A. M., et al. (2006). A practical measure of impairment: Psychometric properties of the impairment rating scale in samples of children with attention deficit hyperactivity disorder and two school-based samples. *Journal of Clinical Child and Adolescent Psychology, 35*, 369–385.

Fabiano, G. A., & Pelham, W. E. (2009). Impairment in children. In S. Goldstein & J. Naglieri (Eds.), *Assessment of impairment: From theory to practice*. New York: Springer.

Fagan, J. R. (2000). A theory of intelligence as processing: Implications for society. *Psychology, Public Policy, and Law*, *6*, 168–179.

Federal Register 34CFR Parts 300 and 301 August 14, 2006, Vol 71 No 156

Fiorello, A. F., Hale, J. B., & Snyder, L. E. (2006). Cognitive hypothesis testing and response to intervention for children with reading problems. *Psychology in the Schools*, *43*, 835–853.

Flanagan D. P., Ortiz, S. O., & Alfonso, V. C. (2008). Response to intervention (RTI) and cognitive testing approaches provide different but complementary data sources that inform SLD identification. *Communiqué*, *36*, 16–17.

Flanagan, D. P., Ortiz, S. O., Alfonso, V. C., & Dynda, A. M. (2006). Integration of response to intervention and norm-referenced tests in learning disability identification: Learning from the tower of Babel. *Psychology in the Schools*, *43*, 807–825.

Fletcher, J. M., Denton, C., & Francis, D. J. (2005). Validity of alternative approaches for the identification of learning disabilities: Operationalizing unexpected underachievement. *Journal of Learning Disabilities*, *38*, 545–552.

Fletcher, J. M., Francis, D. J., Morris, R. D., & Lyon, G. R. (2005). Evidence-based assessment of learning disabilities in children and adolescents. *Journal of Clinical Child and Adolescent Psychology*, *34*, 506–522.

Fletcher, J. M., Lyon G. R., Fuchs, L. S., & Barnes, M. A. (2007). *Learning disabilities: From identification to intervention*. New York: Guilford.

Fletcher, J. M., Lyon G. R., Fuchs, L. S., Barnes, M. A., & Vaughn, S. (n.d.). Comments on proposed DSM5 criteria for learning disabilities. http://www.texasldcenter.org/research/files/dsm5-fletcheretal.pdf. Accessed 12 Aug 2009.

Florida Administrative Code Title XLVIII, Chapter 6A § 6.03018 (pp. 234–235; 321–322) (2009). http://www.fldoe.org/ese/pdf/1b-stats.pdf. Accessed 13 Dec 2009.

Florida Department of Education. (2008). *Statewide response to instruction/intervention (RTI) implementation manual*. http://www.florida-rti.org/RtI.pdf. Accessed 13 Dec 2009.

Francis, D. J., Fletcher, J. M., Stuebing, K. K., Lyon, G. R., Shaywitz, B. A., & Shaywitz, S. E. (2005). Psychometric approaches to the identification of LD: IQ and achievement scores are not sufficient. *Journal of Learning Disabilities*, *38*, 98–108.

Franzen, R. (1920). The accomplishment quotient: A school mark in terms of individual capacity. *Teachers College Record*, *21*, 432–440.

Fuchs, D., Fuchs, L. S., & Compton, D. (2004). Identifying reading disabilities by responsiveness-to-instruction: Specifying measures and criteria. *Learning Disability Quarterly*, *27*, 216–227.

Fuchs, D., Hale, J. B., & Kearns, D. M. (2011). On the importance of a cognitive processing perspective: An introduction. *Journal of Learning Disabilities*, *44*, 99–104.

Fuchs, D., & Young, C. L. (2006). On the irrelevance of intelligence in predicting responsiveness to reading instruction. *Exceptional Children*, *73*, 8–30.

Fuchs, L. S. (2003). Assessing intervention responsiveness: Conceptual and technical issues. *Learning Disabilities Research & Practice*, *18*, 172–186.

Fuchs, L. S., Compton, D. L., Fuchs, D., Paulsen, K., Bryant, J. D., & Hamlett, C. L. (2005). The prevention, identification, and cognitive determinants of math difficulty. *Journal of Educational Psychology*, *97*, 493–513.

Fuchs, L. S., & Fuchs, D. (1998). Treatment validity: A unifying concept for reconceptualizing the identification of learning disabilities. *Learning Disabilities Research & Practice*, *13*, 204–219.

Fuchs, L. S., & Vaughn, S. (2012). Responsiveness to intervention: A decade later. *Journal of Learning Disabilities*, *45*, 195–203.

Fuchs, L. S., Fuchs, D., & Speece, D. L. (2002). Treatment validity as a unifying construct for identifying learning disabilities. *Learning Disability Quarterly*, *25*, 33–45.

Georgia Department of Education. (2008). *Special education rules implementation manual*. http://www.doe.k12.ga.us/DMGetDocument.aspx/Ch_7_IM_Spec_Ed_Elig_REq.pdf?p=6CC6799F8C1371F6BCC5BFB575B75948E5F19BF5D253351EDF800E5355DC38C3&Type=D. Accessed 13 Dec 2009.

Gioia, G. A., Isquith, P. K., Guy, S. C., & Kenworth, L. (2000). *Behavior rating inventory of executive function*. Odessa: Psychological Assessment Resources, Inc.

Glutting, J., Adams, W., & Sheslow, D. (2000). *Wide range intelligence test*. Wilmington: Wide Range, Inc.

Goldstein, S., & Naglieri, J. A. (2009). *Autism spectrum rating scale*. Toronto: Multi Health Systems.

Good, R. H., Kaminski, R. A., Moats, L. C., Laimon, D., Smith, S., & Dill, S. (2003). *DIBELS: Dynamic indicators of basic early literacy skills*. Longmont: Sopris West.

Gordon, M., Lewandowski, L., & Keiser, S. (1999). The LD label for relatively well-functioning students: A critical analysis. *Journal of Learning Disabilities*, *32*, 485–490.

Gough, P., & Turmer, W. (1986). Decoding, reading, and reading disability. *Remedial and Special Education*, *7*, 6–10.

Gregg, N., Coleman, C., & Knight, D. (2003). Use of the Woodcock-Johnson III in the diagnosis of learning disabilities. In A. Schrank & D. Flanagan (Eds.). *WJ III clinical use and interpretation: Scientist-practitioner perspectives* (pp. 125–174). San Diego: Academic Press.

Gresham, F. M., MacMillan, D. L., & Bocian, K. M. (1996). Learning disabilities, low achievement, and mild mental retardation: More alike than different? *Journal of Learning Disabilities*, *29*, 570–581.

Gresham, F. M., Restori, A. F., & Cook, C. R. (2008). To test or not to test: Issues pertaining to response to intervention and cognitive testing. *Communiqué*, *37*, 5–7.

Gresham, F. M., & Vellutino, F. R. (2010). What is the role of intelligence in identification of learning disabilities? Issues and clarifications. *Learning Disabilities Research & Practice*, *25*, 194–206.

Gutkin, T. B., Henning-Stout, M., & Piersel, W. C. (1988). Impact of a district-wide behavioral consultation prereferral intervention service on patterns of school psychological service delivery. *Professional School Psychology*, *3*, 301–308.

Haddad F. A., Garcia Y. E., Naglieri, J. A., Grimditch, M., McAndrews, A., & Eubanks, J. (2003). Planning facilitation and reading comprehension: Instructional relevance of the PASS Theory. *Journal of Psychoeducational Assessment*, *21*, 282–289.

Hale, J. B., & Fiorello, C. A. (2004). *School neuropsychology: A practitioner's handbook*. New York: Guilford Press.

Hale, J. B., Fiorello, C. A., Kavanagh, J. A., Holdnack, J. A., & Aloe, A. M. (2007). Is the demise of IQ interpretation justified? A response to the special issue authors *Applied Neuropsychology*, *14*, 37–51.

Hale, J. B., Kaufman, A., Naglieri, J. A., & Kavale, K. A. (2006). Implementation of IDEA: Integrating response to intervention and cognitive assessment methods. *Psychology in the Schools*, *43*, 753–770.

Hallahan, D. P., & Mock, D. R. (2003). A brief history of the field of learning disabilities. In H. L. Swanson, K. R. Harris, & S. Graham (Eds.), *Handbook of learning disabilities* (pp. 16–29). New York: Guilford.

Hammill, D. D. (1993). A brief look at the learning disabilities movement in the United States. *Journal of Learning Disabilities*, *26*, 295–310.

Hammill, D. D., & Larsen, S. C. (1996). *Test of written language* (3rd ed.). Austin: PRO–ED.

Hawaii Administrative Code Chapter 56 § 8-56-15 (2002). http://doe.k12.hi.us/specialeducation/chapter56/subchapter4.htm. Accessed 12 Dec 2009.

Hawaii Department of Education. (2008). *Comprehensive student support system: Responding to student's needs*. http://doe.k12.hi.us/periodicals/csss/2008/csss0808.pdf. Accessed 12 Dec 2009.

Heaton, R. K., Chelune, G. J., Talley, J. L., Kay, G. G., & Curtiss, G. (1993). *Wisconsin Card Sorting Test, Revised and Expanded*. Odessa: Psychological Assessment Resources, Inc.

Hintze, J. M., Christ, T. J., & Methe, S. A. (2006). Curriculum-based assessment. *Psychology in the Schools*, *43*, 45–56.

Hodapp, R. M., & Dykens, E. M. (2003). Mental retardation. In E. J. Mash & R. A. Barkley (Eds.), *Child psychopathology* (2nd ed., pp. 486–519). New York: Guilford.

Hsieh, P., Acee, T., Chung, W. H., Hsieh, Y. P., Kim, H., Thomas, G. D., et al. (2005). Is educational intervention research on the decline? *Journal of Educational Psychology*, *97*, 523–529.

Hudziak, J. J., Wadsworth, M. E., Heath, A. C., & Achenbach, T. M. (1999). Latent class analysis of child behavior checklist attention problems. *Journal of the American Academy of Child and Adolescent Psychiatry*, *38*, 985–991.

Idaho State Department of Education. (2007). *Special education implementation manual*. http://www.sde.idaho.gov/site/special_edu/docs/manual/Manual.pdf. Accessed 13 Dec 2009.

Idaho State Department of Education. (2009). *Response to intervention-Idaho: Connecting the pieces*. http://www.sde.idaho.gov/site/rti/docs/RTI%20Guidance%20Final.pdf. Accessed 12 Dec 2009.

Illinois Administrative Code Title 23 § 226.130 (pp. 19–20) (n.d.). http://www.isbe.state.il.us/rules/archive/pdfs/226ark.pdf. Accessed 13 Dec 2009.

Illinois State Board of Education. (2008). *The Illinois state response to intervention plan*. http://www.isbe.net/pdf/rti_state_plan.pdf. Accessed 13 Dec 2009.

Indiana Administrative Code Title 511 § 7-40-5(g) (pp. 61–62) (2008). http://www.doe.in.gov/exceptional/speced/docs/2008-08-06-Article7.pdf. Accessed 13 Dec 2009.

Indiana Department of Education. (2009). *Indiana's vision of response to intervention*. http://www.doe.in.gov/indiana-rti/docs/2009-11-14-RTIGuidanceDocument.pdf. Accessed 13 Dec 2009.

Individuals with Disabilities Education Act (IDEA) Amendments of 1997, Pub. L. No. 105–17.

Individuals with Disabilities Education Improvement Act (IDEA) of 2004, Pub. L. No. 108–446.

Iseman, J. & Naglieri, J. A. (2010). A cognitive strategy instruction to improve math calculation for children with ADHD: A randomized controlled study. *Journal of Learning Disabilities*, *44*(2), 184–195. doi:10.1177/0022219410391190.

Joshi, R. M. (2003). Misconceptions about the assessment and diagnosis of reading disability. *Reading Psychology*, *24*, 247–266.

Kamphaus, R. W. (2001). *Clinical assessment of child and adolescent intelligence*. Needham Heights: Allyn & Bacon.

Kansas State Department of Education. (2009). *Kansas multi-tier system of supports*. http://www.kansasmtss.org/index.htm. Accessed 13 Dec 2009.

Kaufman, A. S., & Kaufman, N. L. (2004). *Kaufman test of educational achievement* (2nd ed). Circle Pines: AGS Publishing.

Kaufman, A. S., & Kaufman, N. L. (2004). *Kaufman assessment battery for children* (2nd ed.). Circle Pines: AGS Publishing.

Kavale, K. (2002). Discrepancy models in the identification of learning disability. In R. Bradley, L. Danielson, & D. Hallahan (Eds.), *Identification of learning disability: Research to practice* (pp. 369–426). Mahwah: Lawrence Erlbaum.

Kavale, K. A., & Forness, S. R. (1984). A meta-analysis of the validity of *Wechsler Scale* profiles and recategorizations: Patterns or parodies? *Learning Disability Quarterly*, *7*, 136–156.

Kavale, K. A., & Forness, S. R. (1985). *The science of learning disabilities*. San Diego: College-Hill Press.

Kavale, K. A., & Forness, S. R. (2000). What definitions of learning disability say and don't say: A critical analysis. *Journal of Learning Disabilities*, *33*, 239–256.

Kavale, K., Fuchs, D., & Scruggs, T. (1994). Setting the record straight on learning disability and low achievement: Implications for policymaking. *Learning Disabilities Research & Practice*, *9*, 70–77.

Kavale, K. A., Holdnack, J. A., & Mostert, N. P. (2005). Responsiveness to intervention and the identification of specific learning disabilities: A critique and alternative proposal. *Learning Disability Quarterly*, *28*, 2–16.

Kavale, K. A., Kaufman, A. S., Bachmeier, R. J., & LeFever, G. B. (2008). Response-to-intervention: Separating the rhetoric of self-congratulation from the reality of specific learning disability identification. *Learning Disability Quarterly*, *31*, 135–150.

Kavale, K. A., Kaufman, A. S., Naglieri, J. A., & Hale, J. B. (2005). Changing procedures for identifying learning disabilities: The danger of poorly supported ideas. *The School Psychologist*, *59*, 16–25.

Kaznowski, K. (2004). Slow learners: Are educators leaving them behind? [Electronic version]. *National Association of Secondary School Principals Bulletin*, *88*. http://www.looksmartcollegesports.com/p/articles/mi_qa3696/is_200412/ai_n9483591. Accessed 15 Dec 2009.

Keith, R. W. (1999). *SCAN-C: A test of auditory processing disorders in children-revised*. San Antonio: PsychCorp.

Kentucky Administrative Code Title 707 § 1:310 (2007). http://www.lrc.ky.gov/kar/707/001/310.htm. Accessed 13 Dec 2009.

Kentucky Department of Education. (2009). *System of intervention pyramid*. http://www.education.ky.gov/KDE/Instructional+Resources/Kentucky+System+of+Interventions/Overview/System+of+Intervention+Pyramid.htm. Accessed 13 Dec 2009.

Korkman, M., Kirk, U., & Kemp, S. (2007). *NEPSY* (2nd ed.). Bloomington: Pearson.

Leigh, J. (1987). Adaptive behavior of children with learning disabilities. *Journal of Learning Disabilities, 20*, 557–562.

Lewandowski, L., Lovett, B. J., Gordon, M., & Antshel, K. (2006). The case for clinical impairment in the DSM-V criteria for ADHD. *The ADHD Report, 14*, 8–15.

Lubinski, D. (2004). Introduction to the special section on cognitive abilities: 100 years after Spearman's (1904) "'General Intelligence,' objectively determined and measured." *Journal of Personality and Social Psychology, 86*, 96–111.

Lyon, G. R., Fletcher, J. M., & Barnes, M. C. (2003). Learning disabilities. In E. J. Mash & R. A. Barkley (Eds.), *Child psychopathology* (2nd ed., pp. 520–586). New York: Guilford.

Maine Administrative Code Chapter 101 § 05-071 (pp. 74–79) (2009). http://www.maine.gov/education/legis/071c101emergency.pdf. Accessed 12 Dec 2009.

Maine Administrative Code Chapter 101 § 3.11 (pp. 10–11) (1999). http://www.maine.gov/education/speced/documents/Regulationsasof624.doc. Accessed 12 Dec 2009.

Maine Parent Federation, Inc. (2009). *Response to intervention in Maine*. http://www.mpf.org/RTI%20formatted%20for%20MPF%20Website%203-24-2009.pdf. Accessed 12 Dec 2009.

Mann, L. (1979). *On the trail of process: A historical perspective on cognitive processes and their training*. New York: Grune & Stratton.

Marston, D., Mirkin, P, & Deno, S. (1984). Curriculum-based measurement: An alternative to traditional screening, referral, and identification. *The Journal of Special Education, 18*, 109–117.

Martin, N. A., & Brownell, R. (2005). *Test of auditory processing skills* (3rd ed.). Novato: Academic Therapy Publications.

Maryland Administrative Code Title 13A § 05.01.06 (n.d.) http://www.dsd.state.md.us/comar/getfile.aspx?file=13a.05.01.06.htm. Accessed 12 Dec 2009.

Maryland State Department of Education. (2001). *Identifying specific learning disabilities: Maryland's technical assistance guide*. http://www.msde.state.md.us/SpecialEducation/SLDGuide/SLDGuide-Sig.pdf. Accessed 12 Dec 2009.

Maryland State Department of Education. (2008). *A tiered instructional approach to support achievement for all students: Maryland's response to intervention framework*. http://marylandpublicschools.org/NR/rdonlyres/D182E222-D84B-43D8-BB81-6F4C4F7E05F6/17125/Tiered_Instructional_ApproachRtI_June2008.pdf. Accessed 12 Dec 2009.

Matarazzo, J. (1992). Psychological testing and assessment in the 21st century. *American Psychologist, 47*, 1007–1018.

Mather, N., & Gregg, N. (2006). Specific learning disabilities: Clarifying, not eliminating, a construct. *Professional Psychology: Research and Practice, 37*, 99–106.

Mayes, S. D., Calhoun, S. L., & Crowell, E. W. (2000). Learning disabilities and ADHD: Overlapping spectrum disorders. *Journal of Learning Disabilities, 33*, 417–424.

McMaster, K. L., Fuchs, D., & Fuchs, L. S. (2007). Promises and limitations of peer-assisted learning strategies in reading. *Learning Disabilities: A Contemporary Journal, 5*, 97–112.

Michigan Administrative Code § R340.1713 (pp. 1010–1011) (2004). http://www.michigan.gov/documents/dleg/AACS339.23401_400.20503_297623_7.pdf. Accessed 12 Dec 2009.

Michigan Department of Education. (2009). *Michigan criteria for determining the existence of a specific learning disability*. http://www.michigan.gov/documents/mde/SLD_Final_Criteria_11-2-09_299603_7.pdf. Accessed 12 Dec 2009.

Minnesota Administrative Rules § 3525.1341 (2008). https://www.revisor.mn.gov/rules/?id=3525.1341. Accessed 13 Dec 2009.

Missouri Department of Education. (2007). *Identification and evaluation*. http://www.dese.mo.gov/divspeced/PDF/RegulationIII-Rev-Prop_Feb2007.pdf. Accessed 13 Dec 2009.

Missouri Department of Education. (2008). *State of Missouri guidance for identification of specific learning disability (SLD)*. http://www.dese.mo.gov/divspeced/documents/RtIGuidance08.pdf. Accessed 13 Dec 2009.

Monroe, M. (1932). *Children who cannot read: The analysis of reading disabilities and the use of diagnostic tests in the instruction of retarded readers*. Chicago: University of Chicago Press.

Montana Administrative Rules § 10.16.3019 (pp. 71–73) (2007). http://www.opi.state.mt.us/pdf/arm/16chapter.pdf. Accessed 13 Dec 2009.

Montana Office of Public Instruction. (2009). *Response to intervention: RTI framework*. http://www.opi.mt.gov/pub/RTI/Framework/RTIFrameworkGUIDE.pdf. Accessed 13 Dec 2009.

Muthén, B. (2003). Statistical and substantive checking in growth mixture modeling. *Psychological Methods*, *8*, 369–377.

Muthén, B. (2004). Latent variable analysis: Growth mixture modeling and related techniques for longitudinal data. In D. Kaplan (Ed.), *Handbook of quantitative methodology for the social sciences* (pp. 345–368). Newbury Park: Sage Publications.

Muthén, B., & Muthén, L. K. (2000). Integrating person-centered and variable-centered analyses: growth mixture modeling with latent trajectory classes. *Alcoholism: Clinical and Experimental Research*, *24*, 882–891

Muthén, B. & Muthén, L. K. (2004). *MPLUS: User's Guide* (3rd ed.). Los Angeles: Muthén & Muthén.

Naglieri, J. A. (1989). A cognitive processing theory for the measurement of intelligence. *Educational Psychologist*, *24*, 185–206.

Naglieri, J. A. (1999). *Essentials of CAS assessment*. Hoboken: Wiley.

Naglieri, J. A. (2005). The cognitive assessment system. In D. P. Flanagan & P. L. Harrison (Eds.), *Contemporary intellectual assessment* (2nd ed., pp. 441–460). New York: Guilford.

Naglieri, J. A. (2008). Best practices in linking cognitive assessment of students with learning disabilities to interventions. In A. Thomas & J. Grimes (Eds.), *Best practices in school psychology*. (5th ed., pp. 679–696). Bethesda: NASP.

Naglieri, J. A. (2010). The discrepancy-consistency approach to SLD identification using the PASS theory. In D. Flanagan & V. Alfonso (Eds.), *Essentials of SLD assessment* (pp. xx–xx). New York: Wiley.

Naglieri, J. A., & Conway, C. (2009). The cognitive assessment system. In J. A. Naglieri & S. Goldstein *A practitioner's guide to assessment of intelligence and achievement* (pp. 3–10). New York: Wiley.

Naglieri, J. A., & Das, J. P. (1997). *Cognitive Assessment System*. Austin: ProEd.

Naglieri, J. A., & Das, J. P. (2005). Planning, attention, simultaneous, successive (PASS) theory: A revision of the concept of intelligence. In D. P. Flanagan & P. L. Harrison (Eds.), *Contemporary Intellectual Assessment* (2nd ed., pp. 136–182). New York: Guilford.

Naglieri, J. A., & Gottling, S. H. (1995). A cognitive education approach to math instruction for the learning disabled: An individual study. *Psychological Reports*, *76*, 1343–1354.

Naglieri, J. A., & Johnson, D. (2000). Effectiveness of a cognitive strategy intervention to improve math calculation based on the PASS theory. *Journal of Learning Disabilities*, *33*, 591–597.

Naglieri, J. A. & Pickering, E. (2010). *Helping children learn* (2nd ed.). Baltimore: Brookes Publishing.

Naglieri, J. A., & Rojahn, J. (2001). Evaluation of African-American and white children in special education programs for children with mental retardation using the WISC-III and cognitive assessment system. *American Journal of Mental Retardation*, *106*, 359–367.

Naglieri, J. A., Otero, T., DeLauder, B., & Matto, H. (2007). Bilingual hispanic children's performance on the English and Spanish Versions of the cognitive assessment system. *School Psychology Quarterly*, *22*, 432–448.

Naglieri, J. A., Salter, C. J., & Edwards, G. H. (2004). Assessment of ADHD and reading disabilities using the PASS theory and cognitive assessment system. *Journal of Psychoeducational Assessment*, *22*, 93–105.

Naglieri, J. A., & Reardon, S. M. (1993). Tradition IQ is irrelevant to learning disabilities—Intelligence is not. *Journal of Learning Disabilities*, *26*, 127–133.

National Joint Committee on Learning Disabilities. (1990). *Learning disabilities: Issues on definition.* http://www.ncld.org/index.php?option=content&task=view&id=458. Accessed 6 Oct 2006.

National Joint Committee on Learning Disabilities. (2011). Learning disabilities: Implications for policy regarding research and practice: A report by the National Joint Committee on Learning Disabilities March 2011. *Learning Disability Quarterly*, *34*, 237–241.

Nevada Administrative Code § 388.420 (2009). Retrieved December 13, 2009, from Nevada Administrative Code, Chapter 388

Nevada Administrative Code § 388.420 (pp. 26–33) (2008). http://nde.doe.nv.gov/SpecialEdReports/PP_APR_Improvement_Activities_Revised_Feb2009.pdf. Accessed 13 Dec 2009.

Nevada Department of Education. (2007). Nevada department of special education policy statement response to scientific, research-based instruction. http://nde.doe.nv.gov/SpecialEdResources/SPTechnicalAssistance/LD_Policy.pdf. Accessed 12 Aug 2012.

New Hampshire Administrative Code-proposed §Ed 1107.02 (p. 16) (2009). http://www.ed.state.nh.us/education/laws/documents/1100students-with-disabilities-proposal.pdf. Accessed 13 Dec 2009.

New Hampshire Department of Education. (2009). *An interactive guide to RTI in New Hampshire*. http://www.ed.state.nh.us/education/programs/documents/INTERACTIVEGUIDETORTI-NH.pdf. Accessed 13 Dec 2009.

New Jersey Administrative Code Title 6A § 14–3.5 (pp. 53–59) (n.d.). http://state.rti4success.org/index.php?option=com_state&stateId=135. Accessed 13 Dec 2009.

New York State Education Department. (n.d.) *State Criteria for LD*. http://www.vesid.nysed.gov/specialed/techassist/referrals-evals-eligibility_files/textonly/slide18.html. Accessed 13 Dec 2009.

New York State Education Department. (2004). *Individuals with disabilities education improvement act*. http://www.vesid.nysed.gov/specialed/idea/regents.htm. Accessed 13 Dec 2009.

North Dakota Department of Public Instruction. (2007). *Guidelines: Identification and evaluation of students with specific learning disabilities*. http://www.dpi.state.nd.us/speced/guide/SLDGuide07.pdf. Accessed 13 Dec 2009.

Official Code of Georgia IDDF (5) § 160-4-7-.05 (pp. 18–21) (2007). http://public.doe.k12.ga.us/_documents/doe/legalservices/160-4-7-.05.pdf. Accessed 13 Dec 2009.

Ohio Administrative Code § 3301-51-06 (2009). http://edresourcesohio.org/ogdse/6_-_evaluation/6-7/document#eligibility_determination_-_specific_learning_disabilities. Accessed 13 Dec 2009.

Oklahoma State Department of Education. (2007). *Policies and procedures for special education*. http://sde.state.ok.us/Curriculum/SpecEd/pdf/Default/AmendedPoliciesAndProcedures.pdf. Accessed 13 Dec 2009.

Oklahoma State Department of Education. (2007) *Response to intervention (RtI)*. http://sde.state.ok.us/Curriculum/SpecEd/pdf/Docs_Forms/English/RtI.pdf. Accessed 13 Dec 2009.

Oregon Administrative Rules § 581-015-2170 (2008). http://www.ode.state.or.us/offices/slp/sld_ode_oar.doc. Accessed 12 Dec 2009.

Oregon Department of Education. (2009). *Oregon's response to intervention (Or-RTI)*. http://www.ode.state.or.us/search/page/?id=315. Accessed 12 Dec 2009.

Ortiz, A. A. (1997). Learning disabilities occurring concomitantly with linguistic differences. *Journal of Learning Disabilities*, *30*, 321–332.

Orton, S. T. (1925). "Word-blindness" in school children. *Archives of Neurology and Psychiatry*, *14*, 581–615.

Pennsylvania Administrative Code Title 22 § 14.125 (2008). http://www.pacode.com/secure/data/022/chapter14/s14.125.html. Accessed 13 Dec 2009.

Pennsylvania Department of Education. (2009). Response to instruction and intervention: An introduction. http://pattan.net-website.s3.amazonaws.com/files/materials/publications/docs/RtI-IAnIntro.pdf. Accessed 12 Aug 2012.

Polloway, E. A., Patton, J. R., Smith, T. E. C., & Buck, G. H. (1997). Mental retardation and learning disabilities: Conceptual and applied issues. *Journal of Learning Disabilities*, *30*, 297–308.

Reschly, D. J., & Wilson, M. S. (1990). Cognitive processing versus traditional intelligence: Diagnostic utility, intervention implications, and treatment validity. *School Psychology Review*, *19*, 443–458.

Reynolds, C. R. (1984). Critical measurement issues in learning disabilities. *The Journal of Special Education*, *18*, 451–476.

Reynolds, C. R. (2003). Conceptual and technical problems in the diagnosis of learning disabilities. In C. R. Reynolds, R. W. Kamphaus (Eds.), *Handbook of psychological and educational assessment of children: Intelligence, aptitude, and achievement* (2nd ed., pp. 475–497). New York: Guilford Press.

Reynolds, C. R., & Kamphaus, R. W. (1992). *Behavior assessment system for children*. Circle Pines: American Guidance Service.

Reynolds, C. R., & Kamphaus, R. W. (2003). *Reynolds intellectual assessment scale*. Lutz: Psychological Assessment Resources, Inc.

Reynolds, C. R., & Kamphaus, R. W. (2004). *The behavior assessment system for children* (2nd ed.). Circle Pines: AGS.

Rhode Island Department of Education. (2008). *Specific learning disabilities eligibility criteria*. http://www.ride.ri.gov/Special_Populations/Programs_Services/Attachments/State%20Criteria%20for%20Specific%20Learning%20Disabilities.pdf. Accessed 13 Dec 2009.

Rhode Island Department of Education. (n.d.) *Response to intervention*. http://www.ritap.org/rti/about/overview.php. Accessed 13 Dec 2009.

Rhodes, R. L., Ochoa, S. H., & Ortiz, S. O. (2005). *Assessing culturally and linguistically diverse students: A practical guide*. New York: Guilford.

Robinson, C. S., Menchetti, B. M., & Torgesen, J. K. (2002). Toward a two-factor theory of one type of mathematics disability. *Learning Disabilities Research and Practice*, *17*, 81–89.

Rock, E. E., Fessler, M. A., & Church, R. P. (1997). The concomitance of learning disabilities and emotional/behavioral disorders: A conceptual model. *Journal of Learning Disabilities*, *30*, 245–263.

Roid, G. H. (2003). *Stanford-Binet Intelligence Scales* (5th ed.). Itasca: Riverside.

Rosenbert, M. S. (1997). Learning disabilities occurring concomitantly with other disability and exceptional conditions: Introduction to the special series. *Journal of Learning Disabilities*, *30*, 242–244.

Rourke, B. P. (1989). *Nonverbal learning disabilities: The syndrome and the model*. New York: Guilford.

Rourke, B. P., & Fuerst, D. R. (1991). *Learning disabilities and psychosocial functioning: A neuropsychological perspective*. New York: Guilford.

Rispens, J., van Yperen, T. A., & van Duijn, G. A. (1991). The irrelevance of IQ to the definition of learning disabilities: Some empirical evidence. *Journal of Learning Disabilities*, *24*, 434–438.

Rutter, M., & Yule, W. (1975). The concept of specific reading retardation. *Journal of Child Psychology and Psychiatry*, *16*, 181–197.

Sandoval, J., & Echandia, A. (1994). Behavior assessment system for children. *Journal of School Psychology*, *32*, 419–425.

Schoenbrodt, L., Kumin, L., & Sloan, J. M. (1997). Learning disabilities existing concomitantly with communication disorders. *Journal of Learning Disabilities*, *30*, 264–281.

Schrank, F. A., Mather, N., & Woocock, R. W. (2004). *Woodcock-Johnson III diagnostic reading battery*. Rolling Meadows: Riverside Publishing.

Semel, E., Wiig, E. H., & Secord, W. A. (2004). *Clinical evaluation of language skills-4 screening test*. San Antonio: Pearson.

Shaffer, D., Gould, M. S., Brasic, J., Ambrosini, P., Fisher, P., Bird, H., & Aluwahlia, S. (1983). *A Children's global assessment scale (CGAS)*. *Archives of General Psychiatry*, *40*, 1228–1231.

Shaywitz, B. A., Fletcher, J. M., Holahan, J. M., & Shaywitz, S. E. (1992). Discrepancy compared to achievement definitions of reading disability: Results from the Connecticut Longitudinal Study. *Journal of Learning Disabilities*, *25*, 639–648.

Shaywitz, S. E., Shaywitz, B. A., Fletcher, J. M., & Escobar, M. D. (1990). Prevalence of reading disability in boys and girls: Results of the Connecticut Longitudinal Study. *Journal of the American Medical Association, 264*, 998–1002.

Shepard, A.S. (1989). Identification of mild handicaps. In R. L. Linn (Ed.), *Educational measurement* (3rd ed., pp. 545–572). New York: MacMillan.

Shepard, A. S., Smith, M. L., & Vojir, C. P. (1983). Characteristics of pupils identified as learning disabled. *American Educational Research Journal, 20*, 309–331.

Sheslow, D., & Adams, W. (2003). *Wide range assessment of memory and learning* (2nd ed.). Odessa: Psychological Assessment Resources, Inc.

Siegel, L. S. (1988). Definitional and theoretical issues and research on learning disabilities. *Journal of Learning Disabilities, 21*, 264–266.

Siegel, L. S. (1989). IQ is irrelevant to the definition of learning disabilities. *Journal of Learning Disabilities, 22*, 469–479.

Siegel, L. S. (1992). An evaluation of the discrepancy definition of dyslexia. *Journal of Learning Disabilities, 25*, 618–629.

Siegel, L. S. (1999). Issues in the definition and diagnosis of learning disabilities: A perspective on Guckenberger v. Boston University. *Journal of Learning Disabilities, 32*, 304–319.

Siegel, L. S. (2003). IQ-discrepancy definitions and the diagnosis of LD: Introduction to the special issue. *Journal of Learning Disabilities, 36*, 2–3.

South Carolina Administrative Code § 43-243.1.D (2004). http://ed.sc.gov/agency/Standards-and-Learning/Exceptional-Children/old/ec/stateregs/documents/43-243.1.pdf. Accessed 13 Dec 2009.

South Dakota Administrative Rules § 24:05:24.01:19 (2007). http://legis.state.sd.us/rules/DisplayRule.aspx?Rule=24:05:24.01:19. Accessed 13 Dec 2009.

South Dakota Department of Education. (2007). *Response to intervention: The South Dakota model.* http://doe.sd.gov/oess/specialed/forms/RtI/docs/RTI%208%2016%2007Edition.pdf. Accessed 13 Dec 2009.

Speece, D. L., Case, L. P., & Molloy, D. E. (2003). Responsiveness to general education instruction as the first gate to learning disabilities identification. *Learning Disabilities Research & Practice, 18*, 147–156.

Speece, D. L, & Cooper, D. H. (1990). Ontogeny of school failure: Classification of first-grade children. *American Educational Research Journal, 27*, 119–140.

Speece, D. L. & Shekitka. L. (2002). How Should Reading Disabilities be Operationalized? A Survey of Experts. *Learning Disabilities Research & Practice, 17*, 118–123.

Stanford, L. D., & Hynd, G. W. (1994). Congruence of behavioral symptomatology in children with ADD/H, ADD/WO, and learning disabilities. *Journal of Learning Disabilities, 27*, 243–253.

Stanovich, K. E. (1986). Matthew effects in reading: Some consequences of individual differences in the acquisition of literacy. *Reading Research Quarterly, 21*, 360–407.

Stanovich, K. S. (1988). Explaining the differences between the dyslexic and garden-variety poor reader: The phonological-core variable-difference model. *Journal of Learning Disabilities, 21*, 590–604.

Stanovich, K. E. (1999). The sociopsychometrics of learning disabilities. *Journal of Learning Disabilities, 32*, 350–361.

Stanovich, K. E. (2005). The future of a mistake: Will discrepancy measurement continue to make the learning disabilities field a pseudoscience? *Learning Disability Quarterly, 28*, 103–106.

Stecker, P. M., Fuchs, L. S., & Fuchs, D. (2005). Using curriculum-based measurement to improve student achievement: Review of research. *Psychology in the Schools, 42*, 795–819.

Sternberg, R. J. (1988). *The triarchic mind: A new theory of human intelligence*. New York: Viking.

Stuebing, K., Fletcher, J. M., LeDoux, J. M., Lyon, G. R., Shaywitz, S. E., & Shaywitz, B. (2002). Validity of IQ-discrepancy classification of reading difficulties: A meta-analysis. *American Educational Research Journal, 39*, 469–518.

Suzuki, L.A., & Valencia, R.R. (1997). Race-ethnicity and measured intelligence. *American Psychologist, 52*, 1103–1114.

Taylor, A. B., & Kamphaus, R. W. (2008). *Redefining learning disabilities: An academic impairment model of identification*. Unpublished doctoral dissertation, University of Georgia, Athens.

Tennessee State Department of Education. (2008). *Special education manual*. http://www.state.tn.us/education/speced/doc/80608SEMManualfinal.pdf. Accessed 13 Dec 2009.

Tennessee State Department of Education. (2009). *HEART procedure manual*. http://state.tn.us/education/speced/doc/101409heartprocedure.pdf. Accessed 12 Dec 2009.

Terman, L. M. (1931). The gifted child. In C. A. Murchison & J. E. Anderson (Eds.), *A handbook of child psychology* (pp. 568–584). Worcester: Clark University Press.

The Psychological Corporation. (2001). *Wechsler individual achievement test* (2nd ed.). San Antonio: The Psychological Corporation.

Torgesen, J. K. (1979). What shall we do with psychological processes? *Journal of Learning Disabilities, 12*, 16–23.

Torgesen, J. K. (1991). Learning disabilities: Historical and conceptual issues. In B. Wong (Ed.), *Learning about learning disabilities* (pp. 3–37). San Diego: Academic.

Torgesen, J. K. (2002). Empirical and theoretical support for direct diagnosis of learning disabilities by assessment of intrinsic processing weaknesses. In R. Bradley, L. Danielson, & D. P. Hallahan (Eds.), *Identification of learning disabilities: research to practice* (pp. 565–603). Mahwah: Lawrence Erlbaum Associates, Inc.

Towne, R. L. (2004). Review of the Illinois test of psycholinguistic abilities (3rd ed.). *Mental Measurements Yearbook, 15*, Accession number 15042681 http://search.ebscohost.com/login.aspx?direct=true&db=loh&AN=15042681&site=ehost-live.

U.S. Department of Education, National Center for Education Statistics. (2006). *Digest of education statistics, 2005* (NCES 2006–030), Chapter 2. http://nces.ed.gov/pubsearch/pubsinfo.asp?pubid=2006030. Accessed 6 Oct 2006.

U.S. Department of Education, Office of Special Education and Rehabilitative Services. (2002). *Twenty-fourth annual report to Congress on the implementation of the Individuals with Disabilities Education Act*. http://www.ed.gov/about/reports/annual/osep/2002/section-ii.pdf. Accessed 28 Aug 2005.

U.S. Department of Justice. (1996, July 26). *Americans with Disabilities Act of 1990*. http://www.usdoj.gov/crt/ada/pubs/ada.txt. Accessed 13 Dec 2009.

Utah State Board of Education. (2007) *Special education rules* (pp. 46–51). http://www.schools.utah.gov/sars/lawsregs/docs/rules.doc. Accessed 13 Dec 2009.

Utah State Office of Education. (2008). *Specific learning disabilities guidelines*. http://www.schools.utah.gov/sars/manualsglines/pdfs/sld.pdf. Accessed 29 Aug 2009.

Vaughn, S., & Fuchs, L. S. (2003). Redefining learning disabilities as inadequate response to instruction: The promise and potential problems. *Learning Disabilities Research & Practice, 18*, 137–146.

Vaughn, S., & Linan-Thompson, S. (2003). What is special about special education for students with learning disabilities? *The Journal of Special Education, 37*, 140–147.

Vaughn, S., Linan-Thompson, S., & Hickman, P. (2003). Response to instruction as a means of identifying students with reading/learning disabilities. *Exceptional Children, 69*, 391–409.

Vellutino, F., Scanlon, D., Sipay, E., Small, S., Pratt, A., Chen, R., et al. (1996). Cognitive profiles of difficult-to-remediate and readily remediated poor readers: Early interventions as a vehicle for distinguishing between cognitive and experiential deficits as basic causes of specific reading disability. *Journal of Educational Psychology, 88*, 601–638.

Vellutino, F. R., Scanlon, D. M., & Lyon, G. R. (2000). Differentiating between difficult-to-remediate and readily remediated poor readers: More evidence against the IQ-achievement discrepancy definition of reading disability. *Journal of Learning Disabilities, 33*, 223–238.

Vellutino, F. R., Scanlon, D. M., Small, S., & Fanuele, D. P. (2006). Response to intervention as a vehicle for distinguishing between children with and without reading disabilities: Evidence for the role of kindergarten and first-grade interventions. *Journal of Learning Disabilities, 39*, 157–169.

Vermont Administrative Code § 2362.1(b) (pp. 40–41) (2007). http://education.vermont.gov/new/pdfdoc/pgm_sped/laws/sped_guide_07_0917.pdf. Accessed 13 Dec 2009.

Vermunt, J. K., & Magidson, J. (2002). Latent class cluster analysis. In J. A. Hagenaars & A. L. McCutcheon (Eds.), *Applied latent class analysis* (pp. 89–106). Cambridge: Cambridge University Press.

Virginia Administrative Code Title 8 § 20–81-80 (pp. 54–55) (2009). http://www.doe.virginia.gov/VDOE/Instruction/Sped/varegs.pdf. Accessed 13 Dec 2009.

Virginia Department of Education. (2007). *Responsive instruction: Refining our work of teaching all Children: "Virginia's response to intervention initiative"*. http://www.doe.virginia.gov/VDOE/studentsrvcs/RTI/. Accessed 12 Dec 2009.

Wagner, M., Marder, C., Blackorby, J., & Cardoso, D. (2002). *The children we serve: The demographic characteristics of elementary and middle school students with disabilities and their households*. Menlo Park: SRI International.

Wagner, R. K., Torgesen, J. K., & Rashotte, C. A. (1999). *Comprehensive test of phonological processing*. Austin: PRO–ED.

Wanzek, J., & Vaughn, S. (2008). Response to varying amounts of time in reading intervention for students with low response to intervention. *Journal of Learning Disabilities*, *41*, 126–142.

Washington Administrative Code § 392–172A-03045 (2007). http://apps.leg.wa.gov/WAC/default.aspx?cite=392-172A-03045. Accessed 9 Dec 2009.

Washington Administrative Code § 392–172A-03065 (2007). http://apps.leg.wa.gov/WAC/default.aspx?cite=392-172A-03065. Accessed 13 Dec 2009.

Washington Administrative Code § 392.172A-03060 (2007). http://apps.leg.wa.gov/WAC/default.aspx?cite=392-172A-03060. Accessed 13 Dec 2009.

Washington Office of Superintendent of Public Instruction. (2006). *Using responsiveness to intervention (RTI) for Washington's students*. http://www.k12.wa.us/RTI/pubdocs/WashingtonRTIManual.pdf. Accessed 13 Dec 2009.

Watkins, M. W., Glutting, J. J., & Lei, P. (2007). Validity of the full-scale IQ when there is significant variability among WISC-III and WISC-IV factor scores. *Applied Neuropsychology*, *14*, 13–20.

Wechsler, D. (2003). *Wechsler intelligence scale for children* (4th ed). San Antonio: PsychCorp.

Wechsler, D., Kaplan, E., Fein, D., Kramer, J., Morris, R., Delis, D., et al. (2004). *Wechsler intelligence scale for children* (4th ed. Integrated). San Antonio: The Psychological Corporation.

Wechsler, D., & Naglieri, J. A. (2006). *Wechsler nonverbal scale of ability*. San Antonio: Harcourt Assessments.

West Virginia Department of Education. (2006). *West Virginia response to intervention: An implementation and technical assistance guide for districts and schools*. http://wvde.state.wv.us/osp/RtiImpGuide91906.DOC. Accessed 13 Dec 2009.

West Virginia Department of Education. (2007). *Policy 2419: Regulations for the education of students with exceptionalities*. http://wvde.state.wv.us/osp/p2419.pdf. Accessed 13 Dec 2009

Wiederholt, J. L., & Bryant, B. R. (2001). *Gray oral reading tests* (4th ed.). Austin: PRO–ED.

Wilkinson, G. S. (1993). *Wide range achievement test-3*. Wilmington: Jastak Associates.

Williams, K. T. (2007). *Expressive vocabulary test* (2nd ed.). Bloomington: Pearson.

Willis, J. O., & Dumont, R. (2006). And never the twain shall meet: Can response to intervention and cognitive assessment be reconciled? *Psychology in the Schools*, *43*, 901–908.

Winters, N. C., Collett, B. R., & Myers, K. M. (2005). Ten-year review of rating scale, VII: Scales assessing functional impairment. *Journal of American Academy of Child and Adolescent Psychiatry*, *44*, 309–338.

Wisconsin Department of Education. (2009). *Wisconsin response to instruction/intervention*. http://dpi.wi.gov/rti/. Accessed 13 Dec 2009.

Wisconsin State Administrative Code §PI 11.36(6) (2001) http://www.dpi.state.wi.us/sped/pi11_0701.html#ld. Accessed 13 Dec 2009.

Wong, B. Y. L. (1992). On cognitive process-based instruction: An introduction. *Journal of Learning Disabilities*, *25*, 150–152, 172.

Woodcock, R. W., McGrew, K. S., & Mather, N. (2001). *Woodcock-Johnson III*. Itasca: Riverside Publishing.

Woodcock, R. W., Munoz Sandoval, A. F., Ruef, M. L., & Alvarado, C. G. (2005). *Woodcock-Munoz Language Survey-Revised*. Itasca: Riverside Publishing.

Wyoming Administrative Code Chapter 7 § 4.d.x (pp. 10–13) (n.d.). http://www.k12.wy.us/SE/Docs/CH7.pdf. Accessed 25 Aug 2009.

Wyoming Department of Education. (2011). A model response to intervention framework to identify students with specific learning disabilities. http://edu.wyoming.gov/sf-docs/publications/WY_RtI_Framework_Doc_FINAL_July_27_2011.pdf?sfvrsn=0. Accessed 12 Aug 2012.

Ysseldyke, J., Algozzine, B., Shinn, M., & McGue, K. (1982). Similarities and differences between low achievers and students classified as learning disabled. *The Journal of Special Education, 16*, 73–85.

Index

A. E. B. Taylor, *Diagnostic Assessment of Learning Disabilities in Childhood*,
Contemporary Issues in Psychological Assessment, DOI 10.1007/978-1-4939-0335-1,
© Springer Science+Business Media New York 2014

Printed by Printforce, the Netherlands